The Uncensored History

Michael Freeman

TAYLOR TRADE PUBLISHING
Lanham • New York • Oxford

Published by Taylor Trade Publishing
An imprint of The Rowman & Littlefield Publishing Group, Inc.
4501 Forbes Boulevard, Suite 200
Lanham, Maryland 20706

Distributed by National Book Network

Library of Congress Cataloging-in-Publication Data
Freeman, Michael, 1966–
    ESPN : the uncensored history / Michael Freeman.
        p.   cm.
    Includes index.
    ISBN 0-87833-270-7 (pbk.)
    1. ESPN (TV network)—History. 2. Television broadcasting of sports—
History. I. Title.

GV742.3 .F75 2001
384.55'5—dc21   2001027501

♾ The paper used in this publication meets the minimum requirements of American
National Standard for Information Sciences—Permanence of Paper for Printed
Library Materials, ANSI/NISO Z39.48–1992.

Manufactured in the United States of America.

For my hero,
Alice Freeman

And my best friend,
Kelly Whiteside

Contents

Introduction

A memo from Keith Olbermann, the brilliant but moody former star anchor at ESPN, written in the network's Bristol, Connecticut, headquarters and sent to every on-air member of the staff:

TO: ESPN, ESPN2, ESPNEWS On-Air Staff
FR: Keith Olbermann
RE: Catchphrase Merchandising
DATE: 3/19/97
Ladies and Gentlemen:
For those of you who didn't make it, at the last "Talent" meeting the company, through Jim Noel from legal, mentioned that a process had begun to explore the possibilities of trade- or brand-marking our on-air catchphrases and exploiting them commercially in some fashion.

In response to my question, Noel and Howard Katz said that the process was still in its early stages and thus the question of additional renumeration [sic] was up for grabs, while the intellectual property issues (we said it on their air, therefore they own it) were not.

Apparently the process is a lot farther along than we were led to believe. The following is from the 3/18/97 edition of the *Sports Business Daily*:
ESPN'S FASHION STATEMENTS TO INCLUDE "SPORTS CENTER" PHRASES?
Walt Disney Co. has signed a licensing deal with Pro Player and is "closing another with an unspecified company" in an attempt to "translate the equity of its ESPN brands into successful apparel products," according to Jeff Jensen of *Ad Age*. The Pro Player deal was negotiated by

1

Disney Consumer Products, working in conjunction with ESPN Enterprises. Pro Player's first ESPN apparel products will "hit retail stores around June," and include outerwear, polo shirts, T-shirts, knits, sweatshirts and fleece items featuring the ESPN and ESPN2 logos. Pro Player will also market clothing incorporating ad slogans and signature catchphrases used by ESPN sportscasters, and the company "sees potential" in apparel inspired by the X Games, "targeted at teens and Gen Xers." Although Pro Player will support the program with in-store ads and "is talking" with retailers about merchandising concepts, but "it's possible" ESPN will back the apparel with its own promos. (Ad Age, 3/17 issue)

Apart from the fact that the issue of whether we have any voice in how our own words are used has not been addressed, nor has there been any overture regarding additional recompense for this new and unforeseen use of our names, likenesses, and/or utterances, it occurred to me that many of the catchphrases in question could hardly be considered either our individual, or ESPN's, intellectual property.

It would seem to me that a "Back, back, back" T-shirt might draw some interest from the estate of Red Barber, that a "From Way Downtown Bang" jacket could pique the interest of the estate of Johnny Most—that anything that was created by one of us at another television entity might draw the attention (and the lawsuit) of that previous entity.

My one year of studying Communications Law at Cornell suggests, and a brief communication with my personal attorney (who is a specialist in copyright infringement) confirms, that the company's haste to slap our work on the back of a Pro Player shirt might put us at individual legal risk somewhere down the line. The use or even appropriation of catchphrases is apparently something akin to "sampling" in rap music: It's legal, to a point. Evidently, it's legal for us to say "No Soup for You" or "Cooler Than the Other Side of the Pillow" or to launch into impressions of Bob Murphy, Harry Kalas, Red Barber, Johnny Most, or Ronald Reagan. Whether or not it would be legal for the company to produce apparel quoting us quoting them (directly or merely implicitly) is another matter.

I write all this to you to encourage you to review at your own risk with your attorney and/or agent. Given the misdirection on this issue at the last "Talent" meeting, I do not think we can rely on anybody but ourselves to cover our own legal butts.

• • •

The memo, which infuriated some members of ESPN management, was vintage Olbermann: cogent reasoning seasoned with sarcasm and attitude. Olbermann was no different with cameras rolling—at ESPN, or later as host of his own news talk show on the MSNBC cable network, or now in the sports anchor chair on Fox. His memo also illustrated the growing power of ESPN. The sports network had become so culturally ubiquitous that even the cutesy, signature phrases spouted by the anchors, which helped to make them more popular than some of the athletes they covered, were serious business.

Twenty-one years ago, ESPN was considered a pathetic joke. By the time Olbermann and coanchor Dan Patrick had made "SportsCenter," which combined shtick, superb writing, and great reporting, a must-see for the athlete and fan alike, ESPN was a multibillion dollar business and the most influential sports news vehicle in the world. Some producers in the newsroom, fully aware of the influence the network now held, began to half-kiddingly call themselves "the gods of sport."

Olbermann and Patrick were the top two deities, but it was Olbermann who was the most cantankerous. He wrote other stinging memos that took shots at management—one sent executive Howard Katz into such an angry frenzy he temporarily ceased contract negotiations with Olbermann's agent. It was clear by the winter of 1997 that Olbermann's days at ESPN were numbered. He had grown tired of what he felt were unimaginative bosses who didn't understand what he and Patrick were doing on the concerto that was "SportsCenter." Management, in turn, was weary of Olbermann's myriad complaints. He publicly knocked ESPN's hometown, Bristol, long derided by ESPN employees as a dreadfully boring city. He whined to friends in the newsroom that his six-figure salary was too low and complained about not being appreciated. Almost anyone and everything on the ESPN radar screen was targeted by Olbermann. He was a human SCUD missile. Anchor Suzy Kolber, who worked with Olbermann on ESPN2 in the early 1990s and was sometimes seen crying in the bathroom after a hit from one of Olbermann's poison darts, called him "a baby who would quit, literally quit, at least twice a week, whenever he didn't get his way." No doubt a divorce was coming.

Olbermann was the best writer at the network, in addition to being one of its biggest smart-asses. But there was always something deeper in him than his constant grousing and nuclear ego. "You can't spend thirty seconds with him without being blown away by his intellect," said MSNBC executive Erik Sorenson, who has known Olbermann fifteen years. A dazzling thinker who quietly and selflessly helped several women at ESPN fight sexual harassment, Olbermann was also always one step ahead of management, both frustrating and amazing them. The memo was a taste of his open disdain for management, particularly for executive editor John Walsh and then ESPN president Steve Bornstein, who refers to on-air personalities, called "talent" in television, as "that fucking talent."

But the memo also showed that Olbermann was apprehensive about the future. ESPN was already global, a dominant force in television and journalism, but eager to broaden its reach even further. The network had become one of the best through the tireless work of its founders and then top-notch reporting and Spielberg-like presentation. And now, as Olbermann so deftly pointed out, ESPN was beginning to add a third element: relentless, almost pathological marketing. When ESPN was purchased by Walt Disney Company in 1995, the sports network inherited a genetic disorder—Disney's penchant for marketing a product ten times every millisecond. "If ESPN could market Dan Patrick's ass," Olbermann said, referring to his friend and former prime-time sidekick, "it would try."

ESPN was clearly more than a marketing machine, however. It had become a paradise island in an ocean of mediocre television sports journalism. Its original mission was to provide substance to the sports fan who wanted more than six minutes of highlights and stupid pet tricks on the local news. That hasn't changed. ESPN has taken sports television to a new plane, putting out a better product than all but a handful of its print sports cousins. The network hired reporters Chris Mortensen, Andrea Kremer, Jimmy Roberts, Peter Gammons, and Al Morganti, tops in their profession, who broke story after story. Later, ESPN snagged David Aldridge, Jeremy Schaap (son of author and ESPN "Sports Reporters" host Dick Schaap), John Clayton, Sal Paolantonio, Ed Werder, Steve Cyphers, Mark Schwarz, Greg Garber, Tim Kurkjian, and Shelley Smith to strengthen its reporting. Most of ESPN's reporters and a small portion of its anchors have newspaper experience—a Walsh idea that has flowered beautifully. Its emphasis on hard news is the reason ESPN has broken some of the biggest sports stories of the past decade, such as Nike's exploitation of Asian workers and the thorny issue of athletes and domestic violence.

The network has come a long way from its days of broadcasting rodeos and slow-pitch softball. ESPN was the brainchild of Bill Rasmussen, a creative, and at times flawed, man of uncommon vision. He and his son, Scott, were stuck in traffic on I-84 in Waterbury, Connecticut, on August 16, 1978. Bill had recently been fired from his job as communications director and announcer for the New England Whalers, a semipro hockey team in Connecticut. Rasmussen didn't know it yet, but losing that job was one of the best things that could ever have happened to him. Ideas often come at strange times and now, while sandwiched bumper to bumper on a highway, he and his son would concoct his strangest idea, one that would transform sports on television.

Rasmussen had the notion of buying transponder time on a satellite to broadcast sports twenty-four hours a day, every day, on cable television. At the time, it was a revolutionary idea—and considered patently foolish. Most people had four television channels—five tops—and no one thought of cable as a viable way of reaching the public. Rasmussen disagreed. He purchased some limited time on one of the few cable satellites in orbit, Satcom 1. Several days later, Time Warner, Disney, 20th Century-Fox, and Warner Bros. all applied for a transponder. But Rasmussen and his upstart network were one step ahead.

The first days of ESPN yielded nothing like the current polished product. Rasmussen had the studio built on a barren patch of a tree-lined section of Bristol, because the property was cheap. In the first few years, much of the network was run from midget-sized, crowded trailers. During one of the first live "SportsCenters," a fly landed on the nose of anchor Bob Ley. There were three-foot-deep holes in the parking lot. Anne Bailey, an accountant, remembers that the worst part of working at ESPN was answering phones and having to say "Entertainment and Sports Programming Network" instead of just ESPN. By the time she was finished with that mouthful, the caller was halfway into the conversation. Lynn Johnson, former marketing coordinator, warmly recalls how closely-knit the employees were. "We were so small that anyone who did not go home for Thanksgiving would come to my family's house. My mother was cutting turkey all afternoon. It was accepted because these were the people I spent up to sixteen hours a day with. I saw more of them than my friends or relatives. They were my family."

And a number of them played as hard as they worked. Some used drugs often, and it was not unusual for an employee to snort lines of cocaine off the top of telex machines. There were some producers who gambled away half of their $20,000 paychecks. Gambling by certain ESPN employees even caught the attention of law enforcement at one time and it would bedevil the network through most of its existence.

The love of sports and the feeling that the network was destined for something great prevailed over the vices. "We knew it was going to work; we knew we had something special," said Bob Pronovost, one of the first producer/directors of "SportsCenter." And work it did. Today, ESPN is the largest cable network in the country, available in 76 million homes through more than sixty thousand cable providers. Neither Disney nor ESPN will publicly discuss just how much money the network makes, but industry analysts estimate that in 1998, the last year when data is available, ESPN generated $356 million in cash flow, up ten percent from 1997. Advertising and subscriber revenues totaled $1.1 billion during that same time period. In 1992, when ABC was still sole owner of the sports cable network, ESPN outearned its parent, finishing more than two hundred million in the black, equating to $6.34 cents a second in advertising revenue. The network's profits are more robust now. Nothing else on cable television compares.

About four million households a day watch "SportsCenter." By comparison, the "CBS Evening News" is seen by about 12 million viewers each day and NBC's "Today" show about six million.

The network employs several thousand people and beams its signal over three dozen satellite dishes. It has marketing offices in New York, Chicago, Denver, Detroit, Los Angeles, and Hong Kong. ESPN supplies its product to every continent, even setting up a receiver for eight viewers in Antarctica. It has broadcast deals with all major sports, including the National Football League (NFL) to which ESPN paid hundreds of millions of dollars for broadcast rights. ESPN is as much responsible for professional football strengthening its grip on the American sports fan in the late 1980s as the NFL is for making ESPN a must-watch network for football fans. "ESPN was able to take the draft, the pregame and highlight shows, and other NFL programming to a new level," said NFL Commissioner Paul Tagliabue. "And when they started televising games in 1987, it extended our national reach, turning Sunday's with the NFL from a potential six- or seven-hour television experience into a twelve-hour television experience. All in all, like it has done with other sports, ESPN helped raise the NFL's national profile and prompted other media organizations to match it."

The first day of the 1999 pro football draft on ESPN averaged 2.8 million viewers over seven tedious hours. Wayne Gretzky's final game that same weekend on rival Fox drew six hundred thousand fewer households, despite the appeal of the greatest hockey player ever, the days of hype about his retirement, and the weak competition.

Spinoffs proliferated: ESPN2; ESPN Classic, which reruns old games and features interviews with legendary athletes; and ESPNews, a sports version of CNN Headline News, which employs more than 70 production people, dozens of anchors, and broadcasts hours of live programming daily. ESPN also has 20 networks in 20 different languages internationally. Theme restaurants and an ESPN clothing store at a mall in California complete the empire. When Disney bought Capital Cities, the star-studded media chain, it was ESPN that attracted Disney chairman Michael Eisner. He called ESPN "the crown jewel" of the purchase.

That jewel polished brighter with the 1998 publication of *ESPN: The Magazine,* which has challenged the dominant sports magazine of the last half-century, *Sports Illustrated,* owned by Time Warner. The president of Time Warner said ESPN's magazine was the biggest threat to his company since *Newsweek.* The magazine has been ripped by some media critics for being too cluttered, aimed at 18-year-old kids with Sega-shortened attention spans. Serious journalists decried it as shallow. But just as its parent eventually earned respect, so has the magazine. In 1999, it won best design in the National Magazine awards, the medium's equivalent of the Oscars. ESPN can thank F. Darrin Perry, the brilliant designer stolen away from SI. (The magazine is actually full of SI alumni, starting at the top with former SI managing editor John Papanek.) The magazine also started earning fistfuls of cash, reaching a circulation of more than 850,000 by 1999, up from 350,000 at its launch.

ESPN and ESPN2 alone are valued at more than $10 billion. ESPN's Cinderella story, however, began with losses of $30 million a year and a building without indoor plumbing. ESPN was hemorrhaging so much some at the network feared it wouldn't survive beyond 1980.

But survive it did, becoming not just an icon in sports journalism but an integral piece of American culture, a daily part of the lives of millions who know the theme song by heart: "Da da da, da da da." For many, "Sports-Center" is not just a show, it's an addiction. "If someone surreptitiously took everything but ESPN from my cable television package, it might be months before I noticed," wrote George Will in *Newsweek.*

Further, and perhaps the most convincing evidence of ESPN's relevance is the ABC sitcom "Sports Night," a spoof of ESPN and its anchors, one of whom is former anchor Craig Kilborn. Kilborn turned his ESPN experience into a gig on Comedy Central and now has his own late-night talk show on CBS. The first thing celebrity guests like actress Drew Barrymore say is how much they relished watching the cocky Kilborn on ESPN.

The lineup of "SportsCenter" devotees is long and noteworthy. *Chicago Tribune* columnist Bob Verdi, a close friend of former Bulls superstar Michael Jordan, who often watched himself on "SportsCenter," says he can vaguely remember what civilization was like before ESPN "but I don't care to relive it." Politicians, such as presidential candidate Bill Bradley, and athletes, such as professional basketball phenom Grant Hill, have appeared in commercials promoting the network. Watching ESPN has also become a daily ritual for athletes themselves. Former Met Keith

Hernandez used to watch ESPN to study pitchers around the league. Players and coaches on the Baltimore Orioles begin each day during the season with a baseball breakfast that includes coffee, a danish, and the latest installment of ESPN's "Baseball Tonight." Said San Francisco 49ers quarterback Steve Young: "If you are an athlete, it is a nightly recap of your profession."

Of course ESPN has millions of both casual and hardcore fans who are neither coaches nor athletes. One of them, Joe Grippo from Westbury, New York, who works for the Topps Company, wrote to ESPN's magazine and said that he is such a dedicated fan he moved out of his neighborhood and into a new one "because my cable operator did not offer ESPN2." Andrea Kremer, one of the most visible faces on ESPN and its best reporter, was walking through a Los Angeles airport once when she was stopped by a man and his wife. "I just wanted to tell you," the man said to Kremer, "that I wake up with you every morning." Kremer looked at the man's puzzled wife and said, "Let me explain. . . ."

Governor of Texas and presidential hopeful George W. Bush, son of former President Bush, was in Washington in the spring of 1990 for dinner with his parents at the White House. After dinner, George Jr., flipped on ESPN for live coverage of a Texas Rangers game to watch pitcher Nolan Ryan, who had no bigger fan than the president. The elder Bush had never watched much of ESPN but would later say that watching Ryan on his White House TV that day began an ESPN addiction.

On a boardwalk along the Jersey shore, a vendor sold a T-shirt that read: "Women have PMS, men have ESPN."

The network was even mentioned during an academic scandal involving the University of Minnesota basketball team. Academic counselor Jan Gangelhoff claimed she wrote four hundred papers for players between 1993 and 1998. While writing them, the players were sometimes with her. Other times, she said, they were in the next room, watching ESPN.

The success of ESPN is due mainly to the breadth and depth of its coverage. You want to see if the Dodgers won—watch ESPN. You want to see live updates from the O. J. Simpson trial—watch ESPN. Interested in seeing President Clinton talk about race and sports—watch ESPN. Need a workout? Catch one of the network's half-dozen fitness shows.

"The ESPN approach is that no matter what you are doing in life, they want you to think ESPN," said ABC and ESPN reporter Lesley Visser. "If you are listening to the radio, they want you to turn on ESPN radio. If you're going to read a magazine, they want it to be ESPN's magazine. If you're going to watch television, then you have all of these ESPN channels to choose from."

Perhaps the best measure of a news agency's influence is not just in the stories it reports but the change it effects. It was the racist and outrageous comments of Cincinnati Reds owner Marge Schott to an ESPN reporter that proved to be the last irritant in the eye of major league baseball. Schott said in an on-air interview that Hitler was a positive influence on Germany. Baseball stripped Schott of her ownership privileges for two years and banned her from the team's daily operations. She sold her share of the team. Schott's comments had every major news organization in the country chasing ESPN.

These days it is almost impossible to avoid ESPN's major moneymaker, "SportsCenter," just as it is almost impossible not to be touched by some portion of the ESPN dynasty. Besides the television networks and magazine, ESPN has a radio network and a highly acclaimed Web site. Nine hours of "SportsCenter" air every day. ESPN employees joke that in the winter there is more "SportsCenter" than there are hours of daylight. The longevity of the show, despite constant changes in hosts and time slots, is remarkable. In May of 1998, "SportsCenter" broadcast show number 20,000, which put it ahead of "CBS Evening News" for the most newscasts ever.

Flip through the pay-television galaxy. It's crammed with niche programming chiseled from the larger niches first carved out by ESPN and CNN. ESPN led to the creation of the Golf Channel just as surely as CNN led to Court TV and the Weather Channel. These smaller specialty networks all have a regular evening show in which the news of the day is reported and analyzed. "Whatever ESPN touches," said *Washington Post* columnist Michael Wilbon, "turns to gold."

• • •

ESPN has attempted to hide a grave secret. Behind the well-oiled and smart exterior of the network lurks a troubling history of sexual harassment. ESPN has historically proven to be as hostile a work environment for women as any Wall Street brokerage firm. Throughout much of ESPN's existence, dozens of male executives, producers, anchors, and on-air personalities have been accused of sexually harassing women employees. Investigative reports by ESPN have criticized coaches who were accused of sexually harassing women athletes. As it turns out, a disturbing number of men at the network were abusing their power in similar, if not worse, ways.

ESPN management eventually was forced to either fire, suspend, or reprimand a number of men at the network, often star anchors or admired producers, for inappropriate sexual conduct throughout the late 1980s and into the 1990s.

The harassment ranged from childish locker room humor and sexually explicit e-mail messages to an unnerving incident in which an ESPN male anchor followed one woman producer in his car against her wishes, causing her to file a complaint with management. In another case, that same anchor was accused of attempting to grope another woman producer. He was suspended for three months when a half-dozen women reluctantly came forward and accused him of unwelcomed sexual advances. Two male production assistants sent obscene computer messages to a female counterpart, leading to the controversial firing of one and the suspension of the other. A female production assistant was slapped on the rear end by an on-air personality. Women have been sent lingerie in the mail, have had the size of their breasts discussed openly in the newsroom, and have been propositioned outright for sex.

"The newsroom was all guys, all testosterone, and many of those guys made it clear they did not want women around," said former anchor Karie Ross.

Some of the most disturbing accusations come from Ross, who left a legacy of uncommon courage and bold initiative. Ross was the first woman to vocally attack ESPN's harassment problem after women complained to her about being asked to trade dates for time in ESPN's editing cubicles. When a story is pieced together, it goes through a rigorous editing process, which was done in tiny rooms called editing bays by producers. There were a limited number of these units, and producers and reporters signed up for times, often switching slots depending upon who was on deadline or not. Ross alleged that one male producer in particular would switch times with women only if they would sleep with him.

These are not isolated incidents of harassment; rather, part of an overall atmosphere in Bristol that remains, at times, antagonistic to women.

"I'm pretty comfortable saying that almost every day I worked at ESPN, there was some form of sexual harassment," said a former employee who worked in production both in television and radio at ESPN in the mid-1990s. "I would be walking down the hall and a total stranger would come up to me and say, 'You look really good today and I would love to have a baby with you.' It ranged from comments like that to men making derogatory remarks about me being a woman. Men look you up and down, staring at you. There was one manager who, when he spoke to you, would look you up and down and stop at your breasts and then your pelvic area. Back and forth, back and forth. All those things happened all the time, including getting grabbed on the ass."

In March of 1998, ESPN settled a sex discrimination lawsuit filed by a former sales account executive, who alleged in court documents that she was paid less than her male counterparts with comparable experience, that she did not receive bonuses and promotions because she was a woman, that an ESPN manager took clients to topless bars, and that the network forged documents to portray her as a poor worker. There was also the case of Elaine Truskoski, a secretary who won a ground-breaking sex discrimination lawsuit against ESPN after court battles lasting six years.

The network's lack of diversity behind the camera—in terms of women and people of color—caught the attention of NAACP President Kweisi Mfume. He told *Broadcasting & Cable* magazine in late 1998 that ESPN had as poor a track record for its low numbers of women and blacks in management as any network on television. ESPN maintains it is committed to hiring women and minorities.

"When you look specifically at the ESPNs of the world and the way the structure of an ESPN is, [you] see an outright denial of opportunity there and jobs are not available off camera," Mfume said. "ESPN may be as bad, if not worse, than some of the networks."

Said ESPN's former director of human resources Ricardo Correia: "The issue of diversity, dealing with cultural differences and racial and gender-based differences, is something that has long been talked about at ESPN, but to this day it is not something that anything has ever been done about at ESPN. I'm talking behind the camera."

"So the issue is doing more than just putting a black face on television so that black people who like sports will watch," continued Correia. "The issue is where is it in the continuum of the culture of this company, where people of color, and women, can come in and be exposed to developmental opportunities. Those chances are few and far between . . . and I can't tell you how many blacks left because they were in the same assistant position three, four, or five years and whites had jumped over them."

ESPN's problem with hiring minorities for key off-camera positions demonstrates a split personality toward women. Walsh made a concerted effort to recruit more women to ESPN. Viewers can see a talented collection of anchors and reporters: Robin Roberts, Linda Cohn, Chris McKendry and Andrea Kremer, who has broken a number of key stories over the past decade. Suzy Kolber returned to ESPN from Fox and hosts "Edge NFL Matchup." And ESPN recently hired two female news editors.

However, women who are the nonstars, the grunts who edit and produce, the secretaries who take notes and answer the phones, the sellers of ads have endured a rocky stay over the last decade and more. Many of these problems have never been made public until now, mainly because most women were afraid of reprisals from ESPN, which can be nasty and vindictive against anyone perceived as an enemy. The issue has also been quiet because some at the network do not feel it is their place to discuss such things. "I have daughters, and I have not walked around ESPN with my eyes closed all these years," said Patrick. "I just don't feel comfortable publicly talking about things and issues that do not involve me."

Walsh, who oversees day-to-day operations in the production department, just one area of the network where there were problems, strongly defended ESPN's handling of sexual harassment issues under his watch. Some harassment claims, he said, were exaggerated, and the ones that were not were handled promptly and fairly by the network. "There was a constricted period of time in which we dealt with this issue," Walsh said. "It seemed like the issue was there, we dealt with it, and moved on. It wasn't something that lingered. I felt confident that we did the best that we could do in the quickest possible time that we could do it."

Walsh said the most difficult part of assessing a harassment claim was determining who was telling the truth. Then Walsh added, "There were a couple of [harassment situations] where the men were just nuisances. They were just nuisances and it made the women nuts. It made them crazy. And you spoke to [the men] and said, 'It can't go on like this. We can't have that kind of behavior.' There were no threats, 'If you don't do this, you won't get promoted.' There was a fear of that on the women's part."

"Some of [the harassment] was the kind of odd, quirky, social awkwardness . . . an awkwardness of relating to a female," Walsh said. "Some of it was that. And it couldn't be helped."

Walsh conceded that because of ESPN's rapid growth in the late 1980s and into the 1990s, which included heavy reliance on immature male talent directly out of college, ESPN was perhaps more vulnerable to sexual harassment than many other companies.

A significant number of current and former male and women employees interviewed for this book strongly disagree with Walsh's contention that ESPN's sexual harassment problems were handled quickly and efficiently, complaining that harassment has long plagued the network and that ESPN failed in many ways to control it. During a three-year period in the early 1990s, between seventy-five and one hundred sexual harassment complaints were made by women employees throughout the company, and between twenty to twenty-five of those cases were categorized as serious incidents, according to a former senior member of ESPN management who dealt extensively with sexual harassment at the network. The former manager said serious episodes were categorized as groping, requesting sexual favors in exchange for prime work assignments, or retaliating against a woman for rejecting a male superior's advances. In most cases of harassment at ESPN, the women behind the camera, such as producers, production assistants, administrators, sales personnel, and secretaries, were the victims. The harassers dared not go after the high-profile female anchors.

ESPN says that the former manager has wildly inflated the number of complaints. "That number is totally inaccurate," said the network in a statement. "It would mean that, on average, there was more than one complaint per female employee in studio production, a preposterous supposition."

"We acted promptly and responsibly to every concern brought to our attention," the statement continued. "These situations occurred a long time ago and are not reflective of our workplace today. ESPN was then, and continues to be, totally committed to maintaining an environment for all employees that is free from harassment of any kind."

Walsh stated that between 1989 and 1993 eight women in the production department filed thirty complaints. Walsh said it is impossible to have had seventy-five to one hundred complaints because there were not enough women in production to file that many.

However, ESPN's statement and the statistics Walsh provided pertain only to the production department. In the three-year period stipulated by the former executive, the seventy-five to one hundred complaints over three years were from women who were employed all across ESPN, not just in production. Also, Walsh conceded that his statistics included only formal complaints, and he also acknowledged there were instances when women complained to their various supervisors about a harassment situation, but the problem never reached the stage where human resources took formal action. Thus the complaints were settled off the record. One such instance occurred when an on-air personality three times slapped the rear end of a production assistant. When she spoke to her coordinating producer about what happened, the matter was settled between the three of them, and human resources never processed an official complaint.

In other words, Walsh's statistics include only the instances when women in production filed formal charges and did not include women outside production or complaints in production solved without a formal investigation by human resources. "There was that three-year period when a large number of women across the company complained about being harassed, but wanted to keep things quiet, and things were worked out off the record," said the former executive. "And there was the other group of women who filed formal complaints. The combination of those two groups forms the seventy-five to one hundred complaints. And it was much closer to one hundred."

ESPN's own accounting is troubling in itself. Between 1989 and 1993, when the network says eight women in the production department filed thirty formal complaints, the number of total employees at ESPN remained almost the same over that four-year span. ESPN had approximately eight hundred employees, some two hundred to two hundred and fifty in production, where twenty to twenty-five women worked, the former executive said. So even if ESPN's harassment figures are correct, the network still had seven to eight formal complaints a year emerge from a pool of twenty to twenty-five women in production.

Walsh said the number of harassment complaints in the production department at ESPN is "not unusual for a male-dominated company." Several experts on sexual harassment in the workplace strongly disagreed with that statement. In comparison with ESPN's thirty formal complaints over a four-year period in just the production department, a major metropolitan New York newspaper, during that same time frame from 1989 to 1993, had some 4,000 employees, approximately one-third to one-half of those women, but only three to six harassment cases a year across the entire company, and half of those complaints occurred at the printing plant.

Of course ESPN is not the sole male-dominated workplace to battle sexual harassment. Various studies this decade analyzing women chemical engineers, lawyers, and executives have found that roughly six out of ten reported harassment. Complaints to the Equal Employment Opportunity Commission (EEOC) went from 10,532 in 1992 to 15,618 in 1998.

In 1996 women at a Mitsubishi factory in Illinois were groped, kissed, and called "whores" and "bitches." The company settled an EEOC lawsuit for $34 million. A woman working in the New Jersey Attorney Generals office won $300,000 in back wages and $50,000 for emotional distress after complaining that a supervisor asked her for oral sex and grabbed her breasts and buttocks. A secretary at one of the world's largest law offices, Baker & McKenzie, was awarded $3.5 million after accusing the firm of creating a hostile work environment.

In one form or another, ESPN experienced many of the same problems. An additional problem at ESPN was its uneven punishment. There seemed to be two classes of punishment, one for key employees at the network, another for lower-ranked personnel. Thus some powerful men at ESPN became serial harassers, unafraid of being severely disciplined. Correia explained he has an "eighty percent rule": Eighty percent of most men who are warned about intolerable behavior do not repeat it. But Correia said that at ESPN "the percentage was much lower. It was more like a fifty percent rule."

At ESPN in the early 1990s, three coordinating producers, one of the

higher-ranked positions at the network, were simultaneously either suspended for, or accused of, making unwelcomed sexual advances, according to current and former producers at ESPN. "I think, from talking to
people in management at ESPN now, that management feels a number of
mistakes were made when it came to sexual harassment," said Scott Ackerson, one of the best producers in the business who worked at ESPN and is
now at Fox. "They feel they weren't as aggressive as they should have been."

While one anchor was suspended for sexually harassing women producers, a production assistant was fired, during the same time period, for
a far less egregious episode, leaving some men and women at ESPN to bit-
terly conclude that a double standard existed, one for stars, another for
lower-ranked personnel.

In another instance, a male producer made sexual suggestions to a
woman producer who worked on the same show, "Up Close." After his
advances were rebuffed, the male producer became physically threatening.
He was eventually suspended by ESPN—only to be later reinstated to the
same position. The woman who had been harassed was forced to work
with her harasser.

ESPN struggled with making the transition from a male-dominated
workplace, a "sports locker room" as one woman described it, to one
where women could work comfortably, assured of equal access to key
positions. A senior producer, Barry Sacks, said on more than one occasion,
"Get the broad out of broadcasting." He was joking, but his comment
roiled many women.

In the end, a small group of women challenged the entrenched harassment conditions and changed the ESPN workplace. While Anita Hill was
testifying before Congress about harassment under Supreme Court nominee Clarence Thomas, women at ESPN were staging their own revolt, quietly fighting what can only be called a series of civil rights battles. Some,
such as Ross, spoke publicly at staff meetings of coworkers being sexually
harassed. Others turned in harassers to superiors, risking their careers.
Still others filed lawsuits against the company. And many quit, beaten
down irrevocably by the endless persecution.

ESPN avoided heavy litigation and public embarrassment by compen-
sating some victims with several months of pay, asking them to sign a
waiver agreeing not to sue ESPN, then requesting they leave the company,
a former human resources official said. In effect they were paid off and
told to keep quiet. That partially explains why ESPN has been able to keep
most of its harassment problems out of the news.

Some women did not want their names used in this book, fearing repercussions from the network. Their identities and physical characteristics

were changed (pseudonyms are indicated by asterisks). Several sources refused to discuss harassment issues at the network unless they were protected, and some of the accused would only agree to an interview if their names were not used.

Much of the information for this book emerged from more than two hundred interviews over a four-year period with current and former ESPN employees, including members of ESPN management, anchors, talent, producers, directors, and production assistants. Information from the book was also derived from company documents, handwritten notes, diary entries, and media accounts.

Interviews were conducted with television executives and talent from Fox, CBS, and NBC; commissioners, owners, and executives from major professional sports teams; public relations executives; and attorneys who specialize in sexual harassment and discrimination issues. Court documents also provided crucial information for the book.

Many key participants were interviewed repeatedly, some more than a dozen times. In most cases, interviews were tape recorded, with a few sources taping interviews themselves. (During an interview of two producers, three tape recorders were running simultaneously.) Direct quotations from meetings or conversations came from at least one participant who specifically recalled or took notes on what was said. Quotation marks are not used when a source is unsure of the wording. Thoughts, beliefs, and conclusions attributed to a person came from that person, or someone who knew the source well. Although it is nearly impossible to reconstruct complete conversations and meetings, such recasting was done as close as possible. Some of the interviews were done on "background," which is a common journalistic tool that allows the sources to provide information with the understanding they not be identified. This sort of reporting, used regularly by almost every news organization in the country, including ESPN, was necessary on several occasions because some employees of ESPN—and former employees—were terrified of talking on the record, fearing reprisal from the network. Some were so cautious they would not speak on ESPN office phones but only from their homes or from pay phones. Many insisted no messages be left on their work voice mail because ESPN monitors such messages (which is legal). One producer arranged a meeting in the parking lot of the Bristol Public Library, tucked away in his car. Several other ESPN workers would only meet at a Subway sandwich shop downtown.

ESPN employees, although they work for a news organization, experience a startling lack of freedom in discussing their professional lives. It was no coincidence that seventeen days after Walsh said he would only agree to be interviewed if he could censor what he considered negative material from this book—an outrageous request that was denied—vice president Rosa Gatti distributed a networkwide memo.

"I want to remind all employees of ESPN's long-standing policy," Gatti wrote. "All media communication pertaining to ESPN, its businesses, and industry issues must be channeled through and approved by the Communications Department."

Gatti continued, "This policy exists not to obstruct media communication but rather to ensure that ESPN is represented by the most knowledgeable and appropriate spokesperson in order to provide accurate information and a timely response. Also, do not provide background or off-the-record comments. Such action can affect ESPN and its business."

ESPN reporters obtain substantial information from their sources on background, making Gatti's words hypocritical. In 1993, while battling its own serious harassment problems, ESPN aired a well-reported piece on sexual harassment allegations by women swimmers against their University of Florida coach. ESPN interviewed the women, but hid their faces in black shadows and electronically altered their voices. An ESPN magazine story called "Confessions of a Cheater," detailed cheating in sports and included a first-person account by an anonymous NBA player. The player, who was also shadowed, wrote about punching players "in the nuts."

On "SportsCenter" alone, ESPN has used anonymous sources in its reporting at least two hundred times (Mortensen uses anonymous sources regularly on either his television or Internet reports), and ESPN executives have trashed Olbermann and Fox anonymously for this book.

Walsh, who eventually decided to submit to a brief interview, revolutionized television sports journalism. Under him, ESPN has fearlessly aired controversial pieces that reflect negatively on a personality or team. Occasionally, a story leads to the firing of a coach, the dismissal of a player, or even an NCAA investigation of a college athletic program. When this has happened, the network publicly took its bows for its reports, even when some of them literally ruined lives.

Yet Walsh and ESPN reacted with disturbing arrogance and provincialism when they became the subject themselves. Walsh instructed ESPN anchors, reporters, and producers not to grant interviews for the book, because ESPN did not have editorial control. Only after being told his tactics were to be documented in this book did Walsh release a memo to the staff saying anyone who wanted to cooperate could. That memo was distributed one month after the manuscript was submitted to the publisher (Walsh and ESPN had been told the date it was due). He even fabricated stories about the author and publisher in an attempt to scare employees from cooperating (though in the end many still did). The most unnerving part of ESPN's response was that ESPN and Disney officials conducted aggressive investigations into the author's past, searching for discrediting information.

ESPN: An Uncensored History is a balanced account of a megamedia company formerly mocked for its goofy programming and red ink. ESPN is a major moneymaker, fueled by the star power of its anchors. That collective group took a step back when Olbermann departed in 1997 but remains impressive nonetheless. There is Dan Patrick, one of ESPN's all-time stars; Chris Berman, the forcefully talented, lovable, and uncontrollable anchor; and Robin Roberts, who possesses more poise and natural ability than any other anchor at ESPN. Others include Bob Ley, one of the originals nicknamed "the general"; Charley Steiner, the baseball and boxing expert with a brilliant sense of humor; Jack Edwards, one of the most analytical and ethical journalists at ESPN; Mike Tirico, called the Michael Jordan of ESPN because he makes everyone around him better; and newspoet Stuart Scott, who was once told by management to "not talk so black."

Now ESPN is involved in the biggest fight of its history, facing a serious challenge from Fox, a network described by former ESPN president Steve Bornstein as "a mosquito." With a deep-pocketed owner in Rupert Murdoch, star talent in Olbermann, and ESPN alum Chris Myers, a growing base of sixty-eight million viewers, and a regional concept that emphasizes intriguing local programming, the mosquito doesn't show any signs of being squashed. Fox, along with NBC and Turner, recently agreed to a six-year, $2.4 billion deal for NASCAR's television rights, stealing the motor sport. It was a crushing blow to ESPN. The network and NASCAR used each other to build popularity throughout the last two decades, with ESPN and ESPN2 eventually combining to televise hundreds of hours of motor sports annually, including thirteen Winston Cup, thirteen Busch Series, and twenty-one Craftsman Truck Series events.

ESPN faces another threat: complacency. Can it remain as hungry as it was when Rasmussen, Chet Simmons, Scotty Connal, and Stuart Evey built it with their own hands? "Back then, I guess, there was a tremendous passion for what you were doing," said Bob Gutkowski, a vice president of programming for ESPN in the 1980s. "You only had a certain amount of inventory, and you made sure it translated onto the screen. Now, it's hard for ESPN to have that same passion because of the success and money. As you get bigger, the passion is displaced. Basically, we were fighting for recognition, we were fighting for acceptance, we were fighting not to be snickered at. I think ESPN takes all that for granted now, but that is bound to happen."

Once Fox, which has a showy exterior, puts furniture into its mansion, bulking up with more reputable journalists like Olbermann, dynamic anchors like Kevin Frazier, skilled reporters like Sam Marchiano, and top-notch producers like Ackerson and former ESPN producer Mark Mayer, ESPN will face its first legitimate competition.

If one believes Olbermann, there are already people at ESPN who think Fox will win the war. Those people, according to Olbermann, are trying to jump ship from ESPN to Fox. "We [have received] calls from members of ESPN management looking for work here, and just about everybody on the air has called one of us to try and get a job or at least look at the possibility of it. I am not exaggerating," said Olbermann, who probably is overstating just a tad. "Not Bob Ley, not Robin Roberts, not the people who are entrenched, not Mike Tirico, but everybody else. People I have never even heard of have called me looking for work."

The fact Fox and ESPN are competitors, Olbermann says, is an example of ESPN's smugness and serious miscalculations. ESPN thought the challenge would come from Ted Turner and CNN, not Fox. ESPN was caught completely off guard by Fox, the way the three major networks once were by ESPN.

"I mean, look, we're sitting in a place that shouldn't exist," said Olbermann, pointing to the walls of his Los Angeles–based office. "There were one hundred things they could have done, fifteen of which they needed to do, that could have assured that monopoly forever. The great business decisions? Give me a whole bunch of them and I'll ask you about getting into regionals." Then Olbermann, imitating Walsh's deadpan monotone, said, 'No, we don't have to worry about that regional crap. We're America's only national gathering place for sports fans.'"

"Great," Olbermann said. "Fans are all going to the five-hour open bar, and you've got your little show there. Regionals. They missed that one completely. I missed that one completely. . . . And it was like a clock striking, 'Bong! Oh, I get it now.' They didn't get it."

The Fox star continued his blistering assessment of ESPN management, making it clear he and Bornstein, one of the most fabled executives in sports television history, will not be sending each other birthday cards anytime soon. "Other than Steve Anderson, I don't think any of them are any good," he said. "Dick Ebersol told me when I went to work for him when he was the head of NBC Sports, there is nobody that he would rather see run ABC Sports than Steve Bornstein. The long-term effects of what happens with ABC Sports, we've already seen. They've reduced "Monday Night Football." Clearly, it is not the franchise it once was. Why? Well, he's tampered with it. He married the ESPN product to it clumsily, with bad grace, and was involved in getting rid of Gifford. He could have had a Frank Gifford farewell tour. He could have had a Dan Dierdorf farewell tour. 'Dan we're going to give you one more year on it. We appreciate it. We're going to hype you all the way.' There's a thousand things to do if you sit down and you think of these people as human beings as opposed to 'fucking talent.'"

Berman said that ESPN is a convenient target and that Bornstein, contrary to what Olbermann believes, is most responsible for ESPN's rapid growth in the 1990s.

"It is chic now to bash the network, or to bash me," Berman said. "We are easy targets. I am proud of this network and I wish people would just stop being jealous."

Olbermann is one of the keys to where ESPN—and Fox—go from here. If Fox can keep Olbermann happy, he will continue to lead a passionate fight against ESPN, and draw ESPN viewers away from the network to Fox. He has that much power and appeal, boosted by a five-million-dollar advertising campaign by Fox. If he becomes unhappy, however, the network might experience what ESPN and MSNBC did.

"I think he's happy because Fox executives are stroking his ego and kissing his ass," said Suzy Kolber, who respects Olbermann but was made miserable by his temper tantrums directed at her and others when they worked on the ESPN2 set. "If at any point that ends, he'll be miserable at Fox like he's been everywhere else. . . . He is generally an unhappy person. Which is a shame because he's brilliant, incredibly talented, and it is just a shame that he would have to be unhappy and in turn make other people unhappy."

Right now, Olbermann is stimulated, proving he is worth his multimillion dollar salary. He has brought attention, viewers, and smarts to Fox. He hosted the 1999 major league all-star game with his wit and thoroughness. Earlier that year when Olbermann had reported baseball was considering selling ad space on its uniforms, he quipped, "There's no truth to the rumors that after selling the sanctity of their uniforms, baseball will next offer to sell players' souls."

The year 2000 marks the twentieth anniversary of ESPN's twenty-four-hour sports broadcasting, one of the most significant achievements in media history. Rasmussen never envisioned his modest network becoming the standard by which all cable television is and may forever be judged. Time has dulled his importance in television history. The same can be said for

Simmons, who as president turned ESPN from a ridiculed network into a respected one. Stuart Evey, the Getty Oil executive, made the mix of oil and television palatable to his company, whose ten-million-dollar initial investment made ESPN possible. Ironically, in recent years Evey could not get ESPN officials to return his phone calls, and he accuses Bornstein of trying to wipe his name from ESPN history. Evey has never been mentioned in the company's anniversary guides or television specials.

Few television success stories are as inspiring as ESPN's. In the end, its shrewd, joyous, and sometimes tormented history is the story of the transformation of a tiny cable network into a major player in American sports journalism.

And it's the story of memos like this one from executive Norby Williamson, which was distributed throughout ESPN. Williamson thought employees were spending too much time watching popular television shows instead of working. In Bristol, especially for the lowly production assistant, practically an indentured servant who gets little pay and even less sleep, life can resemble that of a slave in the bowels of a Roman warship. Stop rowing that oar and you risk feeling a whip across your back. It is politely called "the ESPN culture."

Williamson wrote: "Please inform the assignment desk that we should not be putting entertainment shows [such as 'Ally McBeal'] . . . [on the television monitors] so that they can be viewed throughout the building. The last time I looked, we were a sports organization that should have its CP's, producers, Pa's and on-air people concentrating on looking at highlights, reading the wires, and watching games. I hope I don't have to waste your time with another ridiculous and time-wasting issue."

Ironically, ESPN would use a clip from "Ally McBeal" in a story in 1998 on the Boston Red Sox. Maybe Williamson should rethink his directive.

Prologue

The control room is not much bigger than a large walk-in closet, and it's stuffed with people and equipment. The television monitors show the glowing face of anchor Lee Leonard in the studio, flipping through last-minute notes and chatting with the director. A timekeeper shouts the minutes remaining until ESPN goes on the air for the first time, and with each passing second, the tension in the room increases. Ten minutes to go, and a janitor, oblivious to one of the most important moments in television history about to unfold, scrubs some dirty glass doors. He is told to leave but finishes his job anyway. Five minutes to go, the control room receives word the live feeds are fine. Four minutes. Tempers become short and nausea attacks those in the room. There is a controlled chaos as bodies and equipment increasingly shuffle around the tiny studio. At three minutes, the remote truck and the tape room check in. The satellite is transmitting. Everything is go. Conversations shorten to only necessary communications, with answers condensed to "yes" or "no." The time for chitchat ends.

No one speaks until the clock hits 6:58 P.M.

"Two minutes to launch."

Producer/director Bill Creasy orders everyone not involved with the show to leave the control room. Movement toward the exit is minimal because no one wants to miss history. Producer/director Bob Pronovost is actually directing the first "SportsCenter" show. Back then, in the budget-tightened, short-staffed world of ESPN, everyone had two titles and baggy eyes from working fifteen- to eighteen-hour days. Pronovost checks, then rechecks, then checks again the settings on the video machines, the audio levels, the cameras. He has done this fifty times already. It is nervous energy. It has to go somewhere.

Pronovost takes over the annoying time checks. For several seconds, he is fixated on a large clock on the wall. Time seems to move slowly. Pronovost knew he did the right thing by leaving the Hartford CBS affiliate where he was a respected director in a great job at a popular station. He quit Hartford and joined ESPN the same day—sans a pay raise—full of confidence and vigor. When he arrived four hours ago, he noted the offices, more like closets masquerading as trailers, the lack of equipment, and the small staff. He laughed when asked to find plastic bags and to help with the cleanup of the preshow party and winced when people had to use the portable, outdoor, smelly bathrooms because there was no indoor plumbing. When toilet paper ran out, people hopped into their cars, crossed their legs, and raced to use the bathroom at the bowling alley up the street.

His friends wondered aloud if he was crazy to leave Hartford, and as the clock seemed to freeze in place, for a second, Pronovost wondered, too.

When Pronovost snapped out of it, time was running normally again, so he shoots a quick compliment to Leonard through the intercom, telling him he looks good even though Leonard already knows this. He is always the coolest customer in the building. Pronovost reminds the control room there is one minute until air, and he notices someone brushing sawdust off his jacket. The studio is literally being built around them, even now. Other producers swear they hear hammers in the background. Another audio check is fine. Another satellite check is good. *Thirty seconds.* Pronovost barks to stand by on the theme music, then to tighten camera one on Leonard, still as calm as a peaceful lake. There is nothing but static in one communications system, but Pronovost, now in a groove, tells Leonard the assistant director has it under control. The assistant director will be the one—not Pronovost—giving Leonard his cues. The anchor nods. *Twenty seconds until air.* No bodies move in the control room. Everyone fixates on Leonard. To them, he is the most important man in the world. Ten seconds. Get ready to roll theme. Camera one, stand by. Lee, *five seconds.* A nod from Leonard. Still cool. He relishes the idea of introducing a new network to the country. *Three, two, one . . .*

Pronovost: "Take one and roll theme. Cue Lee."

Leonard first sat on a medium-sized stage and introduced the country to ESPN, then joined the raspy-throated George Grande, wearing a garish tie with a big knot, on the gray and orange set, which matched their dreadful red and orange jackets, the colors of Getty Oil, the financial backer. The "SportsCenter" logo is on a wall over their heads and the ESPN logo—the old school one with the thick orange circle around it—is also in view. The set was the vision of television and theater designer Kathleen Ankers, who developed sets for *Roots II,* the *Today Show* and the Bristol Old Vic theater company of London. Just getting it into the building was a chore. The delivery door in the back of the main building had been accidentally sealed by a cinder block wall, so a small group of men carried the hulking set down winding hallways and narrow corridors.

At the time, Ankers's set was considered dazzling. By today's standards, it is awkward, lacking in personality and style. Leonard sinks in the middle of it, still calm, waiting for the theme music to end. He had made a note to himself to smile and look enthusiastic. Leonard had earlier welcomed viewers to the network, now he was welcoming them to the heart of ESPN, where they would get scores and watch sports, some very strange sports. His line is not read from a teleprompter because there are none; rather, it comes from his heart, and goes down in history.

"If you're a fan, *if* you're a fan, what you'll see in the next minutes, hours, and days to follow may convince you, you've gone to sports heaven."

Leonard went on with the broadcast, a never-wavering smile creasing his handsome face. Not breaking a sweat, Bill Rasmussen was twenty feet away in the control room, not believing that this moment had finally arrived. His dream had come true, causing him to actually pinch himself. He had started the first all-sports network. It was there, on the air, despite dozens, no hundreds, of naysayers telling him he would have an easier time starting a colony on Mars than an all-sports cable channel. Who the hell would want to watch sports all day? What would you put on? Twenty-four hours of kayaking and rodeos? Are you kidding? He pinched himself again. Was it a dream? Was this real? Were Leonard and Grande actually on that screen, talking sports?

Just reaching this startling intersection was hard to believe. Rasmussen recalled when he was ten years old, growing up in Columbus Manor, Illinois, in a house his father, William, built himself. He played baseball because all the other kids did—and it was cheap. The Depression gripped the country, so Rasmussen didn't play with fancy bats or expensive gloves. Money was so tight that families were lucky they had enough to eat.

It was a good day when Rasmussen played with a baseball that had only a few scuff marks on it. Most of the time, the seams were falling off. If it was too worn, William tied the loose ends together with black electrical tape. If his baseball bat broke, Rasmussen ran to his father, worried he would never be able to play again. William always calmed him down, promising that anything could be fixed, and then he'd stick a tiny screw in the bat and wrap tape around it. "I don't want you to be ashamed,"

William would say. "You'll learn that there are times you have to make do." William Rasmussen was like that. It was a different time. Even in the bitter, harsh days of the Depression, the Rasmussens never lost hope. It is a characteristic Bill would retain for most of his life, even when times got hard.

Nothing diluted Rasmussen's love for baseball. In high school, Rasmussen listened to the Chicago Cubs on the radio at night. After a couple of innings, he'd reach under his bed for his cracked board game with the little spinner, then play his own game, with make-believe rosters and batting averages. He could play nine innings in ten minutes—that's how quickly his mind worked. His father would peek into his room and watch—imaginary runners, Rasmussen doing his own play-by-play, the Cubs game blaring on the radio. William simply shook his head.

Eventually, Rasmussen played more real baseball and less make-believe ball. Rasmussen always thought of himself as an athlete. He was never cocky about it, but as he entered his teen years, at Gage Park High School in Chicago (two buses and one streetcar from home), he noticed that his muscles were bigger and his legs faster than kids even a few years older. He switched from playing outfield on his high school baseball team to third base, because a coach noticed his talent for catching ground balls. In one game, on a hot weekend in July, Rasmussen fielded a ground ball that moved toward his face at what seemed like one hundred miles per hour. He caught it in midair, making it look too easy.

He went from a scrawny 140-pound kid to a solid 160-pounder, with nimble glove skills who could outrun almost anyone on the field. A scout saw him playing on the Southside of Chicago in the summer of 1950, admiring the way he cleanly fielded every ball without making an error. The scout never doubted that with a little coaching, Rasmussen could become a pro. So the kid who used to play his own fantasy baseball games was a step closer to living out those dreams. The Detroit Tigers invited him to their Class D farm club team, and though he never signed with the club, Rasmussen still thanked his dad. Those taped-up baseball bats had gotten Rasmussen far.

Rasmussen's bid to play professional baseball was aborted by the Korean War. He watched as friends, one by one, were drafted into military service. Always patriotic, he thought earnestly about volunteering, but as more of his friends came back without an arm or leg, or not at all, fighting became less attractive to him. He knew his life would come down to a critical choice: continue to play baseball and be drafted or go to college and receive an exemption from combat.

The idea of getting a college degree had long been buzzing around Rasmussen's head, put there by his father. By his senior year, Rasmussen had shown an aptitude in math and science, which attracted a partial academic scholarship offer from the University of Illinois. His errorless senior season at shortstop had also caught the eye of baseball coaches from a small school in Minnesota. Then his guidance counselor handed him a scholarship application to DePauw University in Indiana. Rasmussen had performed the balancing act of playing baseball and keeping up with his studies well, and teachers liked his enthusiasm. He was in the top ten percent of his graduating class, qualifying him for the scholarship to DePauw.

Choosing DePauw set in motion a series of events that would change Rasmussen's life and lead him to this improbable moment in the control room. There, Rasmussen's body had almost gone limp before he was pulled from his daydreams by a popping sound and then a touch on the elbow. It was his 23-year-old son, Scott, who had just opened a bottle of champagne. Scott, smiling, with tears in his eyes, congratulated his dad. "We did it," Scott said. Little Bill, as some called him, endured the jokes and insults along with his father, so Scott's joy was just as deep.

Pronovost stared at them across the room, happy for the two men, his glance lasting just a second. He didn't want ESPN to come crashing down because of his inattention. He monitored Leonard, who was introducing the network to barely two million homes, and then Pronovost took a phone call from RCA, who said the video and audio were transmitting perfectly over the satellite, which was spinning 22,300 miles above the equator. Pronovost cheated and took another look at the Rasmussens—they were hugging each other.

It was September 7, 1979, a Friday like none other in Bill Rasmussen's life. This day was the culmination of a longtime love affair with sports, and as the clock reached forty-five seconds past the hour, he also weeped. ESPN was his newborn baby.

And it worked.

But for how long? The network's finances were like a patchwork quilt, made up of fickle financial backers and advertisers, and all it took was one slipped stitch and ESPN would unravel. There was another problem, just as immediate. For months, Rasmussen had battled Chet Simmons, the former NBC programming guru, considered one of the best talents in sports television history, and Stuart Evey, the Getty oil executive who controlled the purse strings and regularly let everyone know it. When Simmons came on board, he viewed Rasmussen and his son as amateurs. Rasmussen considered Simmons a product of an arrogant network system. Rasmussen knew that Simmons was gunning for him and soon a fierce power struggle would erupt, pitting Simmons and Evey against his son and him. That was a fight Rasmussen knew he would lose. His stomach tightened again, not from the nervousness of the launch but from the cruel knowledge that his days at the network were numbered, perhaps in single digits.

Rasmussen fixed his gaze on Leonard again, occasionally his thoughts interrupted by someone in the control room coming over to congratulate him. He shook every hand and smiled, but his mind was a thousand miles away.

PART 1

1

One Million Lightbulbs

The Korean War was on the front pages, and communism was threatening to consume the globe, but what really concerned Bill Rasmussen was improving his backhand play at third base. America's attention had focused on the other side of the world as the conflict in Asia continued to grow. Rasmussen became increasingly torn from watching friends fighting a war while he was playing baseball games. A former teammate, the first baseman at Gage Park High School, had joined the Army National Guard in the spring. By the fall, he had been to Korea, was shot in the chest, and hospitalized at a veterans hospital.

Rasmussen looked for a compromise, one that would allow him to serve his country but at the same time not get killed. His solution was to join the Air Force Reserve Officers Training Corps in his second year at DePauw. The Air Force was where he could best use his skill with numbers. And the Air Force liked the idea of an officer who might someday play professional baseball. Rasmussen enjoyed the discipline the military introduced to his life. Around campus, he wore his Air Force blues with pride, and it wasn't uncommon for his classmates to stop him and thank him for his service.

It was baseball, not war, that consumed Rasmussen. At DePauw he played third base and catcher. By his senior year, he had earned a reputation as one of the best defensive players on the team. Rasmussen didn't develop his skills by accident. In his few hours of spare time, he asked friends and teammates to smack ground balls his way, even if it was midnight. There were days he spent hours in the batting cage, and friends used to kid him about how they saw his baseball glove as much as they saw him.

Rasmussen overlooked his record in college as the only player to ever steal home three times, focusing instead on honing his skills, such as improving the speed of his flip to second base for the double play. He still had the fastest hands on the team, but Rasmussen never stopped working to perfect his game.

In June of 1954, Rasmussen graduated from DePauw University, culminating a busy four years. That fall, toward the end of the season, Rasmussen approached his mailbox every day with trepidation. The Air Force had told the cadets to expect a letter in the mail, relaying where they would be stationed. Rasmussen didn't fear being shipped immediately to the front lines—few ROTC graduates faced that. He was terrified, however, of being stationed in a remote part of the world where he couldn't listen to baseball games on the radio or find a suitable field to take some swings.

When the letter came, he wasn't disappointed. Rasmussen was to report to Eglin Air Force Base in Florida on November 15, 1955.

• • •

Eglin was playing a key part in the war effort, with more than four dozen different training divisions preparing pilots for everything from bomber missions to air combat. At any given time, thousands of military personnel were on the base. Rasmussen eventually adjusted to the flow of Eglin, how the pace slowed to a crawl in the afternoon during the blistering summer months and how vital sports was to the collective psyche of the base.

Six months into his stay, Rasmussen had become a sort of cult legend. He was recruited immediately to join Eglin's baseball team by an officer who knew of his athletic background. The team was a good one, composed mostly of former high school and college players from around the country. Just as he had in the past, he impressed his teammates with his solid glove skills and speed. Soon, he was a star on the squad and one of the best players in the Air Force baseball league. The men who watched his games admired how Rasmussen went after a hard-hit ball fearlessly. The women enjoyed his tall, vigorous good looks. Standing nearly six feet with a lean frame, expansive smile, and wavy dark hair, Rasmussen distinguished himself from the other grunts.

Rasmussen delicately balanced the rigid duties of the Air Force, the demands of baseball play and his marriage the past June 25, 1955. Rasmussen had married Lois Ann McDonnell, who everyone called Mickey and who was as patient as she was attractive. The two had met when he was a junior and she a freshman at DePauw—he had waited tables at her sorority house. When Rasmussen had wanted to hurry home from their honeymoon in time for the annual all-star game in July, she understood. Part of her attraction to her husband was his constant energy, which she was fond of saying could power a city. If Rasmussen wasn't doing three things at once, he was bored and miserable. Being around a man with that kind of passion for life was invigorating for Mickey, if at times frustrating.

Rasmussen needed that vitality. He spent most of his days—when not playing baseball or spending time with Mickey—as a contract officer for the armament center. For the better part of two years, Rasmussen procured instruments from the private sector for fighter planes such as the F-89 Scorpion and F-86 Sabre. He and an engineer oversaw military contracts, ensuring the right parts were delivered to the right place.

Between the sometimes painstaking days of sifting through countless pages of documents and the always-cloying military bureaucracy, Rasmussen played baseball. On game days, he was excused from duty at 11 A.M. to go home and rest for that night's game. (Most games were played in the evening to avoid the intense afternoon heat.) For road games, Rasmussen was assigned to temporary duty (TDY). Translation: nap time. While officers marched in parades or drilled in the hot sun, Rasmussen and the other athletes slept in their barracks. Sometimes he felt extremely guilty.

He made up for the slow days by approaching the baseball games with a fierce intensity. They were big events, drawing crowds of 10,000 soldiers and family members, mainly because of the lack of many other activities. He wondered about the stupefying process of people watching sports on any level as long as the games were competitive and fun.

With just as strong a following, the football team was led by strong-armed quarterback Zeke Bratkowski, who later played for the Green Bay Packers. The huge crowds at the games included Rasmussen.

Rasmussen realized he was not a career officer. Air Force life had its rewards, but not the kind Rasmussen was looking for. He received his honorable discharge from the Air Force late in 1956. He left Eglin with his wife, a new baby boy named Scott, and a job tip from Mickey's parents that took the family to Bloomfield, New Jersey. Of course Rasmussen did not forget his glove.

Before leaving Eglin, Rasmussen had made a startling discovery: Not all the parts he procured for the Air Force were used for fighter planes. Instead, some were used to help build the Mercury spaceship. In May of 1961, massive booster rockets from an enhanced Redstone ballistic missile whizzed Alan Shepard past the stars into space. Rasmussen, the officer and a gentle-third baseman, had played a small part in history.

• • •

As he approached his thirtieth birthday, Rasmussen wondered where his life was headed. He rarely thought of his future beyond the weekend's pickup baseball game, but occasionally he considered his prospects for financial security. For now, money wasn't a problem. Working as an advertising assistant in the massive lamp division of Westinghouse in Bloomfield put food on the table. His Air Force contacts constantly opened doors, giving him access to almost any entry-level job he desired. He had chosen Westinghouse because it was near Mickey's parents and easily accessible to the New York area, with its towering buildings, bustling streets, and rich sports culture. Rasmussen had heard about the excellent business program at Rutgers. While continuing to work at Westinghouse, he began attending school at night, and, whenever possible, sneaking off to a batting cage or even playing in a baseball league.

The advertising department of the lamp division was among the busiest in the company. Westinghouse believed that putting money into newspaper, radio, and television advertising was as important as the bulbs themselves. Rasmussen was inundated with product catalogs and network advertising schedules. He liked working with some of the networks, which were at times arrogant, even ruthless, but at least were up-front about their power. Color sets were still years away, but almost every home, rich and poor, had a trusty black and white. Westinghouse considered television the best way of advertising its lightbulbs, so a large chunk of its $3.2 million advertising budget went to promote their product on the little picture box.

Rasmussen did, however, despise the corporate atmosphere at Westinghouse. He became bored and lost patience, despite having more work to do than ever before. "What I really hated was the sense that the corporation knows all and sees all, and they decide if you've done something [to] get an extra chair in your office," Rasmussen calls. "Or you can have a bigger desk in your office or you can have carpet. That's so incidental. The fancy trappings aren't what makes a company, and to see people so engaged in things like, 'If you get to level-three accountant, you get to move to an office down the hall closer to the water cooler.' I hated that."

In May of 1959, tired of the hollow boasts and posturing of his coworkers at Westinghouse, Rasmussen started looking for an exit. He stayed up late, unable to sleep, thinking of ways to change his life, planning the next stage, which he had rarely done before. Rasmussen spoke to Mickey incessantly about a game plan, as though she was his coach and he was still a star third baseman back at Gage Park High School. He wanted something different. He needed something different.

The idea that would change everything did not come as a dazzling bolt in the middle of the night or at some inspirational moment while sitting in his office. Instead, Rasmussen played with his thought for weeks, mulling it over until it became tangible.

Twice a year, Westinghouse held national meetings in New Jersey, with representatives attending from twenty-nine different districts all over the country. Miss that meeting, and one could easily find himself without a job.

At these meetings, Westinghouse executives debated which lightbulbs the company would sell and push for the upcoming season. Dressed in drab suits and ties, the executives discussed lamps the way the Kennedy administration planned naval blockades. Large lamps, small lamps, auto lamps, house lamps, boat lamps, and photo lamps—if it could light up, Westinghouse had it, and debates raged for days. Only after several hundred cups of coffee and many sleepless nights did senior company executives finally approve the lamps they favored and veto the ones in disfavor. By the end of the meetings, Westinghouse compiled consumer catalogs with photos of all the lamps approved, then shipped the catalogs to the regional sales offices.

In 1959 a strike crippled the department that packed and shipped Westinghouse manuals and products. As a result, packing and shipping was relegated to two 60-year-old men who worked part-time and moved with no particular urgency. The thick manuals sat in storage, gathering dust, for months.

After enduring several rounds of the lightbulb World Series, Rasmussen knew there had to be a better way. He took his wife to a diner in Newark and asked her a rhetorical question while chomping on a hamburger. What if Westinghouse wasn't the only company with an archaic or undermanned shipping division? A separate, private company could make millions by contracting for a corporation's heavy lifting. It was a radical idea, one never before tried. Mickey knew as they left the diner that her opinion was irrelevant. Once something rattled noisily in her husband's head, nothing could stop him from seeing it through.

As the decade of wild ideas approached, Rasmussen went to his friend George Waters, the assistant advertising manager, who was always ready to earn extra money. Waters was on the receiving end of the complaints about the tortoiselike shipping department and therefore easily grasped the possibilities of Rasmussen's idea. "That can work," Waters said, "but we'll need one more person."

Jim Millerick, a jewelry salesman and close friend of Waters, got the next phone call. He was just as intrigued. Discussions led to a trip to the bank, where each man withdrew $140 from his checking account to start the business. They then quit their respective jobs to focus on the new venture. The shipping company, the result of thinking on the fly, was called Ad Aid, Incorporated.

• • •

Rasmussen, Waters, and Millerick were touring the eight-hundred-square-foot abandoned storefront shop they had just rented in East Orange. It wasn't a pretty sight, and as they walked across the hard wooden floors, they began to realize just how difficult a job lay ahead. The walls needed painting, the doors were falling off, and there were no phones. "Look at the bright side," Rasmussen said to his partners. "Things are a mess, but it's our mess."

They went to a lumber yard, purchased pieces of plywood, built partitions in the office and then shelves. After sweeping away the dust, Rasmussen visited Westinghouse, whose next round of sales meetings was only a few weeks away. With the approval of his partners, he offered Westinghouse a seemingly absurd deal: Any order, he told them, no matter how big or small, would be shipped from the Ad Aid warehouse within twenty-four hours. An order into Ad Aid on Monday was guaranteed to go out by Tuesday. The Westinghouse managers shook their heads in disbelief and uttered a refrain Rasmussen would hear a lot in the coming years—"There is no way that can be done."

Rasmussen knew how to charm, especially Westinghouse executives. He detailed exactly how he would fulfill his promise. He also stroked their bloated egos by hinting at how good they'd look if the idea worked. They also warmed to Rasmussen's motto: "Right now" as in "We'll get it done right now."

Westinghouse wasn't convinced, but the company figured it had nothing to lose and gave Ad Aid a small order, as a test, after one of its raucous sales meetings. All Ad Aid had to do was pack several hundred light-bulbs, then ship them to local Westinghouse divisions around the country. It was easy enough, but the three men knew there was no margin for error. If the company could not handle a small shipment like this, then larger ones would be impossible. Rasmussen and his partners stayed up all night to meet their guarantee, with Rasmussen calling Mickey on the phone to check in on her, Scott, and their new addition to the family, Glenn.

The lightbulbs went out the next day, just as Ad Aid had promised. Westinghouse was impressed, and they upped the ante with their next frantic order. Rasmussen was asked a simple question: Can you ship one million lightbulbs within twenty hours?

For a brief moment, the life drained out of Rasmussen. But he put up a brave front. "You know my motto," he said. "Right now. One million bulbs or one bulb. We'll get it done."

An agreement was reached. Ad Aid would pack and ship one million lightbulbs to Westinghouse's sales offices across the country.

This time Ad Aid needed help, so Rasmussen and his partners hired one hundred women, mostly housewives, to assist with the packing. They were paid $1.25 an hour, but Ad Aid charged Westinghouse triple, $3.75 per hour. The bulbs arrived from Westinghouse on an overflowing railroad car, and when it slowly pulled in to a docking bay behind the Ad Aid warehouse, the women descended upon it like locusts. They packed the boxes, typed the labels, and stuck them on by machine. At times, their hands were a blur of movement.

After staying up all night, the executives of Ad Aid, a company that was never supposed to work, had boxed, shipped, and mailed more than one million lightbulbs, with help from some of the Newark area's finest homemakers. As Rasmussen watched a forklift load the massive payload onto trucks headed for the airport, Waters and Millerick went over the final totals. Of particular interest were how many lightbulbs had been cracked. Westinghouse allowed only one percent breakage; any more than that, and Ad Aid could lose the lightbulb giant's business.

Rasmussen got the good news from his partners. Just one-half of one percent of one million lightbulbs met their deaths.

Packing and delivering one million lightbulbs, treating each one like a bird with a broken wing, was the best advertising Ad Aid could get. The lack of sleep, especially for Rasmussen, who had returned from his classes at Rutgers at 11:30 at night and was back at Ad Aid by five the next morning, was worth it. Word spread quickly. Bell Telephone called. They wanted help with a massive mailing campaign on telephone prefix changes. The first order was for five thousand, which Ad Aid's ladies' brigade shipped without breaking a sweat. Once the telephone company saw that Ad Aid lived up to its word, as Westinghouse had, Bell placed an order for another five thousand two weeks later. In a matter of months, Ad Aid was shipping 100,000 mailings. The women were earning their minimum wage and the men of Ad Aid fattened their wallets.

Calls poured in from General Electric, General Foods, Ballantine Beer, and S&H Green Stamps. Whenever an executive rang, they started the conversation with "Are you the 'Right now' guys?" Trailers rolled into the loading area day and night.

Ad Aid was making hundreds of thousands of dollars—and growing. A spacious 32,400 feet was added to the company by February of 1960. Soon Ad Aid left its grimy East Orange surroundings, moving to a 30,000-square-foot facility in Newark.

"We were bold, we had guts, and we just made outrageous statements to people," Rasmussen recalled forty years later. "If you wanted a job done, we'd say, sure, we'll do it, even if it was ten o'clock at night. We'd just stay up all night. We hired housewives who could work in the afternoon, in the morning, or on weekends. We had a list of about 130 housewives, and whenever we'd get a job, we would ask our secretary to start calling. We'd tell her we needed fourteen people. They would come in, we'd off-load the truck, and they'd get to work. I think that whole experience was a key one in my life, because it proved that with an idea, you can make it work yourself without the help of some huge corporation."

By now, Rasmussen's confidence was spilling over. He believed there was nothing he could not do.

• • •

In a way, his attitude reflected that of the country's, which was both colorful and smug. A cultural explosion was shaping the way people thought and lived, and Rasmussen sampled as much of the changing times as he could. He went to the movie house with Mickey to watch Audrey Hepburn in *Breakfast at Tiffany's*, smirked at a dance craze called the twist, and read with fascination of the bungled invasion of Cuba.

Sports were changing as quickly as the hemline on women's dresses. The athletes were becoming stronger, more influential, and more bold. They hit the baseball four hundred feet, used their growing stature to make political statements, and played games against our enemy, the Russians. Now fans were not just limited to following their teams by crowding around a radio or picking up the newspaper. The power of television was drastically increasing, and as sports grew, so did the demand of fans to watch as much as possible.

The days of radio leading people through a tragedy or a rousing Notre

Dame football game were over. Television, with its ability to describe a story without words, was more powerful than a faceless voice. Rasmussen watched these flickering images as though the television was reaching only him.

The early 1960s were an exciting time in sports because of television and the abundance of moving stories and images. Elgin Baylor scored seventy-one points against the Knicks in a single game, so impressing the crowd at Madison Square Garden that even Knicks fans applauded. The U.S. hockey team, after upsetting the Russians in an early round, later routed Czechoslovakia by scoring six unanswered goals to win the gold medal. The Chicago Blackhawks won their first Stanley Cup in twenty-three years.

Roger Maris and Mickey Mantle were engrossed in one of the most intense competitions in the history of sports, as the two Yankee teammates battled to break the home run record set by Babe Ruth. By October of 1961, Mantle and Maris were the talk of New York and the country, and though it was an electrifying time in sports, Rasmussen was becoming extremely bored.

Ad Aid was still growing, but instead of enjoying his success, Rasmussen grew restless. He plotted day and night for a way to redirect his career to sports. He started daydreaming again. He knew his window for playing pro baseball had slammed shut years ago, but he could always talk about that sport and others, maybe on the radio at first, then television later. Instead of running a business from an office, Rasmussen wanted to broadcast sports in front of a microphone.

Then one day he stopped fantasizing. He decided to do it. At the end of a busy day at the Ad Aid offices, Rasmussen pulled aside Waters and Millerick and told them he was leaving. Neither man was shocked. They knew Rasmussen would someday get back into sports because he talked about sports incessantly. The only question was when and in what capacity. All that remained to discuss was Rasmussen's compensation package. The three men were pulling in $200 a week each, not a bad penny for the time, and each owned thirty percent stock in the company; the other ten percent went to Rasmussen's father-in-law, who kept the books.

When they first incorporated the company, the partners had agreed that if one of them left, he would receive five months salary plus an agreed upon buyout amount. Rasmussen's last paycheck from Ad Aid totaled $52,000. The money allowed him to pursue his sports fantasies and change his life. He left Ad Aid on October 15, 1962, his thirtieth birthday.

Mickey supported his decision to leave, and when she asked her husband what was next, Rasmussen handed her a classified ad from *Broad-*

casting magazine, a trade publication about the industry. Rasmussen liked reading all the gossip in the broadcasting business, but within the last few months he found himself scouring the help wanted section.

One ad caught his attention. A daytime radio station, WTTT, was being launched in Amherst, Massachusetts, and it needed a combination salesman and sports director. It wasn't exactly a major media market, and the $150 weekly salary was less than he had made at Ad Aid, but this was his chance to get into the sports media business. Rasmussen, undaunted by his lack of broadcast experience, went into the interview full of confidence. "I can sell anything and I know I can do sports, and you're starting a new station, so why don't we all do it together?" His pitch was typical Rasmussen, direct and corny. Like many others, the station manager was impressed with his terminally enthusiastic disposition. He got the job.

• • •

By the summer of 1963, Rasmussen was bronzed from spending many of his weekends sitting in the sun while broadcasting high school games in Amherst. His press box was a card table and folding chair. On windy days, his old baseball glove kept his notes and pencils from blowing away. He took a few minutes before his first broadcast to unravel the mystery of a long, snakelike wire dangling from a pole. After a phone call to the telephone company, Rasmussen climbed the pole, grabbed the wire, stripped it with a pair of cutters, and plugged the wire into the back of an amplifier. That was broadcast central. Rasmussen was his own network, the audience, a grandmother who couldn't make it to the game, a father stuck in traffic, parents who simply wanted to hear their son's name on the radio.

Amherst was a million miles away from the Air Force and his bustling advertising agency, and there were nervous moments when Rasmussen missed the intensity of his past jobs, but those times were few. Broadcasting sports, even if it was high school games, made him happy. Mickey noticed the difference, often remarking on his smiling more, if that was possible.

When Rasmussen had first arrived at WTTT, almost no infrastructure was in place. No sales department or sports staff. Rasmussen didn't even have an office. He started as the station's salesman and sports director. For months, he was the station. Rasmussen broadcast his morning sports show beginning a few minutes before 8 A.M., reading stories almost exclusively about New England sports. Then after his report, Rasmussen hustled around Amherst, selling advertising for $5 a spot on the morning show and $8 for the evening show. He visited the car dealer, the shoe man, and the grocery store manager, and after speaking to a dozen businesses in just a few hours, he arrived back at the studio in time for the noon sports broadcast. Then it was back on the road, banging on doors for most of the afternoon before ending the day in the studio for an evening show.

As fall arrived, Rasmussen was no longer begging grocery store managers to open their wallets, and he had graduated from broadcasting high school baseball games where balls got lost in tobacco barns. Rasmussen had spent the last few weeks in intense negotiations with University of Massachusetts (UMass) athletic officials on behalf of WTTT. The station was desperate to broadcast UMass football games, hoping for a boost in ratings. Agreeing to the idea, the school signed up before the season opener against Maine. Rasmussen was soon a fixture around UMass football practice, grilling coaches and players for information and every piece of gossip. They rarely tired of seeing his beaming face.

As Rasmussen and Dick Page, the school's sports information director, were making the eight-hour drive to Maine for the September opener, Rasmussen went over the lineup in his head, how he wanted to start the show and introduce the complex offense to listeners. Rasmussen would provide the play-by-play, while Page, a patient, friendly sports fanatic, would present the color commentary. They mapped out every detail of the broadcast, with Rasmussen encouraging Page to talk as much as he liked. They both agreed to keep egos out of the mix.

There was one detail, however, that Rasmussen skipped: He had never broadcast a college football game.

UMass beat the Blackbears in a low-scoring game, 14–0. Rasmussen's inexperience never showed. UMass fans called the station to compliment the job the two men had done. Advertisers called, too. The station's ratings started climbing, mirroring the growing influence of the school's athletic program. UMass was not Harvard or Boston College, but it did have a fierce following in dozens of small towns throughout New England, especially in football.

Rasmussen, ever restless, mused over ways of capitalizing further on the soaring ratings of the UMass broadcasts. Football, he concluded, had tapped out. The Minutemen were never going to become Michigan.

The basketball program was another story. Johnny Orr, a brash, overly confident head coach, had been hired by the school several months earlier. Orr was one of the first coaches to bring a relentless, up-tempo game to New England, and Rasmussen was convinced that Orr would win and fill the stands.

This time Rasmussen struck on a new idea: He thought it would be possible to assemble a network that broadcast solely UMass football and basketball, even though Orr's boasts of turning UMass into a competitive Division I program were now only talk. Rasmussen drove to the station one night and rambled through a copy of the rate data service book, which had the address and phone number of every station in Massachusetts. The next day, Rasmussen met with the WTTT brass, explaining his plan to change the format of the station. Despite earning more cash from the increased football ratings, WTTT ended its broadcasting day in early evening because it still could not afford to stay on at night. Rasmussen suggested stringing together neighboring small-watt stations such as WTTT to form a UMass sports network. Quiet villages throughout Massachusetts, especially the western parts of the state, such as Northhampton, Greenfield, Springfield, and Whitensville, all had stations like WTTT. By linking together, these small-town stations would be collectively strengthened—and UMass would quickly, almost effortlessly, broaden its fan base.

Rasmussen approached the athletic department at UMass, where he was always received with a smile and cup of coffee. He was also trusted. The school appreciated his football broadcasts, and the basketball coaches, already in competition with their football counterparts, coveted their own piece of the airwaves. Coach Orr loved the idea, knowing any publicity, even from an unknown giddy radio broadcaster, would help his growing program.

Knowing UMass would sign on, Rasmussen focused on his sales pitch to the station manager. He first made a mental note to use the phrase "run and gun basketball" when pitching the idea. Then he would hit them with how it was a can't-miss proposal. He was selling again. Some managers remained unpersuaded. Others, however, wondered why no one had thought of it before. Four stations in western Massachusetts agreed to carry the games. That feat in itself was a victory.

Rasmussen had secured the cities, he had secured the stations, he even had secured the basketball coach. What he hadn't secured was WTTT. They refused to pay for his venture. They did offer the station as a base, but only if he raised the money for the broadcasts. Rasmussen hit the road again—this time selling advertising in Boston as well as the suburbs. Eventually, he earned the thousands of dollars he needed to start his own mininetwork. But not without more sleepless nights, more time spent away from his family. Rasmussen, as he did with Ad Aid, displayed a single-mindedness that sometimes consumed him. Rarely did he approach anything at half speed, and rarely was he wrong—and he wasn't on this occasion. The network launched in time to carry the first UMass basketball game. It was a hit. Fans adored Orr's style and Rasmussen's broadcasts. That didn't stop Rasmussen from working advertisers in Boston and now New York for more money. He knocked on the doors of S&H Green Stamps and Piel's Beer, his sunny disposition, charm, and Rutgers MBA proving an irresistable combination. Rigid, humorless men fell for the humble Rasmussen, who played the "aw-shucks" routine better than Gomer Pyle. So effective was Rasmussen's pitch that he was able to expand the network to ten stations. By December of 1964, Rasmussen was even considering adding hockey broadcasts.

He didn't know at the time, but his discussions with advertisers, contract talks with his own station, and negotiations with UMass for football and basketball broadcast rights proved critical to his future. The network eventually folded from a lack of advertising, but the experience gave Rasmussen the foundation he'd need to start the biggest project of his life.

• • •

On a lazy Saturday afternoon in May of 1965, Cassius Marcellus Clay, the heavyweight boxer who had America rhyming and opponents dropping, was training in Chicopee, Massachusetts, for his rematch with the bruising Sonny Liston. Clay had removed the veneer of invincibility from Liston after bashing him throughout their first fight, showing he was faster and stronger. By the time of the rematch a year later, the media was begrudgingly calling the captivating Clay by his new Muslim name, Muhammad Ali.

Rasmussen spent weeks trailing Ali, hoping to get a one-on-one interview. His radio network was struggling, but still on the air, with hockey added to its broadcast schedule. Rasmussen began calling those games when Eddie Shore, the hulking Boston defenseman who brought physical hockey to the United States before Bobby Orr was born, heard one of his football broadcasts. Shore was owner of the Springfield Indians, a minor league team on a par with perhaps the bottom teams in the National Hockey League (NHL). Shore ran the team the way he played hockey, with a tough determination, mandating that Rasmussen do the play-by-play his way. Rasmussen chafed at Shore's dictatorial style—it reminded him too much of corporate America—but he wanted to broadcast hockey to expand his talents.

These were quiet years for the underexposed sport, with only six NHL and American Hockey League teams and fewer than one hundred players. Hockey craved publicity, which suited announcers like Rasmussen just fine. They got to know half the players in the league intimately, and, unlike baseball, hockey players welcomed the press, shaking hands and remembering names. The public liked the sport, so Rasmussen had little trouble selling stations on carrying hockey on his network, the only resistance coming from stations close to Boston. They had the Bruins.

Shore and Rasmussen had a convenient relationship lasting five seasons. It warmed soon after Jack Kent Cooke, who would later own the Washington Redskins, took control of the team in 1967. By now, Shore enjoyed his time with Rasmussen, finding him to be a fetching goofball, and Rasmussen gleaned insights into the game from Shore, a Hall of Famer. Their discussions about hockey often lasted hours, leaving them usually the last ones to depart the practice ice.

Between hockey games, Rasmussen gained television experience, a medium that at first confounded him. Rasmussen now had to worry about details not associated with radio: his appearance, his apparel, and his applied makeup, which he could not believe men used. Still, awkward as television seemed to him, he adjusted, and an ABC affiliate in Springfield, Massachusetts, WHYN, hired him for $10 a show to do the weather. It was Rasmussen's first television job, and as if that wasn't difficult enough, he didn't know a low pressure system from a nor'easter. However, he bluffed his way through it convincingly, learning the art of the gliding hand over the electronic weather map. Viewers were sometimes puzzled by Rasmussen's weather forecast of a city where the Indians were playing, and then the score. ("Outside the Civic Center, where the Indians beat the Clippers 4–1, it's thirty-five degrees and clear.")

Viewers were affected in the same way listeners were on the radio network. Rasmussen was hokey, at times silly, and by today's standards, his weather reports would make Al Roker cringe. But Rasmussen showed just enough talent to convince the competing station across the street that he could carry his own sports segment.

When Rollie Jacobs, the fiamboyant sportscaster from NBC affiliate WWLP, accepted a job offer from a Raleigh, North Carolina, station to become its general manager, a move that nearly doubled his salary, the first person Jacobs recommended to his old station was Rasmussen. "He may seem kind of strange," Jacobs told the station, "but there is no one who knows sports like he does."

The station listened to Jacobs, hiring Rasmussen to do two sports broadcasts, at six and eleven in the evening. Rasmussen's life had never been busier, balancing broadcasts for the station and Springfield play-by-play. But he didn't mind, he was back in his element, immersed in sports, his boredom eliminated. His new job gave him access to some of the top athletes in sports. With unchecked glee, Rasmussen talked football with Boston Patriot Nick Buoniconti, basketball with Celtics legends Bob Cousy and Sam Jones, and baseball with Carl Yastrzemski, who warmed to Rasmussen almost immediately.

And of course there was the musical Ali. Rasmussen went to each of his training sessions in Chicopee, watching his speedy hands and quick feet move in an orchestrated blur. When asked why he was a supernova-like celebrity while other boxers were mere media mortals, Ali was fond of saying that he could throw the jive better than other fighters. Ali fascinated Rasmussen because of what he represented. He was the black man's champion, and as the turbulent 1960s came to an end, Rasmussen realized he had met few black athletes, or pontificated much on the radio or television about sports and race.

Before a press luncheon at the Shine Inn, east of Springfield, Ali looked in the crowd of reporters and saw Rasmussen, watching him closely. "You're always smiling," Ali blurted out. Rasmussen, surprised that Ali had noticed him, cheerfully responded, "That's because you're always rhyming." Ali smiled, walked toward Rasmussen, put his arm around him, and then spent more than a half hour, with no microphones or cameras in sight, chatting with the astonished reporter. They circled the training complex and talked boxing, the state of black America, and press conferences. Asked if he really wanted to do those flamboyant interviews, reciting poetry, Ali replied "It's about having fun."

For the next ten years, Rasmussen bounced around the Massachusetts sports world, bobbing from one event to the next. There was the Indians game in Rochester, the UMass football game in upstate New York, followed the next morning by the two-hundred-mile drive in the middle of the night to his job as a physical education teacher at Westfield State College, then the rush home to say hello to the family, which now included a daughter, Lynn, and finally the trip to the station for the evening broadcasts.

Years later, Rasmussen remembered the toll that long hours and traveling took on his family, especially Mickey. "There again you have to think about the people who got married in the forties and fifties," he said. "Then, women were supportive of the husband, and taking care of the kids. It was pretty much whatever I was going to do was fine, but there is no question the traveling still bothered her."

"When I started working in television at night," Rasmussen added, "the kids would eat dinner and my daughter would be confused about how her daddy could be in two places, since I would eat dinner with them, then go do a show. When you are a three-year-old, it's kind of hard to figure out how if daddy was just here, how could he be there on the TV?"

2

ESP-TV

While Rasmussen was learning about color television and the wonder of videotape at WWLP-TV, 3,000 miles away, Stuart Evey, one of the most trusted men in the powerful Getty oil family, received a disturbing phone call at his Los Angeles home in the middle of the night. Years later, Evey would become a pivotal figure in the success of ESPN, but now his focus was on the alarming phone call. It was from Jackie, the wife of George Getty, the man who could never satisfy his billionaire father, J. Paul. Her voice trembled, scaring the usually unflappable Evey.

"Stu, you've got to come over to the house," she said. "George is hurting himself."

Evey bounced out of bed, dressed, and made the half-hour drive to the Gettys', not knowing what to expect. When he got there, George was barricaded in the upstairs bathroom, and Evey was told he had fired a shotgun in the air.

Evey broke the door down, battering it with his large shoulders, and what he saw stunned him. Getty, in nothing but his underwear, was bleeding profusely from his stomach, the result of a self-inflicted wound with a barbecue fork. Evey regained his composure and called the family doctor instead of an ambulance, a move that would ensure secrecy, something the family cherished as much as the crude oil that made them rich. Instead of going to the UCLA Medical Center across the street, Evey was told to drive him to a hospital more than thirty minutes away and register Getty under an alias.

Evey did so against his better judgment. He knew though that this is what J. Paul would have wanted. Any other way and the press would be crawling all over the family. The longer drive, however, diminished George's chances for a complete recovery, and he slipped into a coma. Evey called J. Paul, who was at a dinner reception in London. "Oh, no," said Getty.

The next afternoon, George died, the result of a deadly mixture of alcohol, barbiturates, and blood loss from his stomach wound. This did not surprise Evey. He had become almost numb to the Getty quirks, and later, the family tragedies. When a Getty got caught with drugs, or died, or was kidnapped, Evey was always one of the first called. The Gettys trusted Evey because he handled their affairs with precision and, most important, discretion. He moved up the Getty chain of command quickly and by the early 1970s, Evey was the executive assistant to George, who trusted him with his one-hundred-million-dollar checking account.

As much time as he spent around the family, Evey still never quite understood them; then again, no one did. At one time, J. Paul Getty was the richest man in the world, a status he relished. He loved oil and money at the expense of intimacy and family. Being his son was more like being a business partner than a loved one. J. Paul criticized George if a Getty-owned hotel was missing a few towels or an oil venture didn't produce as expected. George could not handle the pressure, and his death was ruled a probable suicide by doctors.

Another son, Timothy, died from a brain tumor at twelve years old. Ronald Getty was disinherited at a young age, payback after J. Paul's bitter divorce from Ronald's mother. Two sons were left to share the bulk of Getty's estate, worth billions: his fourth son, Gordon, a brilliant musician, and the younger brother, J. Paul, Jr., who spent most of his time in Britain.

Evey earned a reputation as a hard-nosed negotiator who cared deeply about the company. Most important, Evey was a sounding board for George. The two would sit atop the towering Getty offices in Los Angeles and George would complain about life under J. Paul and how impossible he was to please. George showed Evey a letter his father wrote to him. It began, "Dear Mr. Getty . . ."

The family called on Evey again after George's death. In December of 1973, a man was found wandering in the rain near a town in southern Italy. He was covered with bruises, and his right ear had been sliced off with a razor blade. Police identified him as J. Paul Getty III, the 18-year-old grandson of J. Paul. Five months earlier, the local mafia had kidnapped Paul and demanded a three-million-dollar ransom. Initially, the Getty family didn't take the kidnapping threat seriously. Nicknamed "the golden hippie" by the press, Paul's life consisted of orgies and drugs—not organized crime.

It wasn't until an Italian newspaper received a bloody ear in the mail that the Gettys believed the threat. Negotiations with the kidnappers ensued. Evey was by the family's side again, giving advice. In the end, J. Paul reluctantly agreed to provide the ransom money. Paul was released after months of torture, which included being blindfolded and beaten with chains.

By April 1974, Evey, called Stu by most Getty executives, was vice president of the company's diversified operations, overseeing all of their nonoil investments. He was given broad latitude by the Getty's powerful board of directors because he produced results—and they liked his hard-line negotiating tactics with competitors.

Evey could have continued his course of taking relatively few chances with cash-rich Getty, investing the company's money in insurance or hotels. But sitting in the Getty offices in Los Angeles, dressed in his designer sports jacket, Evey poured a shot of bourbon into his morning coffee, something he did almost every day and before a deal. This time he sipped his high-octane brew alone, hatching ways of making money for the company and simultaneously protecting the Getty name from the sad and tragic headlines.

• • •

Back in Massachusetts, far from Evey and the Getty troubles, two men met in the bathroom, which was an appropriate beginning to their relationship.

At 32, Howard Baldwin was the youngest owner in the American Hockey League, and along with the energy of youth came sporadic bouts of arrogance. Baldwin was an athletic man with a thick neck and severe countenance, and his team, the New England Whalers, were in the playoffs. At first, Baldwin had little regard for the importance of carrying the Whalers postseason games on the radio. His opinion changed when other owners convinced him of the vital link between radio broadcasts and ticket sales.

Baldwin knew of Rasmussen and scheduled a meeting for the two at the Eastern States Coliseum in West Springfield. Baldwin was wary of Rasmussen at first. He viewed entrepreneurs as trouble, and Rasmussen screamed the type, the kind of person who flouted the corporate structure coveted by Baldwin. They met at the coliseum to talk business in the bathroom, because the press room was stuffed with bodies. Baldwin was to the point and did not hide his position of strength.

"If you broadcast my games, you will have to do them my way," Baldwin told Rasmussen. "If you don't, you're out."

"I didn't even know I had a job yet to be out of," Rasmussen replied.

He did, and he began working for Baldwin in August of 1974 as communications director and part-time announcer. The frost between Rasmussen and Baldwin was as thick as the ice in the coliseum. They fought over every decision, from how Rasmussen announced the Whaler players to planning hockey legend Gordie Howe's fiftieth birthday party. Rasmussen could never please Baldwin. In one bizarre move that underscored the extent to which the relationship had deteriorated, Baldwin fired the arena announcer and replaced him with Scott, Rasmussen's smart eighteen-year-old son. Rasmussen didn't think Baldwin's interest in Scott was pure. Instead, he believed that Baldwin had hired the callow Scott in the hopes he would fail and be fired, thereby embarrassing his father. That never happened because Scott performed his duties well and kept his job.

The relationship between Rasmussen and Baldwin was typical of the World Hockey League experience. Teams hired and fired coaches weekly, creating an instability that ultimately killed the league. It didn't help that the press treated the World Hockey League as if its players were radioactive.

One of Rasmussen's jobs was to drum up interest, leading Baldwin to blame him for the lack of coverage from the local television networks. When Rasmussen approached United Cable in Plainville, with its measly 9,500 subscribers, the mercurial Baldwin raged that it was a complete waste of time. He may have been right. Cable technology was in its infant stages, and though Rasmussen was beginning to understand the medium better, few in the Whalers organization did, especially Baldwin.

The instability of the Whalers finally caught up with Rasmussen. On a clear Saturday in May of 1978, the beginning of a bustling Memorial Day weekend, Rasmussen's chipper demeanor, after weeks of draining fights with Baldwin, had returned. The hockey season was over, and after deciding to play golf at Farmington Woods in Avon instead of going to a baseball game with friends, Rasmussen looked forward to a relaxing weekend. A few minutes after putting his clubs in the car, and two hours before tee time, the phone rang. It was Colleen Howe, who along with Rasmussen ran her husband's charity enterprises.

"This is not the way I wanted to tell you this," she said, "but I thought you would want to know as quickly as possible. Howard fired you, Bill. He wants you to call him on Tuesday. I'm sorry."

The only thing that surprised Rasmussen was the timing. He could feel this moment coming for weeks but didn't think even Baldwin would fire him before a holiday.

That Tuesday, after shooting par at Farmington, he called Baldwin, something he wasn't looking forward to. When Baldwin answered, Rasmussen asked about his compensation package. Baldwin tersely replied: "There's nothing to really talk about. I'll send your check. If that's not good enough, I won't pay you anything."

Rasmussen was officially fired on May 30, 1978. For the first time since he was a kid in Columbus Manor, he did not have a job.

• • •

Rasmussen spent most of that night in a funk. If his face had dropped any lower, it would have scraped the floor. Scott watched his father sink in and out of depression. Getting fired was a new experience for Rasmussen. His son knew that.

They spent much of that evening thinking about the future, the two of them sitting in the living room, watching television and gulping beers. Even in a time of duress, wondering, yet again, where the next paycheck was coming from, Rasmussen had ideas. The man always had ideas. They rolled around his head, bobbing in and out of his consciousness. The radio network had evaporated, yet thoughts of it nagged him, sticking in his mind. Something about the new cable technology . . . sports . . . New England sports . . . broadcasting. The words didn't have meaning yet because they were nothing more than a random collection of thoughts. He went to bed that night distracted, unable to grasp them completely. Before he fell asleep, he told Mickey to brace herself because another one of those "notions," as she called them, was coming.

The notion came in the form of a voice, not from God, but from Ed Eagan, who called Rasmussen the following morning at home after trying him in the office. Eagan was a stout insurance agent with Aetna, who worked on the same floor as Rasmussen in the Hartford Civic Center. Cable television was still an inchoate technology, and only a handful of men understood its potential. In Connecticut, Eagan was one of them, though his cable operation was not exactly sizzling high tech. Eagan had a personal contract with United Cable in Plainville and when he wasn't selling insurance for Aetna, he was in his Plainville office, which was the size of a large car. Eagan had a passion for sports almost as burning as Rasmussen's, and with Bob Beyus, a fit bicycle enthusiast, the two were planning a series of thirty-minute shows on Connecticut sports. Beyus and Eagan had spent the last several weeks crammed in a van, with a few cameras and some cheap quality video equipment, shooting hot air balloon flights for their opening show. The pictures were grainy, and the video shaky, because whenever the car went over a bump, the cameras rattled. After shooting, Beyus packed the video on the back of his bicycle and peddled it to the cable operators.

After Rasmussen explained his embarrassing dismissal and he listened to Beyus and Eagan talk about hot air balloons and bicycles, his jumbled images fell into place. The room was full of chatter when Rasmussen suddenly interrupted Scott: "What about live sports?" he asked. "Just Connecticut sports on cable. Can we do that?"

The room became quiet. Beyus, the most technically knowledgeable of the group, thought Rasmussen's idea was implausible because individual stations could not afford the production costs of live events. Rasmussen, undeterred, asked about basketball and then the University of Connecticut sports, even women's sports, which had historically posted poor ratings. Rasmussen was selling the room as much as he was brainstorming, and only a few minutes after disparaging Rasmussen's idea, Eagan began to see the possibilities. He tentatively came on board with whatever it was that was forming.

Rasmussen organized a plan. He would speak to the colleges because no one in the room knew the local sports scene like he did. When he was anchoring sports at WWLP-TV, he was inundated with phone calls from agitated athletic directors and coaches from smaller schools who couldn't get their box scores in the daily newspapers. They called Rasmussen about more coverage, and Rasmussen always politely listened, but rarely did those scores get on his broadcast. He would hit those schools first. Scott, unlike his father, was still on good terms with Baldwin, so the Whalers were his responsibility. Beyus would probe United Cable for any interest, and Eagan would spend the night thinking of how to finance what seemed like an impossible dream.

If the group had taken a collective step back to take a good look at themselves, they may have never had the confidence to keep going. Rasmussen was a fired broadcaster, Eagan an insurance agent, Beyus filmed hot air balloon shows, and Scott was the part-time public address announcer for the Whalers. On the surface, they were an unremarkable group. But they were about to begin a remarkable journey.

• • •

Five days later, a Saturday, the group of cable pioneers squeezed into Beyus's undersized office in Plainville early one morning. With some trepidation, each man provided a status report on his work since the last meeting. Rasmussen spoke to the athletic directors at Wesleyan and the University of Connecticut. They were more mildly amused than interested. Baldwin told Scott to come back if the station ever became a reality, although not without sniffing that he doubted that would ever happen. United Cable told Beyus to stick to balloon shows. Only Eagan reported a modicum of good news, saying he could raise $400,000 in financing. Rasmussen and the others were unsure if Eagan could truly get that kind of funding, short of robbing a bank. But they all agreed the venture would cost millions to begin.

Rasmussen was rankled at the slow progress. He was eager to get his idea rolling, but no one outside the room believed an all-Connecticut sports cable station could work.

"At first, we thought people would try to steal the idea," Scott Rasmussen recalled. "Then instead of stealing it, they laughed at us."

They pushed on, propelled by Rasmussen's will. He needed the concept to work more than any of them. The sting of his Whalers experience remained, and his need to make this plan succeed, for now, went beyond his belief in its plausibility. Rasmussen had to prove to himself, to his son, and to his friends that he was no failure.

Rasmussen decided to hold another meeting in two weeks, and this time, he hoped, they would have company. Rather than visit each cable operator individually across the state, peddling his quirky idea, Rasmussen felt it would be more effective to send invitations to try to bring everyone to them. The others agreed, deciding to hold the meeting in the spacious conference room at United Cable. His first rejection of the project notwithstanding, Beyus didn't think there would be a problem persuading the operators to attend. Unlike the major networks, the cable industry was receptive to new ideas, probably because it was relatively new itself.

Rasmussen felt their proposal would be taken more seriously if it had a name. So they met in Scott's condo for dinner and began brainstorming. Rasmussen wanted the words "entertainment" as well as "sports" in the title, because he was still flirting with adding talk-show programming. He blurted out ESP to Scott, Entertainment and Sports Programming network, chuckling at the double meaning. Scott thought the name was bland, but typical of his father's insufferably corny sense of humor. Rasmussen stared at his son across the room, and noting the embarrassed look on his face, grudgingly suggested a compromise.

"We need something that says immediately 'sports network' and when someone sees or hears it, they know exactly what it means," Rasmussen told the group. He wrote the name on a pad that sat on a coffee table in the middle of the room, then slowly rotated the piece of paper to show Scott and Eagan. They weren't sure if they liked the name, but accepted it because they could not think of anything better.

Their Connecticut sports cable channel would be called ESP-TV.

3

"This Is the Stupidest Thing I've Ever Heard"

Cable television was a vast, untamed jungle, and no single conqueror had emerged with the vision to maximize its potential. It had remained a technological underachiever since its inception in the Pennsylvania hills in 1950 until scientists with RCA Americom, one of the leaders in satellite technology, launched a communications rocket from the Kennedy Space Center in 1975. Cable took a giant leap forward, bringing the fantastic possibilities into clearer focus.

But only to a few. The established networks, smug in their dominance, at first ignored cable television, then attempted to stop it once it became clear that cable could fragment their audience. In 1968 broadcasters convinced the Federal Communications Commission to pass several mandates that effectively barred cable from the top one hundred cities, arguing in congressional hearings that cable threatened to undermine the public right to free broadcasting. The networks really feared the fleecing of their pocketbooks. The 1968 ruling was repealed in 1972, but the animosity and distrust between cable and the networks remains to this day.

As ESP-TV began to solidify, the combination of high-quality signal and interesting programming had not been wed on cable television. By the middle of the decade, only a handful of media visionaries grasped the potentially awesome power the medium held, recognizing that cable would some day reach more than a puny ten percent of homes. Ted Turner, the dashing, flamboyant billionaire who owned WTCG-TV in Atlanta and also the Braves baseball team, started his own cable network, airing cheesy old movies and sports. Home Box Office (HBO) in New York, despite occasional references in the cable press as a low-rent operation, was developing a loyal following.

The success of Turner and HBO showed it was possible for nonnetwork, alternative programming to work, much to the distress of the networks. The new satellite technology was promising, allowing cable operators around the country, which by the late 1970s numbered two thousand, to beam their own feeds to the orbiting station and then bounce it back to earth stations. Those stations then sent their signals to individual cable boxes in the homes of those viewers who seemed to like watching movie reruns and Braves baseball.

Public relations for the industry still remained a problem. Advertising revenue was minuscule for cable television compared to the networks, which portrayed cable to advertisers as a wasteland in which dollars were sucked into a bottomless pit. The cable industry did not have a single voice; instead, only a chorus of hundreds of small-time individual cable operators. When the networks ridiculed cable television in the press, the response caused barely a ripple. Cable was a series of fractured islands.

Beyus miscalculated when he told Rasmussen the Connecticut cable operators would be more open-minded than the networks. After experiencing years of abuse from network television, cable developed a deeply embedded inferiority complex, often declaring war on anyone outside their industry. That mentality led to operators taking few risks in cable's early years.

So when Rasmussen walked into their lives with an idea for a Connecticut cable sports station, they didn't know what to make of him or his idea. The meeting was held in June of 1978, and, as planned, in the conference room at United Cable in Plainville. All the dozen cable operators in the state were invited. Most did not come, telephoning in advance that they thought the idea of a sports channel was unworkable. Even fewer would have come had not Rasmussen's friends in cable pleaded on his behalf. When Rasmussen, Scott, Eagan, and Beyus walked into the commodious room, only five people were there, and they were hostile to new ideas.

Rasmussen spoke first, explaining the concept of packaging Connecticut college sports, amateur sports, the Whalers, and maybe some entertainment shows onto one broadcast cable station called ESP-TV. Again, Rasmussen was selling, only this time, he had a bitter and beleagured audience, more difficult to sway than executives at Westinghouse or the manager of a radio station in Massachusetts.

There was resounding doubt about the viability of the concept. Rasmussen's spirit sagged. Then someone asked him if he had spoken to RCA Americom about the satellite. He had not. That never crossed his mind. When Scott asked about the costs of buying time on the satellite, each operator gave a different price, underscoring their own ignorance of the technology. But they knew the future of cable was through spinning boxes in orbit, not solely network television, which consisted of four and five channels and an antenna on top of the box to help with reception.

If ESP was ever going to become a reality, they needed to investigate the cost and availability of RCA's satellites. By not investigating, everyone's time would be wasted from here on.

The pessimism of the meeting unnerved Rasmussen, but he remained unbowed. Beyus was sounding more like he wanted to pull out and go back to riding bicycles. Rasmussen convinced him to stay, at least until he looked into the satellite technology and examined the first piece of programming. Beyus relented.

Rasmussen spent the last days of June trying to reach John Toner, the athletic director at the University of Connecticut (UConn). They had spoken about ESP several times, and Toner was the only person receptive to the idea, thinking it would develop positive press for the school. Rasmussen finally reached Toner that Thursday, telling him they had a name for the company and exaggerating its development, saying in only a matter of months, ESP would be broadcast over sophisticated satellite feeds, and millions across the state would know about UConn sports. Rasmussen was not only selling, he was flat-out lying.

Toner was worked up and scheduled a meeting with Rasmussen on campus several weeks later. Rasmussen knew the meeting was not a commitment to ESP, but acting like it was, he told the others at Beyus's office at United Cable that it was time to call a press conference to announce the launch of ESP to the public. Scott was not surprised by his father's suggestion, even though it was clearly premature. That's how he had watched him live his life. Taking chances and experimenting with ideas was Rasmussen's way. Most of what Rasmussen had done in his life had worked, so Scott wasn't about to argue. Eagan had no qualms about alerting the news media. Beyus did, but he was outvoted by the others.

The only matter left to discuss was finding a permanent place to conduct business. United Cable offered to rent them a small office, about the size of a living room, for $100 a month. They moved in on Monday after buying some plywood from a local lumber yard and nailing it to old doors. The group now had desks.

• • •

Rasmussen called members of the press with whom he had developed relationships over the years while working in radio and television and with the Whalers. Almost forty reporters were invited to the press conference to be held in the hotel ballroom at the Holiday Inn in Plainville on June 26, 1978. Rasmussen was hoping at least half would show.

Four did—none of them from television.

When the reporters walked into the ballroom, they saw Rasmussen, Scott, Eagan, and Beyus sitting nervously at a table in the front of the room. A tray with a half-dozen cans of Coca-Cola provided the only refreshments for a room without a working air conditioner. In addition to the humid air, the room was stuffy with doubt.

The ESP founders had further developed their game plan, telling the four reporters they hoped the first broadcast would be the UConn-Navy football game on September 16, 1978, a Saturday. They envisioned covering almost every school sport and would charge $18 per subscriber for the package. As Rasmussen continued, a reporter in the back of the room sneered. Others were leaning over in their chairs, making jokes to each other about the absurdity of a cable sports network.

"I remember being one of the people laughing," said Bill Pennington, who worked for a small Connecticut paper at the time and is now at the *New York Times*. "I thought, 'This is the stupidest thing I've ever heard.'"

Lou Palmer, a respected radio announcer at WTIC, sarcastically reminded the group that NCAA rules prohibited televising college football on Saturdays. Rasmussen said their plan was to tape-delay the contests to show later that day or during the following week. Palmer scoffed at the idea of anyone wanting to watch old games. Matt Buchler from the *Journal Inquirer* asked about the number of charter ESP customers. Rasmussen, by now skilled at evasion, said that thousands of flyers had been mailed to UConn school alumni and ESP expected a significant response. Of course, Rasmussen had no idea how many would respond. For all he knew, the alumni might react the same way as the reporters—with skepticism.

"We stood up there and told them we were going to do all this stuff and they looked at us like we were completely insane," recalled Rasmussen. "One reporter flat out said, 'Sports on cable? That will never work. No one will watch.' Lou Palmer was there, and he had doubts, but he eventually came to work for us. We had no believers in that audience and they were chuckling at us. They discounted us so much that nothing was reported in the papers. We were looked at as these crazy guys."

The press conference ended after only twenty minutes. The reporters left not as converts but as doubters. The ESP board was left alone to digest the event. It had been too much for Beyus, who snapped.

"This is goddamn madness," he told the others. "I'm out."

Beyus promised to rent them any equipment they needed, then left the ballroom, flailing his hands in exasperation. Now only three partners remained, but not one of them was in despair; with Beyus gone, there was one less to share the pot.

• • •

The embarrassing press conference behind him, Rasmussen decided to incorporate ESP, which was stunningly simple. The group hired attorney Bob Hempstead from Hartford, a friend of Eagan's. He authored the needed paperwork, and Scott, emptying his checking and savings accounts, provided the $91 fee for registration. On July 14, the company was formally incorporated, with Eagan listed as the president, because his lawyer had handled the transaction. Rasmussen and Scott were listed as vice presidents.

They met later that day, and that's when it hit the remaining three: None of them had any money. Lack of funds became a chronic problem, threatening to derail the company on numerous occasions in the future. But for now, back in their United Cable offices, they plotted their next steps.

The money from Ad Aid was long gone, but Rasmussen still had enough capital to keep ESP barely afloat, using his personal credit cards and borrowing from family members and friends to maintain ESP on life support for a while. The immediate need for cash was to pay the bills: rent, utilities, travel expenses, corporation taxes, stationery. So Rasmussen took an advance from his Visa card, totaling $9,400. He paid the necessary bills and then split what was left, about $4,000, between Scott and Eagan.

Scott always looked for ways of saving money to maximize ESP's financial resources. For instance, he wired their office phone through the receptionist's desk at United Cable for ESP to sound more professional to a caller (they couldn't afford their own secretary). When they went to lunch, the phones were put on hold so that callers got a busy signal instead of a constantly ringing telephone. Even though business was nonexistent, ESP always wanted to give the impression that it was rolling.

ESP did not, however, skimp on business cards. Each man carried four cards at all times, and they were each listed as a vice president of a different department. Their title would depend on whom they were meeting that day. If it was a programming meeting, then any one of them could be vice president of programming. Or marketing. Or finance. They changed titles the way some changed shoes. The fourth card was always left blank, in case creative title-making was needed.

As another sweltering July hit Connecticut, ESP was ready to make a major play. It was time for the men who thought everyone else was wrong to finally start proving they were right.

• • •

Al Parinello was RCA's best salesman, but these days he felt as if he couldn't sell a snow cone to a man dying of thirst. He sold satellite time. Even though RCA's bird was in orbit, the company struggled to persuade businesses to invest in its transponders, the small boxes tucked away inside the orbiting satellites that provided basic feeds to the cable boxes on the ground. Business was so lukewarm, RCA started reevaluating its satellite investment.

Under this cloud, Parinello drove from city to city, always with the same result: interest but no commitment. Then he got a phone call from Rasmussen in his New York office. Rasmussen didn't need to be sold, he wanted time on the satellite. Parinello had doubts about a sports network, but he was enticed by Rasmussen's confidence. Besides, Parinello was desperate; he would meet with anyone.

Rasmussen refused to talk to Parinello in ESP's shabby office, with its splintered desks, tacky chairs, and hijacked phone system. Rasmussen paid United Cable $20 to rent its conference room, which featured comfortable leather chairs and a large mahogany desk.

Rasmussen and Scott greeted Parinello in the conference room. Parinello was impressed. In front of him were two men dressed in stylish jackets and ties, speaking eloquently about their proposed sports network. They appeared to be solid businessmen—though Parinello was struck by Scott's apparent youth. Rasmussen always believed in the efficacy of glibness and appearance. But he also knew that ESP would eventually have to demonstrate substance, which posed a problem with his near-empty checking account. He needed to stall RCA long enough to secure financing for ESP, so until then, he planned on charming Parinello, fooling him really, into thinking he could afford the steep fees for satellite time. If Parinello ever discerned the truth, Rasmussen knew that ESP would evaporate into nothing more than talk about what might have been.

The group got down to business quickly. Parinello gave them a basic education on Satcom 1, talking as he would to a room of fifth graders. Then the talks turned to money, the main purpose of Parinello's visit but the source of anxiety for Rasmussen.

Despite a meager demand for cable, RCA charged a stiff price for access to its satellite. Parinello discussed a number of options, most of which ESP could not afford. The one Rasmussen thought they could, called by Parinello the "moderate" transponder, turned out to be still too high: $1,250 a night for five hours, seven days a week.

Throughout the meeting, Rasmussen remained composed, never revealing to Parinello the panic churning in his stomach. ESP would need a bank loan of hundreds of thousands of dollars, if not several million, to afford the transponder. Originally, Rasmussen believed ESP should buy two or even three satellites for future expansion. Now he realized acquiring only one would require even more imaginative financing.

Rasmussen, smiling falsely, thanked Parinello for coming, his mind already exploring ways of obtaining the money. Parinello headed for the door, then suddenly he stopped and turned. "There is something else you should know," he said. RCA had another transponder, one that sent its signal twenty-four hours a day, each day, and cost $35,000 a month with a five-year lease. When Rasmussen was in the Air Force, he could rapidly work out mathematical calculations. On this day, he didn't even try, his mind locked on raising the needed money for the satellite.

Parinello drove back to New York without a deal. Rasmussen met at Scott's condo to rehash the meeting. Because he had inherited his father's aptitude for numbers, Scott calculated the math in his head and concluded that it was $107 cheaper a month to rent a twenty-four hour transponder than one with only a five-hour window. Parinello's last-minute aside had changed the course of their thinking. Instead of broadcasting Connecticut sports just a portion of the day, Rasmussen and Scott were intrigued by the possibility of all Connecticut sports, all the time.

They debated the merits of both transponder plans until late that night. Rasmussen was concerned with the daunting task of filling ESP-TV's around-the-clock menu. Scott argued that the programming would follow, with the novelty of all-day, all-night Connecticut sports bringing in viewers. Scott's view barely edged out those of his slightly skeptical father and Eagan.

The next day, Rasmussen phoned New York. When Parinello answered, the vice president of ESP-TV was so geeked he forget to say who he was, merely blurting out "We'll take one," as if ordering a cheeseburger from a drive-through restaurant.

"You'll take what?" asked a surprised Parinello. He recognized Rasmussen—his inimitable zeal giving him away—but had no idea to what he was referring.

"We want the twenty-four-hour transponder," Rasmussen replied.

Parinello was ecstatic, reminding Rasmussen there was no money down and the first payment was not due until 90 days after the contract was signed. That gave Rasmussen a little time to raise the money, but not much. Parinello asked for written confirmation of their telephone conversation. Rasmussen was happy to oblige. His order came a few weeks later with a simple letter.

Dear Al,

Please consider this letter our order for a five (5) year, full-time pre-emptible transponder on RCA Satcom 1 effective January 1, 1979.

Be advised that our site clearance allows access to odd numbered transponders 1, 3, 5, 7, 9, 11, 13, 19, 21 & 23.

It is understood that the rates for this service are as follows:

Year 1	$410,000
Year 2	460,000
Year 3	515,000
Year 4	575,000
Year 5	645,000

I will appreciate an early confirmation of your receipt of this order.

ESP-TV had its transponder. They received confirmation from Parinello in a return phone call a few days later. He told Rasmussen how lucky ESP was to have submitted its application then, because if it had arrived only a few days later, they might have been left out. After a *Wall Street Journal* story predicted the cable industry was about to explode in popularity, thanks to satellite links like Satcom 1, monster media companies suddenly started banging on Parinello's door. The man who once could not get a return phone call was now fielding applications from Time, Inc., Walt Disney Co., 20th Century-Fox, and Warner Brothers Communication RCA assigned its transponders on a first-come basis, and because ESP was among the first to submit an order, it was guaranteed a transponder. Parinello complimented Rasmussen on his perfect timing.

When RCA announced the transponder winners, an executive at 20th Century Fox, sitting alone in his California office and reading the *Los Angeles Times,* saw Rasmussen's network listed. "What the hell is ESP and where is Plainville, Connecticut?" he asked himself.

4

A Long Night

Rasmussen had long wanted to fix the air conditioning in his 1975 light blue Mazda GLC, and while he and Scott were stuck in a three-mile backup on Interstate-84 near Waterbury, he really wished he had. A two-car pileup had stopped traffic, and Rasmussen and Scott were both extremely irritable. It was August 16 and Rasmussen's daughter, Lynn, was celebrating her birthday near the beach in Ocean Grove, New Jersey. Rasmussen and Scott had been discussing, then arguing, programming to broadcast on the transponder and how it would be paid for. Rasmussen kept prying ideas from Scott, and for the first time in years, Scott raised his voice in exasperation at his father.

"Dad, play football all day for all I care," he bristled. "I'm just sick of talking about this."

Rasmussen understood it was the heat talking, not his son. Yet, his idea made sense. He asked Scott, "Why not?"

The traffic began to move, inching along. It was two o'clock in the afternoon, well over ninety degrees.

"I mean, why not," Rasmussen continued. "Why can't we just have college games on all day. Not just Connecticut, but all sports. What's wrong with football all day?"

Scott straightened in his seat and began to envision the possibilities. The one seemingly unshakable problem was the stranglehold CBS and ABC had on most major college sports broadcasts.

Rasmussen was ready. Besides showing the games on a tape-delayed basis, which the NCAA permitted and had been their plan with UConn, perhaps ESP could persuade the NCAA to allow their network to show the games not wanted by the big networks. In other words, the leftovers.

"What the hell are you talking about?" Scott said.

The traffic was moving faster, maybe ten miles an hour, and Rasmussen's mind was speeding up with it. ESP would broadcast the sports the networks never touched, such as college hockey, volleyball, and swimming. He wanted to do a nightly, half-hour studio show, just like the networks, and sports updates at least five times a day. They would buy their own fleet of remote trucks, even if they were overpriced. The traffic began moving smoothly. Rasmussen pushed the pedal on the Mazda, and the two men were cruising at sixty, but they barely noticed, especially Scott, whose irritation disappeared with the breeze. He took a legal pad from a bag in the back seat and started recording his father's ideas.

They would need studios, recognizable talent, and production crews. Scott figured an initial staff of at least eighty to ninety. They would outline the presentation of their new idea for a complete sports network—all sports, all the time, not just Connecticut—to a banker or an investor. The NCAA would be their hook, but it would not be easy convincing a powerful conglomerate to believe in a fantasy like ESP. After all, not a single brick had been laid or even a dollar invested. And ESP was still broke.

That did not stop Rasmussen and Scott from continuing to outline their future. They arrived in Ocean Grove around five that evening. Rasmussen gave Lynn a kiss and wished her a happy birthday. Scott hugged his sister and told her she was an old lady. They both then went into the kitchen and grabbed plates of meatballs and helpings of birthday cake. They sang "Happy Birthday" to Lynn, then retreated to a corner of the house, where Bill opened the throttle again and Scott scribbled frenetically. Mickey looked at her two men and shook her head.

The trip home was faster and cooler. They got to Rasmussen's condo in Connecticut around midnight. Neither of them was tired. Needing a caffeine boost, they opened two sodas. Scott began to draw the main ESP building. He sketched the studios and production facilities, forgetting to draw the stairways and bathrooms.

Rasmussen emphasized the need for a main sports show to compete against the network news and to tie the programming together. His early name for it: "SportsCentral."

Approaching half past two in the morning, Scott petered out, but Rasmussen had one more detail to work out. Where would the studio be built? He remembered something ESP's landlord at United Cable, the helpful Jim Dovey, had said regarding an abundance of cheap property available in

Bristol, Connecticut. Without even seeing it, Rasmussen decided that would be the site—it was available and it was cheap.

It had been a grueling but exhilarating day. In a span of fourteen hours, Rasmussen's vision for sports television had changed drastically. ESP as a simple station showing only Connecticut sports had taken a dramatic, improbable leap in thought to a 24-hour, all-sports cable network. This ambitious plan had not evolved, it had sprung, full-blown, from the mind of an excitable man baking in a traffic jam.

• • •

Friends who had known Rasmussen for years saw a change in him in the months after that bizarre yet fruitful trip to New Jersey. Usually affable, Rasmussen conversed with economy, as if he did not have time to talk.

Truth is, he didn't. His obsession with the new direction of ESP left little time for anything else, including sleep. Scott pursued the financing for the start-up. Rasmussen tackled an even more difficult task. He had to convince the NCAA that his network, which didn't yet exist, was good for college sports. The NCAA was known for its close-minded approach to new ideas and was fiercely loyal to the networks, which for years had belittled cable to many college athletic directors.

Rasmussen spoke again to Connecticut athletic director John Toner, informing him about ESP's new direction. Toner expressed his misgivings about a national all-sports cable network, but he was intrigued enough to steer Rasmussen in the right direction, which was the fifteen-member NCAA television committee. Toner then told Rasmussen that two members of the committee would be key: Walter Byers, the executive director of the NCAA, who commanded respect from everyone, and committee chairman J. O. Coppedge, the Naval Academy athletic director, known by midshipmen and the television committee as tough but fair.

Rasmussen quickly made headway, setting up a September meeting with Coppedge, who traveled to Connecticut for Navy's game against the Huskies. They talked for fewer than five minutes in the lobby of a Ramada Inn. Coppedge did not overplay his hand, refusing to dismiss Rasmussen but also not encouraging him. For Rasmussen, the meeting was confirmation enough. Just getting Coppedge's ear was a victory in itself.

The NCAA had to break soon because ESP was on the verge of financial collapse. A bank turned down Rasmussen for a $25,000 loan, causing him to grovel to family members for money. RCA called shortly after, wanting to know when it could expect its deposit, which was due in just over a month.

Scott had learned a few things about bluffing from his father, so he immediately took the offensive. "Did you send us a bill?" he said. "Have we not paid our bill? Are you questioning our integrity?"

Scott's reaction was dangerous. Instead of simply saying they would mail the payment soon, he overreacted—which should have aroused further suspicion at RCA. But like so many strangely auspicious moments in ESP's early days, this too took an unusual turn. The RCA financial executive, concerned about losing an account, became flustered, saying he would get back to Scott, and then hung up.

ESP could not survive in this manner much longer. It needed a quick influx of cash, enough to tide it over until Rasmussen got his chance in front of the NCAA.

• • •

The man across the table from Rasmussen and Scott cradled a pipe in his hand, his steely face staring at Rasmussen, who was making his pitch about ESP. J. B. Doherty was a no-nonsense ex-Marine officer, the antithesis of Rasmussen. He rarely smiled, but his clear thinking made him a valuable partner in the K. S. Sweet investment firm. He took neat notes during the meeting in the company's Pennsylvania office, and then told Rasmussen they should meet again toward the end of September.

Rasmussen came to the second meeting with plenty of allies, as if he was planning a Normandy-like attack against Doherty. With Rasmussen were Scott and Eagan, and also Beyus, who remained disenfranchised from ESP but agreed to help.

The group sat in the K. S. Sweet conference room debating ESP's potential for more than ten hours, breaking only to eat pastries and then sandwiches for lunch. Doherty had his doubts, as just about everyone did, but unlike everyone else he could also comprehend the limitless possibilities of the venture. Therefore at the end of the day K. S. Sweet agreed to provide initial funding of $75,000, analyze the amount needed to start ESP-TV, and create a proposal for potential investors.

As Rasmussen walked to his car, his ever-present smile broadened. He had rescued his dream one more time. This would not be the last near-death experience for ESP. In the months to come, the company would play this game of brinksmanship many times. Rasmussen's will, ability to persevere, and knack for scheming his way through land mines, however, always kept his company one step ahead of the grim reaper.

Doherty went to work on ESP, thinking of ways to attract investors willing to pony up $10 million, the minimum Doherty and the firm estimated was needed to start the network. Meanwhile, Rasmussen focused on the NCAA. His idea was far from a realization, but it was a step closer. What ESP needed now was programming. It needed sports.

• • •

Rasmussen drafted a two-page proposal for his first meeting with the NCAA. It was six paragraphs and almost embarrassing in its simplicity.

PURPOSE   ESP-TV intends to complement rather than compete with current NCAA television contractual arrangements. We propose to extend football's national television coverage to more schools and to add many other sports, including every championship, to our nationwide network. This additional coverage will further enhance the Association's stated goal of advancing the overall interests of intercollegiate athletics and provide national exposure to more institutions and student athletes than ever before possible.

CONCEPT   ESP-TV will televise nationally a minimum of five hundred (500) NCAA Division I, II, and III men's and women's athletic events via RCA Satcom 1 to earth station–served cable television systems. Each event to be broadcast at least twice to maximize exposure. Highlight packages, commercial network action segments, and extensive NCAA and member institution promotion to be an integral part of ESP-TV's effort.

MARKET   Satellite technology has provided the greatest potential market growth possibility since the introduction of network television. Current market estimates indicate nearly 12,000,000 viewers can be reached via Satcom 1, with the number expected to double during the next year. Studies have shown that cable viewers are among the nation's heaviest users of television programming.

SCHEDULE   ESP-TV proposes to work very closely with the NCAA to develop schedules in all sports that will maximize our mutually stated goals. We plan to air NCAA events daily from September through June within parameters mutually established by the Association and ESP-TV. The NCAA will continue to receive national coverage during July and August with highlight shows, features of individuals and individual institutions, summer programs, and previews of the upcoming year.

MECHANICS   ESP-TV headquarters in Bristol, Connecticut, will transmit all programming via a ten-meter dish to RCA Satcom 1, which in turn will deliver the signal to authorized earth stations throughout the continental United States. The majority of the programming will be videotaped on location and returned to ESP-TV headquarters for broadcast. ESP-TV is currently accepting bids on seven complete remote trucks and will station these units strategically throughout the country to provide the most modern pickup facilities for each Association event.

COMPENSATION   The nature of the cable television market is such that dynamic geometric growth is expected during the next several years. Concurrently, advertising participation and rates will increase dramatically. This dual growth should be reflected in any compensation agreement. To fairly compensate the NCAA, we propose a payment that will directly relate to the monthly number of subscribers receiving the programming and a percentage of all advertising dollars generated by any NCAA event televised under this proposed agreement.

Rasmussen felt that a simple, direct approach was better, at least for now, than an encyclopedia full of far-fetched boasts. The NCAA committee was sharp. They would see through any fanciful claims.

Still, the proposal contained classic Rasmussen bluffs. He was not close to purchasing a dish to transmit ESP-TV's signal. The indication that in a year, twenty-four million people would be cable subscribers was considered a wildly high estimate by even the most ardent cable supporters. And noticeably absent from the proposal was the ten-thousand-pound gorilla—ESP's plan to finance such a grand concept.

That was not missed by NCAA executives in Rasmussen's first meeting at the organization's headquarters in Shawnee Mission, Kansas, in mid-October. The meeting was brief, with Byers, the most influential member of the NCAA, not present. Instead, Dennis Cryder, who oversaw television production, spoke to Rasmussen. He doubted the NCAA would ever opt for cable but promised to pass along the proposal. Cryder said the NCAA would meet with Rasmussen in December, some two months away. Rasmussen was crestfallen because he wasn't sure if ESP could last that long without a significant financial backer. Cryder rejected his entreaty to move the meeting up. Then the final blow: The entire process could take up to a year, Cryder told him.

Refusing to submit to depression on the flight home, Rasmussen prepared for ESP-TV's first broadcast. He took out a notepad and scribbled down his thoughts. ESP needed a test show that would prove Rasmussen and his rag-tag group could at least put on one show. The next day, he was back on the UConn campus, speaking to Toner about broadcasting two Huskie events, a soccer and a basketball game. By the end of the week, Lou Palmer, who in July had ridiculed ESP during Rasmussen's first press conference, had been recruited from WTIC radio to do play-by-play for the test show, along with Arnold Dean. Peter Fox was ESP's first producer and Bob Ronstrum, the former Whalers comptroller, was hired to handle the small payroll.

Meanwhile, Doherty had approached seven major investors regarding ESP and had been rejected by each. ESP was still cash-strapped, causing Doherty concern with the cost of a test show, which could approach tens of thousands of dollars. He was not pleased either with the increase in staff, because that meant a larger payroll. But after some throat clearing, he approved fronting the money for both the show and the staffing, then told the group the good news, K. S. Sweet was adding $50,000 because the original monies had already dried up.

ESP's practice telecast was set for November 17. The group worked tirelessly to prepare, their headquarters a borrowed production truck. Fox prepared the pregame stories, Rasmussen helped with the graphics, and Scott spent hours on the phone asking dozens of cable companies to preview ESP free of charge. Some declined, but many others accepted, finding the price was right.

The UConn basketball team won its exhibition game against Athletes in Action, which was broadcast live. Palmer was characteristically sharp. During the soccer game, which bored Palmer, he was at least enthusiastic.

Technically flawed and at times resembling a grainy home video, the test nevertheless was a major hit nationally. ESP ran a message across the bottom of the television screen asking viewers to contact the company and report where they were calling from. Viewers in twenty-six states, including Juneau, Alaska, flooded the tiny Plainville office with phone calls. In all, 850,000 households picked up the test show from Satcom 1. Two UConn graduates watched from Fort Myers, Florida, then after the broadcast, breathlessly called Toner to express how happy they were to see Connecticut sports on television. It was the first time they had contacted their alma mater in twenty years.

Toner was convinced of ESP-TV's potential and would later prove a valuable ally in convincing the NCAA of the same. Rasmussen was even more sold. He always suspected people would watch almost any athletic competition. Now he was certain of it.

• • •

A continent away, in late November of 1978, Evey was in Hawaii, doggedly trying to close a deal on Getty's behalf for a gorgeous beachfront hotel. It was owned by K. S. Sweet. Evey had spent most of his time negotiating with Doherty, whom Evey found to be direct but pleasant.

The sale failed to go through, but that did not sour cocktails with Doherty, who hours ago had switched his thoughts from the hotel to ESP. Doherty was desperate for some action on ESP, so figuring he had nothing to lose, he asked Evey if he was interested. Getty was the eighth and final company on his list, no doubt the longest shot of them all. Getty was oil, and oil was always cautious about putting money into anything except drilling holes. Doherty remembered that the night before, Evey had mentioned Getty was loosening the noose on its nonoil side. Evey had a few drinks in him then, just as today, so he wasn't sure if Evey really meant it.

"What do you know about satellites and cable television, Stu?" Doherty asked.

"I don't know a satellite from a goddamn fire hydrant," said Evey.

Doherty explained what was happening in the faraway world of Connecticut with a sports station called ESP-TV. Evey had never heard of ESP, or a guy named Rasmussen. But, the idea of a sports cable channel enticed Evey, and that was not the bourbon speaking. He could not explain why, it just did.

Doherty was at first perplexed because the mention of ESP and cable television usually drew curious stares. Evey, however, listened intently. The Getty executive had no idea what ESP was or how cable worked, just that he needed another drink and first thing the next morning, he would start making phone calls.

• • •

To Rasmussen, the Los Angeles Getty tower seemed to stretch endlessly into the California sky. He was a long way from the closet-sized office shared by three people in Plainville, which had earned the nickname the "crisis control center" because there were always crises and little control.

When Rasmussen met Evey, he was struck by his aristocratically handsome looks and professional attire. Evey's hair was perfectly combed, showing just a touch of gray on the sides, his white shirt starched, his dark tie in a precise knot.

Rasmussen was nervous for the first time in months. He was back in the corporate atmosphere that gave him hives, and he could tell almost immediately Evey was the kind of high-powered company man who had driven him to entrepreneurship. But right now, Evey was the pivotman who would determine whether ESP went on the air or into oblivion.

The meeting started promptly at 9 A.M., and Evey asked if Rasmussen wanted coffee. Evey already had his in hand, spiked with a shot of bourbon. Wendel Niles, a Hollywood producer, had his coffee black, minus the alcohol. Niles knew as much about cable television as Evey did, which was nothing, but he served as Evey's security blanket, even if it was a thin one.

Rasmussen outlined where the project stood, and dropped somewhat of a bombshell on the two men. In addition to wanting $10 million, ESP needed the funds by December 31, only 23 days away, because that was the deadline for the installment payment to RCA for the satellite.

New ideas traveled through the Getty corporation the way blood pulses through a hibernating bear. Getty was a huge, unwieldy behemoth. Even oil ideas, the lifeblood of the company, sifted slowly up the burdensome chain of command. A nonoil project was bound to proceed with the speed of molasses, and Evey knew ESP would never receive approval in three weeks.

Evey briefly paged through Rasmussen's fifteen-page proposal, then told him it needed scrutiny by his financial advisers at Getty. Rasmussen headed back to Los Angeles International Airport and his first appearance before the NCAA television committee. As soon as Rasmussen left, Evey called his advisers, which consisted of only one person, George Conner, the financial manager for the nonoil division who had a quick mind and hearty work ethic. Evey gave Conner a copy of Rasmussen's proposal, and several hours later, they met at the LA Club, perched on top of the Getty building. Evey had a scotch and water and eagerly awaited Conner's thoughts.

"Your instincts are correct," he told Evey, "this has promise."

Evey ordered Conner to examine it further, which meant Conner had to delay his Christmas vacation to Tulsa, Oklahoma, where his family was waiting. There were computer models to run, fiscal projections to make, and good old-fashioned detective work to begin. Conner did not know it, but the pile of other projects on his desk would be shifted to others in the division, and for the next three and a half years, he would dedicate his life to ESP.

Evey started his own intense analysis. Unknown to Rasmussen, an investigator from Getty was hired to scrutinize his background, primarily to rule out that Rasmussen was a fraud. Evey phoned dozens of friends, including Art Keyler at Time-Life, who put him in touch with Richard Munro, the head of HBO. Evey told Munro he thought ESP could be the HBO of sports. Munro snickered. "I can see all kinds of problems . . . I don't think I'd ever touch that," Munro said.

When Munro headed Time, Inc. in the mid-1980s, he rebuffed the efforts of *Sports Illustrated* publisher Bob Miller to make a bid for ESPN when it was on the selling block. Munro's position was wrong then, and it was wrong that day when Evey called, but his was a common perception. No one thought ESP could work, except for Rasmussen and his merry men and now Evey, an emphatic convert.

Rasmussen's relationship with Evey would decline after their cordial meeting in December, sinking into hostility just a few months later. Nevertheless, the two men had done something unusual. Rasmussen convinced an oil company to at least ponder the possibility of investing in cable television, and Evey, the eyes and ears for Getty, had the open and astute mind to listen.

• • •

While Rasmussen and Doherty played a five-minute video presentation for the NCAA at the Los Angeles Airport Marriott, with the organization's executive director, Byers, sitting quietly in the back of the room like the godfather, Scott was in snowy Bristol, Connecticut, trying to find a home for ESP.

Bristol was the last place Scott ever expected to build a sophisticated, enterprising sports network. The city was once the clock-making capital of the world. During the Second World War, factories built ball bearings for tanks and fuse elements for bomb parts. Smoke, not skyscrapers, dominated the skyline.

When Scott arrived toward the end of December 1978 on his second trip to Bristol, the dreary atmosphere hadn't changed much. The town was in the clutches of a crippling depression, with twenty-five percent unemployment. He passed somber faces on his way downtown to meet with officials from the redevelopment agency. They had expressed what was now an obligatory doubt about ESP yet were mildly pleased with a company considering a move to their city.

ESP agreed to pay $18,000 for a flat, grassy, tree-lined parcel of land, less than an acre, between Middle and Birch Streets. The astonishingly cheap cost of the land ended any speculation that ESP might settle in Manhattan, where office space would cost ten times as much.

Scott eased the city's leaders of their concerns, primarily by explaining that the satellite dish would not fry birds or small kids. He had a more difficult time pacifying their persisting anxiety about ESP's capability to raise payment for the land. Consequently, the city had one demand: At the next board meeting in thirty days, ESP was to make full payment for the land or lose it. Other investors were interested, they claimed, and though Scott doubted them, ESP could not afford to lose such reasonably priced property. Scott agreed that when he was next in Bristol, a check would be in his hand.

Making the promise was easy; keeping it, however, would be more difficult because K. S. Sweet had stopped funding ESP. Bristol might as well have asked for $18 million. It looked hopeless—until another act of divine intervention. On the day of Scott's promised payment, almost a foot of snow buried Bristol during a brutal snowstorm, forcing the meeting to be rescheduled to February, a month away. ESP remained on life support. Scott thought to himself: "God must be a cable man."

• • •

A cold, hard December had come and gone, and ESP still had no commitment from Getty, or the NCAA. Rasmussen and Scott were $80,000 in debt, having borrowed money from their families just to eat, gas their cars, and prevent eviction from their homes. This winter had been the most frightening time for the men and their idea. Not only was ESP falling apart, but their personal finances were as well.

On rare occasions, the stress caused Rasmussen to withdraw, barely speaking to Mickey or Scott. Usually, however, Rasmussen blithely marched on, ignoring or refusing to dwell on his financial plight. During this time, he decided that limiting ESP to discussions with only the NCAA was not tactically wise, so he approached professional sports.

Val Pinchbeck, the National Football League's director of broadcasting, was in his Park Avenue office in Manhattan when Commissioner Pete Rozelle buzzed him. "Val, I need you in here, there's a guy coming to meet with me," Rozelle said. "His name is Rasmussen, and he is starting an all-sports network." Rozelle trusted Pinchbeck on all television matters, and he wanted Pinchbeck's insights on Rasmussen's proposal.

Rasmussen made his pitch in Rozelle's office, but he failed to change their perceptions of cable television. "Pete and I said to ourselves, 'How many homes can something like this reach?'" remembered Pinchbeck. "There were serious doubts."

It was the same thing with professional baseball, basketball, and hockey. No league wanted to commit limited resources to a medium with only marginal potential.

These failures sent Rasmussen back to his original plan, which had been to woo the NCAA at all costs. The NCAA remained leery of ESP because it had little to offer other than promises and dreams, and to the powerful NCAA, both were worthless. Cash is what counted, and Rasmussen had none to offer in exchange for broadcast rights. When the NCAA asked how he planned to finance his network, he responded with vague generalities or slyly attempted to change the subject. In late January, Byers finally entered the negotiations. "We don't want to be used," the NCAA executive told Rasmussen. "It sounds like you are looking for a hunting license. We give you what you want, and then you go hunting for customers."

Rasmussen was surprised at Byers's directness. He was also embarrassed at the way Byers had exposed him and his plan. That is exactly what he wanted to do. Rasmussen needed product before he could make people believe in ESP. Doherty tried to convince Byers otherwise but had no luck. On the face of it, Byers just couldn't agree to the proposal. At that point, Rasmussen, desperate, decided to go for broke. He looked squarely into Byers's bespectacled eyes and declared: "If you are worried, I have an idea that will appease you. Name the bank, and we'll put 50 percent of the agreed contract price in an escrow account by July 1. Does that help?"

Doherty and Conner froze, incredulous at what Rasmussen had just promised. The others did not agree with Rasmussen's view that the success of ESP required onerously unfavorable or reckless deals and if necessary, lies. But Rasmussen was willing to do whatever it took to get ESP on the air.

Byers eventually came around, not because of Rasmussen's exhortations but because of George Conner's and, more specifically, Getty's presence. By mid-February, Byers authorized contract discussions. For the first time, Rasmussen felt he could see the finish line with the NCAA.

In the middle of a February meeting in Shawnee Mission, Conner called Rasmussen from Los Angeles, and after excusing himself from the room, Rasmussen got the good news—the Getty strategy committee had tentatively approved funding for the ESP project, as it was called within the oil giant's offices. Conner asked Rasmussen to leave as soon as he could for Los Angeles. Once Byers learned of the commitment, he told Rasmussen the NCAA would likely sign on as well.

"In the span of about ten minutes, two things I had been fighting months for happened," Rasmussen remembered.

He met with Evey in his offices the next morning. There were still top-ranking Getty officials Rasmussen had to meet. One was the stoic Harold Stuart, a member of the Getty board of directors. Any project in the Getty pipeline had to pass through Stuart, who worried, as others throughout the oil giant, about the upside of cable television. He trusted Evey, however, and $10 million was a pittance.

What Rasmussen did not know was that he would schmooze Stuart at

30,000 feet in the Getty corporate jet. Stuart and two other executives were flying to Odessa, Texas, to attend the Oil Hall of Fame, and they wanted to get a feel for Rasmussen. After leaving the Getty offices, Rasmussen traveled to the Los Angeles Airport, then boarded the plane. Stuart and the other executives grilled Rasmussen for more than three hours. In his element, Rasmussen handled their questions with ease.

Once on the ground in Texas, Evey directed Rasmussen to the limousine carrying the wives of the executives, while Evey climbed into another limousine with Stuart. Rasmussen had no idea that ESP's fate was being decided in the fifteen-minute ride to the Midland Hilton.

"What are your thoughts?" Evey asked Stuart.

"He seems like a nice man, but I don't know if I would trust him to run a business," Stuart said.

"You don't have to trust him to run anything," Evey replied. "I'll be running the project."

"That's good," said Stuart, "so let's go ahead."

Rasmussen was waiting to register at the front desk when he saw Evey approaching, with a stern look on his face. Rasmussen tensed. But as Evey got closer, his expression changed.

His words were simple. "Congratulations. ESP is a go."

Seventeen years after he left Ad Aid, Inc., nine months after he was fired from the Whalers, and only days after a close call with bankruptcy, Rasmussen finally had his network.

• • •

Several days after the Texas flight, Rasmussen was back in Los Angeles on the elevator in Getty's corporate building and heading to Evey's office on the eighteenth floor. He was exhausted. In the past forty-five days, he had flown to Kansas City eight times for meetings with the NCAA and to Los Angeles six times for talks with Getty. Rasmussen was seeing airplanes in his sleep.

Rasmussen was not emotionally ready for the transformation he saw in Evey as the two men sat down to sign the final agreement. The Getty executive, knowing he had all the leverage, moved hostilely to take advantage of it, shedding whatever good-guy image he may have projected to Rasmussen during the courting process. Rasmussen and Evey had a verbal agreement that Getty would own eighty percent of ESP, Rasmussen and the others, the remaining twenty percent. In effect, Getty was buying the option of funding the network for as long as the oil giant desired. That could be for three weeks or three years. Getty could pull out anytime after the initial ten-million-dollar investment.

The terms were oppressively unfavorable to Rasmussen and his group, but they needed Getty's money, and Evey knew it. Evey picked up the agreement document, holding the inch-thick papers in his hand and began waving them in Rasmussen's face, his salty demeanor exacerbated by his morning shot of bourbon. Rasmussen could smell the alcohol on his breath.

Evey took off his glasses and grabbed the papers as if he was squeezing Rasmussen's privates.

"Well, we're giving you all this money, and I think we're going to change something," Evey said. Then he slammed his fist on the desk for emphasis.

"We're going to adjust this so Getty owns eighty-five percent, not eighty," Evey said, his voice rising. "It's eighty-five percent or no deal." There was another stipulation: The fifteen percent left for Rasmussen and the others could not be sold unless Getty approved. In other words, Rasmussen could not make money from his own stock unless he had permission from Getty.

Evey had one more demand. He wanted Ed Eagan, who had stuck through countless ESP crises when others fled, out of the project. Evey disliked Eagan because he spoke his mind. "He's not part of the package," said Evey. "Either he's out or the deal is off." Eagan, later learning of Evey's decree, somberly remarked, "I guess this is what's called taking one for the team." He left the company.

Evey said he does not remember the meeting playing out that way, though he does not deny asking for the changes. Rasmussen demurred. "That meeting was the first time I saw his ruthless side," Rasmussen said. "Those kinds of things happened throughout. We would have meetings and if he didn't like the way things were going, he would become very dramatic, very nasty. It was just his style. He never, ever let us forget who was the boss."

Although Evey acted harshly, even petulantly, he did what any good executive would do: He maneuvered the best deal for his company. "Stu could be rough," Conner recalled, "but the bottom line is, he had an open mind. If there was your typical executive sitting in Stu's office instead of Stu when Rasmussen came into the picture, the network would have never happened, or maybe happened much later. I'm convinced of that. Stu made it possible, even if he was difficult."

Rasmussen signed the new papers. The tense meeting did not temper his excitement. Getty wired several hundred thousand dollars to Plainville for deposit into the ESP account, the first time it had money in months. Rasmussen wrote Doherty a six-figure check to repay K. S. Sweet's interim loan to ESP. They had breakfast later that morning. "Well, we did it, can you believe it?" Doherty asked. Rasmussen took a sip of his orange juice. "Yes, yes I can."

The two men who had spent almost every day together for the past six months then shook hands, with Rasmussen flying back to Connecticut and Doherty to Pennsylvania. They never saw each other again.

5

NBC North

The agreement between ESP and Getty caught the media and sports establishments off guard, because Rasmussen and Getty had kept their discussions secret. The reaction was predictable. The networks downplayed ESP, saying it would never work because not enough homes were wired for cable; the print media was more bullish, but still wondered who would watch sports all day; and cable pioneers, such as Ted Turner in Atlanta, kicked themselves for not coming up with the idea first. Turner and ESP would soon begin an intense rivalry, the millionaire cable operator and Evey at its nexus.

Whether you were a believer or not, one fact remained undeniable. Getty money gave ESP credibility and the resources to honestly test the idea. The *Bristol Press* began covering ESP regularly after the announcement. *Sporting News* declared: "The biggest television sports story of the year emerged from little Plainville, Connecticut, the other day. Big Oil has diversified into the industry."

Evey, Conner, and Rasmussen moved quickly to sustain the momentum. Evey didn't think Rasmussen could build the network from the ground up, so he turned to his friend, Hollywood agent Ed Hookstratten, for advice, meeting him at a golf course in Palm Springs. Evey wanted to hire someone, preferably with a network profile, to run ESP and hoped Hookstratten could help put together a list. Serving as Getty's accounting eyes and ears, Conner arrived in Plainville on a Monday morning, the only hiccup in his plans being a statewide search by Connecticut state troopers for his Hertz rental car. The front license plate had been stolen and used in a robbery. Rasmussen, liberated from pursuit by police or creditors, flew to

Shawnee Mission to sign a two-year agreement with the NCAA. ESP was now free to broadcast dozens of collegiate sports, some live, some tape-delayed. The official announcement of the NCAA agreement, the first time college sports had delved into cable, brought more press to ESP. Almost overnight, the network had made itself a force in the sports broadcasting business, one competitors couldn't ignore for long.

Sitting in his NBC office at 30 Rockefeller Plaza, Chester Simmons was amused at the sudden and voluminous media attention directed at ESP. Once ESP started grabbing headlines, he had made his opinion clear throughout NBC: An all-sports cable station would die quickly. No television sports executive commanded respect like Simmons. His opinion meant something, which was why an Associated Press reporter was in his office now to ask his thoughts on sports and cable television, particularly ESP.

"My immediate concern is with the dilution of the product," he told the reporter. If cable does work, Simmons continued, then the glut of sports may hurt everyone.

"It probably won't come to that," Simmons said, "because cable sports networks won't work. There are not enough people watching cable. I think this sports network is doomed, to be honest."

Simmons was a network man—perhaps the smartest of all network men. He helped launch what was then the preeminent television sports show, "The Wide World of Sports," on ABC. He left for NBC and then sprinted up the chain to sports president, making the network one of the first stops for sports.

His relationship in recent months with NBC, however, had soured because of the network's lukewarm reaction to Simmons's new contract demands. It was a position NBC would later come to regret. For now, rumors swirled that Simmons was unhappy and wanted out of NBC.

Back on the ninth hole in Palm Springs, Ed Hookstratten, one of the most connected and influential agents in the film industry, wanted a piece of ESP without actually joining the network. He and Evey had been friends for years, and Evey knew that Hookstratten would be a valuable asset in bringing stars to the network, both in front of and behind the camera. Evey put him on retainer for $50,000 a year, just enough, as Evey told him, "to put a little Getty Oil on your shingles."

Hookstratten laughed and made good the money immediately. He identified two prominent personalities who could transform ESP: Simmons, who was indeed fed up with NBC because talks for a new contract were not going well, and Jim Simpson, the thirty-year-old NBC broadcaster whose face was recognized in most living rooms in America and who was also looking for a change.

That was the kind of star power Evey coveted. If ESP could recruit two respected giants in the industry to join the infant network, additional credibility would follow. He told the super-agent to covertly make contact with Simmons and Simpson.

ESP was making strides on another front as well. Rasmussen had decided on a date and time the network would air its first show: September 7, 1979 at 7 P.M., less than six months away. They would have to triple their efforts to make the date.

Construction on the ESP building began in late March. Conner, with a new rental car, established the accounting system and hired the first employees since the Getty purchase. Conner reported the daily happenings of ESP to Evey. Meanwhile, Evey worked on trying to rent two remote production trucks instead of buying them as Rasmussen wanted. He had rejected the hiring of an Academy Award-winning producer who wanted $1 million to produce the first show.

In May of 1979, the same year that the Big East Conference debuted and Indiana State's Larry Bird and Michigan State's Magic Johnson thrilled the country with their performances in the NCAA final, ESP added a key source of revenue. Anheuser-Busch signed a $1.38 million contract with ESP, the largest single advertising contract in cable history. Rasmussen celebrated by having a Budweiser with Scott.

The contract was a boon for the network and brought a flood of favorable publicity. ESP was on its way—or so it seemed. What few knew at the time was that the initial ten-million-dollar investment from Getty had been feverishly spent. Building a studio, hiring producers, purchasing remote trucks and other equipment had drained the money. When Scott turned in financial projections to Evey, showing larger losses than Evey wanted the Getty board to discover, Evey, frustrated by the mounting costs, ordered, "Change the numbers. I can't show Getty those numbers." Scott did, and instead of showing a ten-million-dollar loss, the reports to Getty falsely showed the network losing half of that.

Evey knew he could not cook the books forever. The losses were mounting too quickly. He had underestimated the cost of building a headquarters, about $3.5 million, and the jump in payroll funding, in excess of $1 million. Evey had to ask for more money. After spending a week on the telephone softening up Getty board members to the idea of an increased budget, working them like an adroit politician, Evey flew to Los Angeles, Rasmussen and Scott in tow, to meet with the Getty board. Rasmussen and

Scott, sitting before a boomerang-shaped glass table, fielded dozens of pointed questions from the board members. Thirty minutes into the interrogation, Evey interrupted.

"Gentlemen, when I first came to you with the concept of investing in a cable television network, I told you that our geological studies showed that there was a reservoir, and I was requesting funds to develop that reservoir. Today I am here to tell you when I said that, I was absolutely correct with one exception. Not only is there a reservoir, but the hole is much bigger than I ever anticipated."

"Gentlemen," he concluded, "I need more pipe."

By artfully putting his request in terms the oil men could understand, Evey drilled a hole through their resistance. Some board members still objected, and intense debate continued for over an hour until Harold E. Berg, the new, straight-shooting chairman, ended the discussion. "I think we can make money on this network," he told the quiet room. "If not, we can cut it off at $35 million and write it off as drilling a bad hole. So let's vote."

They did, and ESP had its money. Though not told how much they were given, ESP knew it had enough to go on the air and stay on for at least a few years. Several more times over the coming years, Evey would romance the Getty board for additional ESPN money. And each time they would ask, "How much more pipe?"

Getty executives were sometimes puzzled by Evey's passion for ESP. But they didn't know Evey. Evey was drawn to the possibility that ESP could develop into a powerful, visible network, one that would make him a star and for which he'd get all the credit. His interest in ESP stretched deeper, though. Evey, before anyone else, thought ESP would grow into a massive money-maker. He envisioned it as a "major lift" network, part of a basic package that cable operators could use to get into a viewer's home. Once there, the cable companies could entice viewers with the pay-movie channels like HBO and Cinemax, where the real profits were.

Years later, Evey would be proven correct.

There was an increased bounce in everyone's step after the Los Angeles meeting. Rasmussen shelved his traveling, media interviews, and immediate planning to concentrate on the network's name, which he felt needed to be changed. Rasmussen wanted something with four letters, not three, to distinguish the sports channel from the Big Three networks.

In his condo, Rasmussen sat down and began drawing. He added "network" to ESP for a four-letter acronym, then drew an elliptical circle around the name. He gave his design to the printer. When it came back, the circle was perfectly drawn. Rasmussen liked what he saw. So did Evey and Scott.

It was July 13, 1979, a Friday. Rasmussen's network had its final name: ESPN.

• • •

Rasmussen knew snagging a cherished prize like Simmons from under the nose of NBC would be like finding gold at the bottom of the sea. What he didn't know were the Byzantine turns the pursuit would take.

NBC still gave no definitive answer to Simmons in his request for a new contract, and Simmons was becoming increasingly agitated. He viewed ESPN as a viable option after several clandestine phone calls to industry insiders revealed that ESPN could work. When Hookstratten, and later Rasmussen, made contact, Simmons was more open to the idea than his previous public quotes indicated.

Simmons wanted to meet face-to-face with Rasmussen in New York and set up a longer meeting in Bristol. When Rasmussen called Simmons at his NBC office in New York in June, Simmons whispered into the phone that he would call him right back. Simmons did. He instructed Rasmussen that they could meet in New York but Rasmussen was forbidden from coming to 30 Rockefeller, just in case an NBC executive recognized the new father of sports cable. Simmons was unhappy with his negotiations with NBC, yet he did not want to lose NBC as an option. So when Rasmussen arrived in New York, he avoided the entrance of the NBC building and the security guards, instead, walking to a pay phone two blocks down the street from where he called Simmons, and the two ducked into a quiet restaurant nearby.

The conversation was brief. Simmons said he wanted to see how the construction of the main studio was progressing in Bristol, but he refused to stay at a hotel in the small Connecticut city, fearing a paper trail. Rasmussen suggested they meet in the parking lot of a McDonalds near the ESPN site, then drive to the studio construction area. Simmons agreed. "Ronald McDonald had no idea how big a part he played in ESPN's history," Rasmussen joked.

They took separate cars from McDonalds because Simmons was nervous someone would see them together. Rasmussen drove his car, Simmons and his wife drove in theirs. The site was still mostly a mixture of dust and metal. In the middle of the site, a long piece of steel stuck straight up, with an American flag on top, flapping in the wind. Simmons surveyed what was before him and turned pasty. "When are you guys going on the air?" he asked.

It was a common question, but Rasmussen was sticking to the September 7 date, just eight weeks away. As they walked around the mud-caked site, Rasmussen showed Simmons the planned location of the reception, studio, and office areas. Rasmussen assured Simmons that they would make the date because they had to. Otherwise, ESPN would lose credibility with cable operators. Simmons remained skeptical. He stared at the dirt and steel and, like always, did not mince words. "You will never go on the air by then," he said, realizing how far away he was, in both miles and philosophies, from the mighty NBC offices.

Simmons's trepidation irked Rasmussen, who decided, at that moment, he did not like Simmons. Rasmussen wasn't even sure if Simmons was the right man to run ESPN. But he was Evey's man, and that's all that mattered.

Doubting Simmons's ability was one of the few errors in judgment Rasmussen had made up to this point. Not only was Simmons the right man, he was the perfect man, and his influence on ESPN would prove to be deep and invaluable. For now, ESPN was a piece of clay, and it needed a stern, smart executive with hands of stone to mold it. Rasmussen was too soft for that job—Simmons was not.

Simmons was more enthusiastic about ESPN than he let on to Rasmussen. Simmons felt, frankly, that Rasmussen was a lightweight who knew nothing about running a network. Besides, Simmons knew who signed the checks, Evey. It was time to meet him.

• • •

Simmons's paranoia escalated as he and Rasmussen set up a meeting in Los Angeles with Evey a few days after leaving Bristol. Simmons demanded they leave on a late flight, minimizing the number of people he'd encounter. They agreed on a 9:30 P.M. flight from JFK Airport, meeting in the back of the Ambassador's Club in the TWA terminal. Then they moved to an empty portion of the concourse, watching as passengers boarded their flights. Simmons was smoking, rattling off questions to Rasmussen, still expressing doubt about debuting in early September. Fifteen minutes before the plane pulled from the tarmac, they boarded.

Simmons was temporarily calm, relieved that no one had seen him. Then the last two passengers boarded. Merlin Olsen, the hulking ex-defensive end from the Los Angeles Rams, and John Brodie, the former quarterback for the San Francisco 49ers, saw Simmons and immediately went to him to say hello. Then the athletes sat down—directly in front of Rasmussen and Simmons. One of Simmons's most effective moves at NBC had been to recruit ex-athletes to provide color for the broadcasts, and Simmons had hired both Olsen and Brodie. They revered him, spending most of the six-hour flight turned backward in their seats, chatting with him, and brow-beating him about why he was flying to California. Simmons introduced Rasmussen only as Bill and never mentioned he was from ESPN.

"Chet, if you are flying across the country, something big is going on, let us in on it," Olsen said.

"No, no, no, just routine stuff," Simmons responded.

After narrowly escaping being sacked by Olsen, Simmons met with the Getty Oil vice president in his office the next morning. Simmons sized up Evey quickly. "He made it clear how valuable he was to the company, how much the Getty family liked him. . . . He had an air of confidence," Simmons recalled years later. "Basically, Evey was a star fucker. I think he liked the whole idea of being in sports, around the stars. He liked the celebrity of it. I think it juiced him."

Evey asked Simmons how he'd run the network, the talent he would recruit, and his vision for ESPN. No job offer followed, but the meeting went well. Simmons was clearly interested in the job; Evey was clearly interested in Simmons. That left Rasmussen wondering where he fit in. He was beginning to feel as if he had no control over his own creation.

Rasmussen flew back to Connecticut and Simmons to New York. Several days later, in Plainville, the telephone rang in Rasmussen's office. It was Evey. He wanted to begin negotiations with Simmons, but before he hung up, he barked into the phone, "We'll pay him $175,000. That's it. If he doesn't like it, he can fuck off."

Simmons had one last request before officially joining ESPN. Rasmussen held the title of president, but Simmons refused to be called executive vice president. Evey played umpire, asking Rasmussen if he would mind the title of chairman of the board while Simmons was named president. It was more of an order than a request. Rasmussen reluctantly accepted.

The announcement did not come until later, but Simmons was hired on July 18—and for more money than Evey had decreed, $200,000 plus per year. Simmons then made the first of several key moves, stealing Scotty Connal, a thirty-year veteran of NBC. Connal was the best production man in the business. It would be his job to bring producers, directors, and technicians to ESPN.

Simmons's departure caught NBC by surprise, forcing them to scramble for a replacement before the impending Moscow Olympics. "Losing Chet and Scotty could not come at a worse time," an anonymous NBC executive told the *New York Times*. Simmons talked bravely to the press and to colleagues, predicting that ESPN would some day be a premier network. Privately, he suffered buyer's remorse. After the announcement, he and his wife went to the Bahamas for a week. Simmons lay on the beach, rehashing his decision.

"I remember being on this beautiful beach, the sand and waves, this great scenery, and all I could think about was, 'God, what have I done? Have I ended my career by going to this ESPN?'" Simmons said later. "I think I knew in my heart that we were entering a new era of television. But at the time, the networks were laughing at us."

Simmons may have had doubts, but his hire brought incontrovertible credibility to ESPN. His name meant as much to the network as Getty's money and signaled the beginning of open warfare between cable and the networks. If the best in the business, Simmons, believed in something that on the surface seemed as absurd as an all-sports cable station, then the networks had better stop flipping their noses and start paying attention.

In Plainville, the Simmons announcement galvanized the ESPN staff, which totaled twelve. At dinner that night inside the White Birch Inn, a small group toasted the beginning of something special. Rasmussen raised his glass of soda, smiling, but inside he felt strange, almost empty.

Rasmussen knew what was happening. His title as chairman of the board meant nothing, relegating him to the role of queen of England. Getty not only owned most of ESPN's stock, the corporation controlled his as well. In a few devastating motions, like a sword cutting through flesh, Rasmussen's power had been sliced away. His own network, his creation, was easing him out.

• • •

Simmons's office at NBC was big enough for a family of four. He had a large comfortable leather chair and an expansive, gleaming desk. By late summer, ESPN was still operating out of Plainville while the main offices were being built in Bristol. Rasmussen and Scott, once a heartbeat away from the poorhouse, were accustomed to living in spartan surroundings, so they never blinked at their closet-sized digs in Plainville. Simmons was another matter. His tiny desk was shoehorned into a tiny room. If Simmons wanted to back up from his desk, he had to ask Scott to move so he could get out.

Feeling pinched, Simmons left the office and checked into the Farmington Motor Inn, which later became a base of operations for ESPN. At one point, the seventy-two-room motel was crammed with nothing but ESPN workers, and Simmons and Connal stayed up until four in the morning in Simmons's room, eating pizza and planning the future of the network. The immediate goal was recruiting bodies. Evey wanted a nonunion work force because that would save millions of dollars in payroll expenses, leaving Simmons little choice but to fill the staff with twenty-year-olds directly out of college. Working at low pay and with no union ties, they had the muscle and energy Simmons knew would be needed to get on the air by the date promised the cable operators.

Connal was only slightly more discriminating. He began all his interviews by asking applicants the section of the paper they checked first. If the answer was anything other than sports, the interview usually ended there.

The result was a lean, hungry work force that resembled the eventual viewers. Every person had an insatiable appetite for sports and few minded staying up all night, night after night, to birth the show. The few who did not adapt quickly to the harrowing pace were either fired or quit. It was Darwinism in all its gratifying, cruel glory.

Of course some positions could not be filled by a snot-nosed rookie, and for those spots, Simmons buried his face in the NBC telephone directory. Jim Simpson wanted out of NBC, so Simmons courted him. He hired technical talents and accounting experts from NBC as well, including Barry Black, an NBC unit manager and jack of all trades. Connal recruited Reggie Thomas to head engineering.

These raids concerned NBC, but they didn't realize how much talent Simmons had hijacked until it was too late. Finally, after more than two dozen defections, an executive with RCA, the parent company of NBC, tracked down Simmons at the Farmington Inn. "Look, Chet," he said, "when you left we gave you a nice settlement package and I'll be blunt. If you keep stealing our people, you might lose some of those payments." Unfazed, Simmons continued to ring the NBC switchboard. He could get practically anyone he wanted because he carried so much weight in the industry. By the end of summer, after dozens of defections, the press started calling ESPN "NBC North."

On-air personalities were easy to acquire. Simmons and Connal scoured the Connecticut and New York areas for local television anchors and radio reporters who were willing to work cheap. They didn't have to go far to find Lou Palmer, who was already working at the network. George Grande was plucked from a CBS affiliate in New York. Tom Mees was hired after quitting as sports director of WECA-TV in Tallahassee, Florida, and Bob Ley joined the network on just its third day after finishing a stint as a soccer stadium announcer.

Producer Fred Muzzi, who once fell into a ditch in the dirt parking lot and was covered up to his chest in mud, and another producer, Stephen Bogart, the son of Humphrey Bogart and Lauren Bacall, came aboard. Pronovost was identified by Connal. Steve Anderson, the son of Dave Anderson, the Pulitzer Prize-winning columnist from the *New York Times,* was hired as a production assistant, as was Bob Rauscher. Ed McMahon, Johnny Carson's sidekick, called about a job for his son. He got it. Rosa Gatti, a cable doubter at first, was hired for public relations. Gatti was the first woman sports information director at a major college but left her secure job at Brown University. Simmons had liked how she ran the NCAA hockey tournament.

The first round of Simmons and Connal hirings brought six producers/directors, six associate producers, and six production assistants to ESPN. The new group of cable renegades worked from early morning until sunset, setting up equipment, scheduling programming, and working with RCA to coordinate satellite coverage. Though exhausting, there was almost a spirituality to their work, a sense that something special was gaining momentum. And no one wanted to disappoint the peerless Simmons.

In the weeks before the first broadcast, Simmons spent most of his days on the telephone, rarely traveling to the ESPN building, which now at least had a few walls. On one of those trips, a Thursday morning, he watched as a truck brought the first of the dual ten-meter dishes, the key to everyone's dreams, onto the ESPN complex. As Simmons stood there in a trance, a six-foot-five, beefy man, plodded through the muddy lot, his shoes caked in brown guck, walked up to Simmons, and told him how nice it was to see him. Simmons recognized the deep voice from conversations on the telephone but not the face at first. A time would come when the face of Chris Berman would be one of the most recognizable on television. Today, however, he was simply the guy with the booming voice who Simmons instantly liked because of his exuberant personality. Simmons wanted to hire him immediately.

• • •

Berman had dreamed of becoming a sportscaster since he was eight. In Rye, New York, his hometown, all the kids played baseball on his lawn.

They nicknamed it "Berman Stadium," where he played first base and did color commentary imitating the quick-tongued style of Red Barber.

Berman had a high IQ, using his intelligence to enter Brown University. He was immediately drawn to the campus radio station, where he announced sports and honed his wisecracking skills. From a beat-up red station wagon, he reported the traffic, light to moderate, except when it was moderate to light.

After graduating from Brown, he was hired by a five-thousand-watt radio station in Waterbury. He then added weekend anchor duties at WVIT-TV. He traveled to every Connecticut athletic event possible, feeding his appetite for sports while feeding his stomach with free press box food. Berman was a regular at the Tuesday gatherings of the media that covered Yale football. The school paid for a lush meal at a five-star restaurant near the campus, seducing the sportswriters with prime rib, salmon, juicy salads, lobster bisque, and cheesecake. Berman was always there, but he rarely asked any questions, instead listening and munching on his steak. Local reporter Bill Pennington once asked Berman why he even bothered to come. "Hey," Berman replied, "it's a free lunch."

Berman read about ESPN in the Connecticut press. When he phoned Simmons, he was told simply to show up. Berman typified ESPN talent from those days: young, energetic, bright, and willing to do whatever management asked, even if that meant working sixteen-hour days or anchoring at two in the morning.

Berman signed with ESPN on October 1, 1979, for $16,500 a year. His first assignment was the 3 A.M. show with Tom Mees. Meanwhile, in early August, with just four weeks remaining until the first broadcast, Simmons gathered the troops for a pep talk. The staff was now up to thirty-two, and they could barely squeeze into the Plainville conference room where only two months earlier Rasmussen often had sat alone wondering if his idea would ever get off the ground. Simmons stood on a platform, above everyone, implicitly asserting dominion.

"I know it has been a brutal pace so far and we've worked ourselves to death," Simmons began. "All I can tell you is I am dedicated to making this work. I was around for the start of the ABC network and then the rebirth of NBC. I've seen it all and I can tell you I feel better now than I ever did at those other places. We will do it."

Simmons stepped down to heavy applause. Despite the passionate speech, he remained privately concerned that they would not make it on the air by September 7. Late one afternoon on August 25, Simmons pulled Connal aside and asked him if it was still possible.

"I'll let you know in twelve hours," Connal said.

Connal probed his people, surveyed the entire complex, and picked over every detail of production, arriving at an inescapable conclusion.

Exactly twelve hours later, he reported back to Simmons.

"Let's do it," Connal told him.

6

"You Have to Be a Son of a Bitch"

The night before the launch, Scott could barely sleep, tossing restlessly in his bed. He finally got up at five o'clock, surrendering to the increasing mixture of excitement and anxiety. As Scott dressed, a strange nausea developed in his gut. He and his father had worked thirteen excruciating months to get to this day, and now that it was here, something didn't feel right. He wanted to go back to bed. Instead, he made his way toward the studio.

Gaping holes still marred the foundation, and bulldozers continued to move mounds of earth. Incredibly, ESPN was going to do its first show with the studio only three-quarters built. Inside, the set still had not arrived, wires dangled from the ceiling, mosquitoes buzzed through the building, and a small family of skunks wandered an abandoned corridor. The production assistants had given one of them a name—"Stinky."

Simmons was frantic, and even Connal, his close friend and confidant, could not calm him down. Simmons barked at Rasmussen for making the commitment to this day in the first place. Rasmussen, who had become accustomed to Simmons yelling at him, walked away. But even through anger, Simmons maintained clarity, directing his staff with the precision of an air traffic controller.

Rasmussen taped a piece on how a satellite transmission works, and as evening approached, Creasy and Pronovost rehearsed with Leonard and Grande, who had written the show's script on two old manual typewriters. Connal shunned teleprompters because he knew the scant programming and highlights would lead to plenty of ad-libbing on the air. Connal wanted his anchors to look as if they were conversing, not parroting a script.

Simmons tried unsuccessfully to clear the jammed studio, which was crowded with NCAA officials, members of the media, and others. George Conner, who had worked nonstop since arriving from Getty, finally relaxed.

One hour before the debut, Rasmussen and Scott snuck away to spend a few minutes alone. They walked to the back of the complex, where their only company was an unoccupied bulldozer. They weren't sure what to say to each other, and at first there was just small talk and smiles. Rasmussen then grabbed Scott and pulled him close. They cried together for several minutes. They then went back to the studio.

• • •

7 P.M.

Anchor Grande glances admiringly at Leonard, who is introducing the taped Rasmussen piece on satellites. He knows he is watching a professional. The first ESPN sports wrap-up show is only seconds old, but he likes the pace of it so far. Grande can tell if a broadcast is going to go sour in the first few minutes, and at that point, everything was smooth, so he relaxes.

It takes just two minutes for Grande to fall out of his comfort zone. In the background, people on the set and in the control room can hear rumbling noises outside that sound like a large truck. It's the bulldozers, still shoving earth around the construction site. No one has bothered to tell them to stop plowing.

Before someone can alert the construction workers, Simmons and his staff face a more serious dilemma. Colorado coach Chuck Fairbanks stands on the field before his game against Oregon and waits to do a live interview. In his ear, Leonard hears nothing but static, and on the monitors, Fairbanks's lips are moving, but there is no sound for almost a minute. Simmons cradles his head in his hands.

Outside, the bulldozers are still barreling around the lot. One of them rolls out of control and collides with a production trailer, flipping it several times. Inside, technicians are tumbling around like socks in a dryer. Fortunately, the trailer lands upright; after checking for broken bones, no one decides to seek medical attention. The show must go on.

With a polished ease, Scotty Connal oversees the rest of the show, which goes without a glitch. At 7:30 P.M., ESPN broadcasts a collegiate sports preview, and then 30 minutes later, ESPN shows a live slow-pitch softball game between the Milwaukee Schlitzes and Kentucky Bourbons. Stuart Evey and Simmons wince every time the Milwaukee team makes a play, since that means the broadcaster must mention the word "Schlitzes." ESPN's big sponsor is Anheuser-Busch. "Every time I heard that Milwaukee team mentioned, I shivered, I just shivered," Simmons remembered.

A live wrestling match follows at 11 P.M. and then the first thirty-minute highlight show, called "Sports Recap," at 11:30. Leonard and Grande are back on the air, wrapping up the highlights at midnight. The 7 P.M. show and the college preview are rebroadcast, followed by a tennis tournament from Monte Carlo. ESPN goes off the air about four in the morning.

The show was piped onto television monitors back at the Plainville Holiday Inn, and when ESPN concluded its groundbreaking evening, a celebration ensued in the small ballroom. The dreams of the two Rasmussen men, the open-mindedness of Evey, and the guidance of Simmons and Connal converged to make ESPN a reality.

Simmons was as proud of the past eight weeks as he was of anything he had accomplished at NBC. He drank a Bud and lit a cigar. Then he climbed up on the platform. The room became quiet. "It was a good first night," he said. "But don't forget, you've got to do it tomorrow night, and the night after that, and the night after that. So go home and get some rest."

Simmons knew the greatest perils were yet to come. Putting on sports every day, all day, had never been done before. That would be the real challenge. Tonight was just the beginning.

Simmons's reality check failed to dull the overwhelming feeling of accomplishment. Launching ESPN was certainly not on a par with sending a man to the moon or developing the microchip. It was, however, in the spirit of these seminal events. What started as a fanciful idea had with equal measures of determination and stubbornness become a reality. In a matter of a few years, it would be a cultural phenomenon.

• • •

But first, at 7 A.M. on September 8, there was munster hurling.

Two million Americans had ESPN on their cable systems, and probably only a handful of them knew what they were watching early this morning as men wearing short skirts ran around a field playing a version of field hockey. It was the type of odd alternative programming that would define ESPN for years.

The rush of the first day wore off surprisingly fast for the weary staff.

Simmons slept three hours and then was back in the studio by six that morning. He could not help but chuckle at what was beaming out over the air. At 8 A.M. there was a rebroadcast of a wrestling match, followed by Irish cycling, and then a "Sports Recap." Then came more slow-pitch softball, Korea against Japan in volleyball, a special about marathons, and then UConn against UCLA in soccer. After that game, Toner received more phone calls from excited alumni, and Simmons joked with Connal, wondering if it was too late for them to crawl back to NBC.

It would not have been an ESPN broadcast day without a mishap. This time it was not lost audio or killer bulldozers but a traffic accident. A small sedan crashed into a nearby telephone pole, which fell onto ESPN's power supply, knocking out electricity to the station for several minutes before backup generators kicked in. Pronovost wondered what could happen next.

Meanwhile, Berman, whose commanding voice could often be heard from one end of the newsroom to the other, even when the bulldozers were at their loudest, was already into a habit of tormenting producers by appearing only several minutes before air time. Berman anchored the late-night "Sports Recaps"—he would do so for four years, mostly with Tom Mees—and for some reason, one Wednesday night in June he was feeling particularly frisky while reading the scores. After reading name after name of athletes, he came upon baseball player John Mayberry. Instead of just blandly reading his name, as previously, Berman, completely spontaneously, began what would become a trademark. He blurted out, "John Mayberry, R.F.D." Berman continued the broadcast, unsure if the audience understood what he had tried to do, or if they thought he had gone too far. Berman got his answer when he heard Pronovost laughing heartily in his ear. The man operating the camera guffawed so uncontrollably the picture shook. Berman may not have invented the use of nicknames—there are tapes from the 1930s of The Detroit Tigers announcer Ty Tyson referring to a pitcher as Luke "Pied Piper of" Hamlin—but no sports broadcaster's career ever benefited more from creative nicknaming than Berman's.

The press portrayed ESPN as an alternative to three minutes of sports on the stuffy local stations. The *Bristol Press* began its love-hate relationship with the network by publishing a flattering editorial: "It would be premature to say that ESPN represents a threat to the existing big three television networks, but the possibilities are clear. An independent station with the right to beam its programs through a communications satellite can offer alternative programming without affiliating with one of the major networks. The potential now exists for decentralization of television broadcasting, dominated by ABC, CBS, and NBC for three decades. Stations such as the local ESPN are among the first to test the new options opened up by the proliferation of communications satellites. They are trailblazers and it will be interesting to monitor their progress."

Connecticut Magazine featured a lengthy article on Rasmussen. He was on the cover, one foot planted on top of a television, as if he were taming the cable jungle. The headline read: "Why are ABC, CBS, and NBC Afraid of This Man?" *Newsweek* said ESPN was "television's most ambitious project" and claimed the network's all-sports diet would be a source of marital discord because husbands would hunker down and watch sports all day. Red Smith, still the most notable sportswriter of the time, interviewed Simmons and wrote a complimentary column.

Some media analysts remained skeptical, suggesting ESPN was a novelty. On Wall Street, advertising analysts declared ESPN would never turn a profit because cable lacked staying power and viewers would tire of constantly watching sports. Before ESPN, the three major networks combined got by with eighteen hours of sports coverage per week. Analysts reasoned: Who would want to watch more sports than that?

Even Lee Leonard was not completely sold. Seven months after that incredible first day, he left ESPN for another cable startup, CNN.

Sports Illustrated, with its power and prestige, chimed in with perhaps the most important piece on ESPN, predicting, "ESPN may become the biggest thing in TV sports since 'Monday Night Football' and nighttime World Series games." The feature included a large picture of Rasmussen, plus a quote from Scott that described viewers who stayed up to watch sports at 3 A.M. as "sports junkies." (Later media reports would credit Scott for first publicly coining that phrase.)

It was a significant chunk of publicity for the incipient network. Everyone at ESPN was high from the story. Scott was in Bristol, poring over the *Sports Illustrated* article, when the phone rang. It was Evey. He was screaming. "That was the worst piece of shit article I have ever seen," Evey yelled. Scott stayed calm and realized that Evey simply was angry that neither his name nor Getty's had been mentioned.

Evey and Scott's relationship had completely deteriorated because Evey felt Scott contributed nothing to the network. As for the senior Rasmussen, he had a two-front war to wage: Evey and Simmons. His relationships with each of the men had reached a critical point, swelling as a star does just before going supernova.

"I didn't like Chet because he came on like gangbusters," Rasmussen recalled. "He was always screaming, throwing stuff against the wall. He was very dramatic. The very, very first day he came on board, he said, 'I don't want you talking to any newspapers. And we'll have none of this self-aggrandizement.' I didn't like that, because ESPN was in constant contact with the cable industry, and the cable industry had a real anger toward the networks because the networks had treated them so poorly. They did not trust Chet. And Chet said to me once, 'We're going to show these cable shit-kickers how to run television.' We needed someone who was not so arrogant, who could deal with the cable industry, and I knew more about the people in it than Chet."

Whenever the media wanted to do a story on ESPN, Rasmussen got the first and, sometimes, only call. He was the more interesting part of ESPN's rags-to-riches tale, the entrepreneur who turned television upside down. Simmons at one point got so frustrated with Rasmussen getting all the attention, Rasmussen claims, that Simmons ordered the receptionists at ESPN to tell anyone who called for Rasmussen that he was not in the office, even if Rasmussen was sitting right there.

Simmons and Evey tell a different story. They say the reason they were upset with Rasmussen had nothing to do with jealousy over a lack of media attention for themselves. They assert that Rasmussen was a loose cannon who made promises to cable outlets behind their backs and hired people on a whim without saying a word. The last straw for Simmons was when Rasmussen announced, without first consulting anyone at the network, that on September 1, 1980, the network would go to twenty-four-hour broadcasts. Evey, Simmons, and Connal felt ESPN needed much more time and many more resources to reach that point.

Evey claims Rasmussen would tell an athletic conference that their championship could be on ESPN, then announce to the cable press a deal had been struck. The news would travel on the wire at light speed, and Getty's stock would get a positive bump. But there often was no deal, only talk of one. Then Evey would receive calls from Getty attorneys asking what the hell was going on in Bristol.

Rasmussen, added Evey, did something even worse than make cock-eyed statements to the press. Rasmussen was allegedly trying to sell portions of his ESPN stock to buyers, including cable moguls like Ted Turner, knowing the stock was tied up by his agreement with Getty. Evey and a Getty attorney had received so many requests for Rasmussen's stock, Evey said, including one from Turner, that the company had to compose a form letter to handle the inquiries, which numbered dozens. Rasmussen denied this, saying Turner had paid him $100,000 to talk about selling the stock.

Simmons couldn't have cared less what Rasmussen did with his stock.

He simply felt it was time for Rasmussen, and his son, to leave the network. "We had some pretty tough times between us," Simmons remembered, speaking of Rasmussen. "We had some pretty good shouting matches about what he and his son were doing unilaterally. How he was trying to get involved in certain things. His son, I don't know what he was doing there, other than the fact he was his son. They both had little understanding of what should happen next. We were totally miles apart. . . . And Evey was not all that taken with Bill. He looked at Bill as this little guy from Connecticut who had the idea, now it was time for someone else to execute it. Now, it's time to go bye-bye."

"Unfortunately, when you do these things, you have to step on some toes and you have to be a son of a bitch," Simmons continued. "I finally had to be the son of a bitch who had to drive the final nail because I couldn't work this way. You needed just one guy to run the company. Put the responsibility in my hands. I want it in my hands. I don't want the other guy out there, doing what he wants to do, freelancing. It had to come to an end."

It was a harsh reality but the truth. Rasmussen was not equipped to take ESPN to the next level. Simmons was. So Simmons met with Evey in Connecticut, and the subject was Rasmussen. Simmons wanted Rasmussen at least to step aside, perhaps leave the company entirely. "This has got to end," Simmons complained. "He and I just can't work together." Evey agreed but wanted Rasmussen to stay aboard for a little while longer, because he felt the publicity of firing the founder might tarnish the network's developing image. They would meet with Rasmussen and define his role, but Scott would be asked to leave immediately.

On the Sunday following the launch, Rasmussen, Evey, and Simmons had lunch. Evey was blunt. "This meeting is to clarify something. I want Chet to be in charge. Do you understand that?" Rasmussen had expected this confrontation, but he was still surprised by its harshness. Burning inside, he said little.

Later that week, Evey asked Scott to fly to Los Angeles for a meeting. Scott and his father knew what Evey wanted. "Just promise me something," Rasmussen said to Scott before he left, "you will not say anything rash." Scott promised. He took the elevator to the eighteenth floor and met with Evey in his office. Evey said Scott could stay in Getty public relations and keep his current salary, about $75,000 a year, or stay with ESPN and take a pay cut. Scott hated both options and quit, quietly, with dignity. As Scott got up to leave, Evey said, "One more thing. You can keep your company car, but I want the license plate." Scott's plate read "ESPN1" and he was fond of it. He said no and kept the tag (which now hangs on a wall in his living room). Scott flew back to Connecticut, went to his office in Plainville, cleaned out his things, and left the network on September 18, 1979.

Scott remained intensely bitter over his departure and would not go back to ESPN for nineteen years. One day he decided his children needed to see what was once one of the most important things in his life.

"If it were not for my kids," Scott said, "I would have never gone back." He later tried to start an all-sports radio network that went bankrupt and currently runs a successful polling service.

The bloodbath at the newly minted station continued, as each of the original executives had his turn in the ring with Evey. Bob Chamberlain, who for a short time headed rights and acquisitions, was let go outright. So was Jon Foley, who worked in public relations. Bob Bray ran ESPN's payroll and was told he could stay if he took a fifty percent pay cut. He declined. Peter Fox, who produced some of the early ESPN shows, was fired a few months after his friends. Evey wanted everyone to sell their stock back to Getty; some did.

Rasmussen, defanged after that breakfast, stayed with ESPN for one year, mostly touring cable shows, proudly boasting about the network that had cast him aside. The media, oblivious to the turmoil behind the scenes, still wanted to interview Rasmussen, and he even received an occasional phone call about programming. Oklahoma coach Barry Switzer finally returned a call Rasmussen had made three weeks earlier regarding Switzer taking part in a college football show. Switzer said he wasn't interested in ESPN because he felt such a small network could do nothing for the powerful Sooners. Another man wanted ESPN to pay him to put rooftop platform tennis on the network—not even ESPN was that desperate.

Rasmussen quickly bored of his role as cable ambassador. He anxiously called Simmons one day in Bristol to tell him he was leaving the network, then phoned Evey in Los Angeles. As part of a settlement offer, Evey wanted Rasmussen to turn in his stock in exchange for $250,000. The offer was low, since it was clear the stock was worth several times that, at least. "No way that will work," Rasmussen said. Evey conceded. Rasmussen got $250,000 and kept his stock.

Rasmussen, like Scott, owned a company car, a 1978 Cadillac. Evey first said Rasmussen could keep it. Then Evey, out of spite, changed his mind and deducted its worth, about $5,700, from the final settlement, a fitting end to their convenient, and then later contemptuous, relationship.

There was not a dramatic last day at ESPN for Rasmussen nor a final, teary-eyed glance at the ESPN building. There wasn't even a going-away party. Rasmussen just faded out, like a lost satellite signal.

"I would go back to sometimes visit friends," Rasmussen said recently. "I felt good about what I accomplished there. I was never bitter and I never looked over my shoulder. I did my part. I guess it was just time to go."

7

Snake Eyes

Several months after Rasmussen's low-key exit, Getty finance wizard George Conner was in a deep sleep in his room at the Farmington Motor Inn, dreaming of the time he worked only nine-hour days at the Getty offices. The phone rang, breaking the silence of the night. It was 3 A.M., and a man from RCA was on the line, his voice cracking.

"We're going to have to take you off the bird," he told Conner.

Conner sat up straight in his bed. He had become used to the way RCA called Satcom 1 "the bird." He had also become used to the way its representatives sometimes exaggerated problems. But this time, Conner could tell from the man's hurried tone of voice, as well as the time of night, this was no false alarm.

A crucial U.S. Army communications satellite was spinning out of control in orbit. Satcom 1 had the latest technology, so Uncle Sam, which can take control of civilian hardware, wanted it. That meant ESPN would be forced to go off the air indefinitely. As Conner was relayed the horrific news while sitting in his pajamas, his heart stopped pumping.

Later that morning, the blood was coursing through his body again. The army had reestablished attitude control of its bird, and ESPN was saved from a military coup. It never went off the air. "From that day on, my biggest fear was that the Russians would shoot down the satellite," Conner recalled.

These were frenzied, sometimes terrifying days for the network. There was a constant fear that everything could come crashing down any day. Maybe Satcom 1 would burn up in orbit, essentially ending ESPN, or Getty, pumping $12,000 a month into the network, would tire of losing

100

money and pull out. Or maybe Ted Turner's CNN, the little station that could, which debuted in 1980 and featured its own half-hour sports show, would run ESPN off cable by stealing its viewers. CNN did have talent on its sports side. Keith Olbermann made his cable debut on the network as a fill-in for another reporter. His first interview was with New York Mets manager Joe Torre. CNN of course had no idea what it had in Olbermann or three years later in March when they hired another great talent named Dan Patrick.

Even after ESPN went to twenty-four hours of continuous broadcasting on September 1, 1980, something Rasmussen never got to savor, a stinging sense of dread sometimes filled the newsroom. That fear produced a raw, anything-goes mentality, which sometimes worked in a positive way. The tension stimulated creative juices, leading to intelligent and at times witty programming, which loyal viewers loved. The fear of extinction also brought the staff closer. They ate pancakes together at the White Birch, hamburgers at Hamps (nicknamed "Cramps"), and cold cuts and chips at the company Christmas party, which almost everyone attended. In March, Simmons invited employees to his home for Passover. ESPN teams competed in softball leagues and Saturday flag football games in Bristol. ESPN wasn't so much a company as it was a close fraternity.

"We felt like we were fighting this war against the doubters," said Berman. "We were in the bunker. Everyone knew everyone."

Yet, the closeness could not erase the profound stress a twenty-four-hour network imposed on a small staff. That stress sometimes produced unhealthy, even dangerous, addictions. Some producers, directors, and talent eased the burden of broadcasting twenty-four hours a day with a limited staff and equipment by using drugs heavily. A few pacified their insecurities as members of an upstart network with sex parties and late-night orgies, sometimes in the ESPN main building and trailers. And a number gambled incessantly to defeat the boredom of living in Bristol.

Some acted as though each day at the network was their last, even after Anheuser-Busch, in October, extended its contract with ESPN to five years for $25 million. It was hailed by the press as the most significant achievement in cable television history, and to some degree it was, but the network was swimming in so much red ink, the money was a raindrop landing on top of an ocean of debt.

ESPN was able to overcome its self-inflicted wounds by the tireless work of Simmons and Connal, who slaved to bring ESPN up to network standards. To show the rest of the staff they were there to stay, Simmons sold his house in Greenwich and moved to West Hartford, and Connal bought a home in Bristol. Connal had a minuscule technical budget compared with the big-three networks; still, he managed to produce decent live broadcasts mostly by being resourceful. His favorite phrase was "We have to make our two cameras look like five."

Simmons concentrated on programming, the most difficult job at the network. The pro sports still were unconvinced of ESPN's viability. The Simmons name, however, opened some doors. A year earlier, NFL owners had voted 28–0 against allowing ESPN to carry portions of the draft, fearing no one would watch. Simmons traveled to New York to meet with Rozelle—the two were friends from Simmons's NBC days—looking for an NFL ally. "Pete, we're going to do something no one has ever done before," he said to Rozelle.

Intrigued, Rozelle leaned forward in his seat. Simmons laid out his plan to carry the entire draft live on ESPN. Rozelle looked dumbfounded, then asked, "Why would you want to do that?" Trusting the instincts of Simmons and NFL broadcasting director Val Pinchbeck, who thought it would be a wise idea, Rozelle worked the owners, who trusted him. On April 29, the first live coverage of the NFL draft was hosted by Grande and former soccer announcer Bob Ley. Televising the draft would turn out to be one of the shrewdest decisions ESPN ever made. Eventually, because of the behind-the-scenes work of Tom Odjakjian, an ESPN programmer, and Jim Steeg with the NFL, both ESPN and pro football agreed that the draft should be moved from Tuesday to Sunday to augment fan interest. Ratings tripled.

Simmons wanted programming that the big three were afraid to touch. He and Connal emphasized this quirky predilection to every producer who joined the network. It seemed as if one additional producer or director a day was cramming into the offices. They all had the same profile: young, white, male, college educated (usually on the East Coast), limited television experience, and a willingness to work cheap. And each new hire learned quickly how to operate with limited REM sleep. Producer and director Bill Creasy, hired by Simmons from the CBS affiliate in New York, brought in Steve Bornstein from a public access television station as a programming assistant. Loren Matthews was a director of broadcast promotions for the New York Mets, and after a brief stint in ESPN's promotions department, headed to programming. Odjakjian came from the Eastern College Athletic Conference. The three men would later prove among the most crucial hires in the history of the network.

Connal, public relations maven Rosa Gatti, the programming staff, and others would meet in Simmons's office (or the White Birch or the conference room) to debate what to put on the air. Programming was not based on Nielsen ratings, because the ratings didn't exist for cable until late

1982. Instead, programmers relied solely on their guts and the advertisers preferences.

The programming arguments, heated at times, often lasted hours. Sometimes they were over small things, like whether ESPN should run its fitness shows on New Year's Day for all those overweight, perennial resolvers. Some wanted to pit the top two Ivy League schools against each other in a live football game, which they wanted to call the Elite Bowl. It was voted down.

Outside Simmons's office, Bornstein, sporting a full beard and short Afro hairstyle, was rising rapidly through the production ranks, owing to his matchless work ethic. He sometimes spent seven straight hours on the phone, looking for tapes of games—any games—to fill airtime. Most of the time was spent chatting up college athletic directors and coaches. He would start the conversation by asking if they had a hockey game that night. If so, the next question was always "Can we get a tape?" If that answer was yes again, the game was on the air the next night, then rebroadcast two or three times.

They aired tapes of Australian rules football, auto races, high school lacrosse, a world Frisbee championship, tractor pulls, obscure ping pong and golf tournaments. The TV screen for more than three million potential viewers showed rodeo matches, water skiing, wind surfing, horse steeplechase races, and even women mud-wrestling in bathing suits. Bornstein liked the idea of putting on the running of the bulls from Spain, so ESPN did. The network purchased the rights to a tennis match in Italy and dubbed the tape with commentary from Palmer, who was in an air-conditioned room in Bristol but simulated his attendance at the match by complaining about the heat "here in Rome."

Odjakjian replaced Bornstein, who moved up the programming ladder, as manager of program scheduling. Odjakjian played a hunch. When Steve Sabol began NFL Films, a football video library, he showed his highlights, which spanned decades, mostly on old projectors at Elks clubs. Sabol operated out of a kidney dialysis center on 13th and Vine Streets in Philadelphia and had built a cult following, including Odjakjian. In the fall of 1980, Odjakjian called Sabol about putting his films on ESPN. Sabol loved the idea, even cutting his fee considerably after realizing the cash-strapped circumstances of the station. To Sabol, it was an investment, like sticking a few dollars in a money market account.

Odjakjian's only request was that he wanted the telegenic Sabol as host. Sabol promptly expressed doubts about his television-hosting abilities. "Don't worry about that," Odjakjian said, "because no one is going to be watching anyway."

Sabol's show first aired in the early morning hours. In just a few weeks, he started receiving letters of thanks from thousands of men working the graveyard shifts and from fathers tuning in while feeding their babies at two in the morning. Odjakjian had underestimated the show's popularity.

NFL Films became such a viewer favorite that Odjakjian lobbied to use some of Sabol's films during ESPN's Monday night football show, which preceded ABC's show. He was opposed vigorously by others at ESPN, who thought such a move would benefit the competition more than it would ESPN. But Odjakjian, quickly making a mark inside the network for his superior instincts, figured it was foolish to fight the tide of millions running to their televisions sets to watch the big Monday night game. Instead, why not make ESPN part of the party? Odjakjian got his wish, and Sabol's films went on to become one of the most recognizable pieces of programming in ESPN history.

In June of 1980, ESPN aired a college baseball game between Hawaii and Miami, that July the first Canadian Football League game. With its strange rules (three downs instead of four), oblong field, and inferior players, the networks thought the CFL was poison, but ESPN embraced it. The Hambletonian horse race was in August. There was skiing, a live boxing match between Frank "The Animal" Fletcher and Ben Serrano, and professional bowling.

In the programming department's trailer, the staff kept a photo of a Trident submarine on the wall. Someone had written over the original print: "Coming to ESPN: submarine racing." It was their inside joke. ESPN was willing to put almost anything on the air to fill time, and with the military's permission, even submarine races might make it.

Simmons constantly checked the network's pulse and, being no fool, realized that ESPN could not survive on downhill skiing alone. He wanted to emphasize its strength—college hoops. So ESPN decided to broadcast the early rounds of the NCAA tournament, which the networks ignored. That March, ESPN aired 455.5 hours of college basketball or related programming, which brought a tired smile to the face of Simmons. The first night of the oversized NCAA tournament menu, ESPN ran five live rooms, or what some directors called hot boxes. Each one controlled a different contest, and at times, because ESPN was new at handling multiple simultaneous games, there were moments of chaos, like late switches or audio problems. Connal always seemed to know what was needed to avoid the next glitch, sometimes admonishing the guilty party, other times gently touching a shoulder with his large hands to reassure a stressed-out director.

"He was a hockey player, a tough guy, but a very fair guy," recalled producer Stephen Bogart, who was hired by Connal for $12,000 a year.

Simmons's attention ranged from acquiring programming to attacking the problems of "SportsCenter," which were numerous, none looming larger than the lack of top highlights. ESPN had no reciprocal agreement with the networks to share clips, so instead of Dallas Cowboys-Washington Redskins highlights, ESPN was stuck many times showing a punchless UConn highlight or Boston Red Sox game filmed by a local Hartford station.

The dearth of highlights led to some awkward, and at times, exalted, "SportsCenter" moments. Anchors were forced to ad-lib for minutes at a time because of the lack of video. Sometimes they filled the vacuum with hackneyed praise of a favorite athlete, rhapsodizing, for instance, about the heroic qualities of Joe Montana. Other musings were more beguiling. Berman invented the "Swami," an over-the-top clairvoyant whose predictions were wrapped around clever writing and robust humor. Viewers loved it. Once after sitting down for a meal in Newport Beach, California, the waiter asked, "What does the Swami want for dinner?"

Berman flourished when asked to wing it, his quick mind recalling vital statistics about a player and his splendid wit sending the studio, and presumably the audience, into crippling laughter. And fans were still tuning in to watch the nicknames. Berman was receiving suggestions from producers and also viewers, who filled his mailbox with letters.

Grande could also deftly fill the picture voids. During an 11 P.M. "SportsCenter" in the winter, producer Muzzi yelled into Grande's ear, "We're four minutes short! Talk about the National League for four minutes!" Four minutes is a decade in television, but Grande handled it gracefully, mesmerizing the audience with a thoughtful comparison of National League and American League pitchers. Sometimes the time-killers were written in the script as a "two-shot talk about it."

Simmons was proud of his anchors, but long stretches of talking heads, without highlights, underscored the gaps in ESPN's coverage. He knew "SportsCenter" would never succeed unless the highlights improved. Simmons once again drew on his stature in the business and waded through his vast Rolodex. He approached the networks, seeking permission to use their highlights on ESPN. NBC agreed on the condition he stop swiping NBC employees. He did. Simmons made a different pitch to ABC. "We don't have anything you want now, but I guarantee you, one day we will." ABC, sensing this was more than just bravado, agreed.

NBC and ABC so readily agreed to open their video cupboards because they did not view ESPN as serious competition. CBS did, constantly rebuffing Simmons's requests. The network's stubbornness vexed Simmons, pushing him to defiance. One afternoon in Bristol, an ESPN producer came to his office wanting a highlight from a New York Giants football game on CBS. "Just take it," Simmons said.

ESPN did, using it on the late "SportsCenter" that night. The next afternoon, Simmons's phone lit up with complaints from CBS officials. He ignored them and kept stealing the highlights. CBS relented several months later, realizing that fighting Simmons was a waste of time, as taking legal action would be. By hook or by crook, Simmons had gotten his network the sexy video nuggets needed to make "SportsCenter" more attractive.

• • •

In June of 1982, the San Francisco Giants and San Diego Padres were playing a late-afternoon game, oblivious that three thousand miles away the "SportsCenter" newsroom was riveted on the action.

The game was scheduled to start promptly at 7:30 P.M. Eastern time but began twenty-five minutes early because of an unannounced special promotion. Dozens of faces in the ESPN newsroom stared at the live feed as the first pitch was thrown at 7:05.

"The rest of the country did not know the game had started early, and certainly the bookmakers in Connecticut didn't know about it," Pronovost said. "So we're watching this game, and the Giants have scored six runs in the top of the first. Everyone in the newsroom and in the control room is on the phone, calling their bookies, betting five grand, ten grand, whatever. When people say we were betting our salaries back then, they are right."

Pronovost continued, "The fourth inning, it's 6–2. The fifth inning, it's 6–3. The sixth inning, it's 6–4. Chris Berman was working that night, and just a few seconds before we go on the air, I say to Chris, who knew what was going on, 'Chris, I have a little update for you.' You can see he's getting a little nervous now. So bottom of the ninth, San Diego ties it, and the game goes into extra innings. Guys are walking around, tense, barely able to do their jobs. I remember being in the control room and I saw the final come across. We all lost, 7–6."

Berman, who had been growing a mustache but was told to shave it by management, was well into the 11 o'clock show when Pronovost chimed in his ear, giving him the score. Berman did not skip a beat, staring into the camera and saying with a long face, "In a game that was not exactly of passing interest around here, San Diego beat the Giants, 7–6." A profound, almost audible depression swept through much of the newsroom.

Berman said he could not recall the story but did not doubt its authenticity, because he remembered a similar incident involving a college basketball game that began earlier than scheduled. The denizens of the newsroom again wagered heavily on it once the home team jumped to a large lead, and again they lost.

Pronovost was not a heavy gambler, but many were. ESPN producers, directors, and anchors had access to information few did: players hiding injuries, coaches changing game plans, instantaneous news on any contest around the country. With the information age still in its infancy, ESPN employees had a technological jump on most fans.

Being privy to that kind of information had a corrupting effect on some. Employees thought they knew more about sports than anyone, making any bet a good bet. "It went in phases," explained Sal Marchiano, who came to ESPN in 1981 as an anchor and boxing expert. He never gambled. "At first it was, 'I must be an expert.' Then it was, 'If I know so much, I ought to bet and make money.' Then came the gambling. It was rampant in Bristol. Everyone was betting their asses off. It was an epidemic."

"You get 25-, 30-year-old people heavily into sports, you're going to get a lot of gambling," producer Bogart said. "It was almost as if it was part of the work. Because we became so knowledgeable about sports, you begin to think, 'This is easy.' Of course it never is, that's why they call it gambling."

Some slapped down $1,000, betting on whether a player was going to make a catch. Others bet all of their $20,000 salaries on single games. People lost their families and homes. Gambling permeated the network to such a degree that ESPN attracted the attention of the Connecticut State Police. After a series of raids across Connecticut in the early 1980s, investigators with the organized crime unit noticed a high number of phone calls from ESPN's offices to bookmakers around the state. Antigambling unit officials contacted ESPN management, warning them to control their employees or there could be arrests, according to former ESPN officials. (A spokesman for the state police said he could neither confirm nor deny any warnings that might have been made, because many of the records from that period have been destroyed. However, it is common for Connecticut investigators to warn high-profile companies if there is evidence of employees making illegal bets, the spokesman said.)

Pronovost remembers another instance when he wanted to make a bet. He called his bookmaker, and a strange voice answered the telephone.

"Who's this?" Pronovost asked.

"I'm a Connecticut State Police officer, who is this?"

Pronovost quickly hung up. The next day, he called the bookmaker again to follow up on an earlier bet. "I called last night and a cop answered the phone," he said. The bookie apologized, saying he had been raided.

Bristol's isolation and quiet nightlife contributed to the gambling problem. With few social outlets in town, gambling served as a way of bringing excitement to an otherwise work-oriented existence.

"Being in Bristol was like being on 'The Rock,'" said Marchiano. "People got too close to the subject. Everybody in the same room, every night, this crush of work. Never going anywhere, no sex life, people got wacky. People were young and foolish. I never got into gambling because I saw what happened to certain sportscasters. My whole attitude was, 'This is stupid, stupid.' But other guys didn't see it that way."

The same could be said about drug use at the network, another way a number of employees at ESPN eased the pain of sometimes lonely lives. In 1981 cocaine use, a national problem, infiltrated ESPN. Some directors supervised live shows while buzzed. At house parties in Bristol, a few producers would snort cocaine until four in the morning, stay up all night, work all day, and then use cocaine again that night.

"There was a lot of blow going around the newsroom," Bogart said. "There was a ticker machine outside 'SportsCenter' that had so many razor blade nicks in it from people using razor blades to cut up their cocaine, they had to replace the top of the machine."

As many others at ESPN, Bogart spent around $400 a week on cocaine. Eventually, the drug took its predictable toll on his body and mind. He stopped eating and lost weight, slept little, and as a result, suffered declining strength. Like dozens of others who worked at ESPN in those days, Bogart would later receive treatment for cocaine and alcohol abuse. He has remained sober for more than ten years. Some others sought therapy for gambling addiction.

Somehow, the gambling, drugs and interoffice romances had little effect on the product. ESPN was clearly getting better, even if it was still losing bushels of money. The network continued to hire top people for anchor and analyst slots, and technological and programming upgrades started reshaping, albeit slowly, the image of ESPN from a network watched solely by geeks with too much time on their hands to a network for the hardcore sports fan. During its coverage of the 1980 March NCAA Tournament, ESPN introduced the "cut-in" format in which it would quickly cut from one game to the next. On the programming side, ESPN added "Sports Talk," which was television's first national sports talk show featuring audience participation, as well as live coverage of a NASCAR race.

Colleagues started noticing what Simmons and Connal were building. In May of 1980, while attending the National Cable Television convention in Dallas, the indefatigable Evey was approached by a representative of Ted Turner, chairman of TBS, who wanted to explore a merger between CNN and ESPN. The two secretly negotiated for months, with Evey dispatching Roger Werner, hired by Getty as team leader of a study group to examine improving ESPN's bottom line, to research Turner's network. Werner reported to Evey that the Turner organization was saddled with significant debt, and he recommended against a merger. Also, Werner discovered that Turner wanted a position on the Getty board, a highly unlikely prospect. The merger never materialized, yet Turner's interest was a signal event for the network, the first time competitors recognized the promise ESPN held. The failed merger also triggered the intense rivalry between Evey and Turner.

By May of 1981, ESPN climbed over the 10 million-household mark, and by the end of that year, 13,609,478 homes were wired with ESPN. Along with the increased exposure came innovations that pushed the television envelope. The network sent four reporters—Mees, Berman, Marchiano, and Ley—to each regional site of the NCAA tournament. On the Monday following the weekend games, each would provide a wrap-up of the action from his regional site and then toss it to the next reporter before Berman ended the wrap-ups by tossing it to the studio. The segments often ran longer than twenty minutes. No network had ever tackled such a complicated maneuver for a sporting event, but for hoops addicts, it was nirvana. The basketball buffet signaled the beginning of what would become ESPN's massive event coverage packages.

The network was feeling so good about itself that in August, against Simmons's wishes, Evey decided ESPN would post the one-million-dollar bond needed to enter the bidding process for the television rights to the 1984 Olympics. Evey knew ESPN lacked the resources to compete with the big networks for a jewel like the Olympics, but he calculated that the bidding alone would bring priceless publicity. Evey's instincts proved correct. The press hailed ESPN's bid as smart, bold, the actions of a maverick company. After milking the publicity, Evey notified the Olympic committee of ESPN's withdrawal from the bidding process, and Getty got its money back.

Under the fearless guidance of Simmons and Connal, ESPN withstood the rampant gambling and drug use to establish itself as a player in sports broadcasting. Encouraged to take chances, producers fed a growing appetite among the public for sports. These were heady, unruly times at ESPN.

"People still had long hair then," Bogart said. "Sex, drugs, and rock and roll. Coke was still a good drug. It was a party. The whole thing was a party. ESPN was a party. The idea was a party. The whole sports thing was a party. But we did a great job. We worked hard, we played hard, we were visionaries, we were doing something special. Above everything else, we wanted to succeed."

8   Simmons's Final Roar

Late one afternoon, in the middle of the talent-hiring explosion, which ESPN could not afford, Simmons came crashing into Evey's office in Bristol. Simmons had spent the last three hours at a small college basketball game and discovered someone the network must have as an analyst. Evey listened to Simmons, then examined the budget, confirming what he already suspected. The network could not afford another announcer. Evey's relationship with Simmons had become more prickly in recent months, however, and Evey did not want to further alienate Simmons. So he begrudgingly made room in the budget for Dick Vitale, who was hired as a college basketball analyst for $150 a game.

Each night ESPN welcomed a new station, from Ohio to Arkansas to Alaska. Sometimes Pronovost's lists were so long, there were too many to read on the air in one night. But it was the new faces walking around the cramped newsroom who really sent an electrical charge through the building. After seven and a half years, Greg Gumbel, afraid of being typecast at WMAQ in Chicago as the local sports guy, left his high-rise apartment, and also his newscasts that got a forty share every night, for a house in Simsbury, Connecticut. Gumbel knew the main reason he was hired was his black skin, but he also knew that alone would not secure his position indefinitely. He seamlessly adjusted to the idiosyncrasies of Bristol: few people of color within a thirty-five mile radius of the studio, neighbors who visited on horseback, and an abundance of snowblowers, which no self-respecting Chicagoan would ever own. In only a short time, Gumbel earned a reputation as a professional and friendly anchor, one of the best ever at ESPN.

Sharon Smith, the second woman anchor ever at ESPN, arrived shortly after Gumbel and was a godsend to the gambling addicts at the network. A horse-racing maven who astounded her colleagues by picking the right horse 85 percent of the time, Smith assignments were the source of keen competition among the producers, at least those with an urge to gamble. Smith never placed a bet herself, deeming it unprofessional. Another female hire, Gayle Gardner, grew up in Brooklyn. The daughter of a liquor salesman and housewife, Gardner used to cut out paper dolls while watching Y. A. Tittle quarterback the New York Giants. She was instantly credible to viewers, a difficult feat for women in sports at the time. Perhaps the best writer of the early anchors, Gardner never hesitated to reproach an editor if a story was sloppily handled. Men at ESPN who had temper tantrums were viewed as demanding and even professional; male coworkers muttered "bitch" behind Gardner's back.

"I would work as hard as I could, not to let people down," Gardner said, "and I expected people to work as hard as I did. As a woman, there was more pressure on me, and I couldn't make a mistake, so I was extra cautious. I asked people to check and recheck things, and some men did not like that. In reality, there were more men who yelled and screamed than I ever did."

Gardner was told her ESPN career would start with a few simple live score updates in the evening. The network pulled a switch immediately after she walked into the building, and she anchored the hour-long NFL program by herself.

She didn't know what to expect after the show and returned quietly to her desk. "Well, no one said I was terrible," she thought. The phones at the network started ringing only seconds after she signed off, with callers asking who the hell was that woman and when would she be on again.

Simmons hired Marchiano, who had the best combination of skills and hair in the business. ESPN needed a New York voice to appease rich Manhattan advertisers, and there were few broadcasters in New York better known than Marchiano. He was one of the most knowledgeable men in the country on boxing and also knew Joe Namath's home phone number. In addition, he was the favorite broadcaster of the New York Rangers. ESPN considered Marchiano, like Gumbel, a pivotal hire, so he received an initial six-figure salary, unheard of in the minimum wage world of ESPN. Marchiano earned the nickname "six-figure Sal," but he was worth the handsome paycheck. He hosted the Thursday night fights show, the first weekly boxing program on cable, which became so popular that the network added a second show on Saturday night.

Some new anchors could not adapt to the no-frills Bristol environment or the intense workload and crumbled under the pressure. One pulled down his pants in the middle of the newsroom as a joke after a long, stressful day. He was fired forty-eight hours later. A woman sportscaster arrived the same morning as Gumbel and lasted only a year. She was too inexperienced and couldn't cope with the ever present mishaps. Anchor Jimmy Myers liked the network but was almost killed one afternoon. Before shooting a sports update, he plugged in the stage lights only to witness the cheap electrical system surge uncontrollably. The socket exploded, sending Myers reeling backward. He was taken to the hospital, then released in good health. ESPN asked him to report to work the next day.

"Jimmy, what the fuck are you doing here?" Marchiano asked. "You should sue these motherfuckers."

"I don't want to do that," Myers said, still looking a little drained from his near-death experience, "I just want to work."

Berman, Grande, Mees, and Ley saw themselves as ESPN lifers, or ESPN lasters, which meant they would stay around as long as ESPN did. Gardner, Gumbel, Marchiano, and others viewed ESPN as a stepping stone to a major network job. But all of them were in love with ESPN, which is why so many stayed for at least three or four years despite the crazy hours and occasional annoying questions from friends who wondered what ESPN was and why they couldn't get it on their regular television.

None of the anchors knew of management's strategy to develop Berman, Gumbel, and Gardner as the core stars of the network for the next ten years.

Soon, each anchor fell into a specialty. Grande, an anchor and director, did baseball and was named senior announcer of "SportsCenter" by Connal, the only time in the history of the network someone held both positions. Berman gravitated toward the NFL. Marchiano was the boxing expert. Smith could look at a horse and name its mother and three distant cousins, Mees was a hockey fanatic, Ley favored college basketball, and Gardner was adept at all sports but favored football.

Gumbel believes no anchors had more fun nor produced a better product than that group of early talent. The shows were looser and the egos more manageable because ESPN was still considered a distant fourth from the networks in sports coverage. The group became close, spending hours together in the newsroom. They sat only a few feet from each other at small, wooden desks, the splinters sticking Gumbel in the knee or running Gardner's stockings. The newsroom was so short of space that NFL producer John Wildhack and several others had to put their desks in a narrow hallway nicknamed the bowling alley.

Space at a premium, smokers had to take their breaks outside in the shadow of the twin dishes. The outdoor smoking ceased once the technicians warned that too many close encounters with the satellite dishes could cause sterility.

Berman, with his overwhelming presence and booming megaphone of a voice, had a positive effect on the other anchors. "When we were on the air, his words came screaming out of his mouth," Gardner said. "I realized it was a good thing. Most people need to bring their energy level up. He was all over the wall. He was enthusiastic. You didn't feel a competitive thing, but you felt like you could be out there more. A year into ESPN, because of Chris, I had no inhibitions."

The technical miscues that still crept onto ESPN's broadcasts frustrated the anchors, but they also served as a bonding agent and created a playful atmosphere. Thus, when one of them became tongue-tied, they were able to laugh good-naturedly at themselves and each other. Mees once called the Lakers the "Los Angeles Leakers" and Gumbel accidentally said tennis star Chris Evert "won in straight sex." Gumbel and Lee both broke up on the air.

Mees, like Gumbel, was extremely well liked. The staff constantly poked fun at him, especially his high-pitched voice. While in a commercial break during a late show in June, Muzzi, who by now had cleaned himself off after falling into that muddy hole, called Mees's home answering machine and recorded the outgoing message. Just as Mees was coming back on the air, Muzzi played Mees's own voice from the home machine into his ear, breaking Mees up on the air.

"Tom was the sweetest person on the planet," remembered Gardner. "He was always there, working very hard. He was always called 'solid Tom,' but he was always much better than he was ever given credit for."

The close-knit anchors and producers, well into 1982, soon had more sports to play with. After months of negotiations between ESPN vice president of programming Bob Gutkowski and National Basketball Association (NBA) lawyer David Stern, who believed that ESPN would someday dominate sports, the network signed an agreement with the NBA for forty regular season and ten playoff games that year and in 1983. And the NCAA, that October, awarded the network more college bowl contests, like the Liberty Bowl.

As the programming expanded and the costs increased, Evey desperately sought ways to trim the fat. He quietly laid off a handful of members of the production department. When Bornstein's name was surprisingly added to the list, Evey, aware that Bornstein was one of the few people in production with children, overruled the move. Bornstein's job was safe.

The year was shaping up to be a busy one for Evey. Another network was expressing interest in getting a piece of ESPN, and his conflict with Simmons was escalating. In fact, they had reached critical mass. It was fitting that in the summer of 1982, ESPN was named a codefendant in a divorce case in Austin, Texas; the wife charged that the network was instrumental in ruining her marriage by providing too much sports coverage, which her husband gleefully enjoyed. Fitting, because Evey and Simmons were headed for a bitter separation of their own.

• • •

In May of 1982, Mees was broadcasting the 7 P.M. "SportsCenter," wearing a tie that did not quite match his jacket, when the outside line rang in the control room. It was Evey, who was at his Los Angeles home hosting a small group of friends. They were all watching "SportsCenter."

Connal picked up the line and when he heard Evey's voice, he rolled his eyes in disgust. He'd been through this routine before and knew what was coming.

"At the next commercial break, I want that tie on Tom changed," Evey said. "It doesn't match, it's ugly, and it better be gone soon."

Evey slammed down the phone, then turned to his friends and started laughing with them. They waited until the next commercial break and laughed even harder when the screen showed Mees reading the scores wearing a different tie.

Evey had placed meddling phone calls to the control room many times before. Once during a busy show in Bristol, while the Getty man was hosting one of his typical star-studded parties and consuming his normal four or five drinks, Evey was asked by a guest for the Dodgers score. Evey called Bristol and sent the director scrambling through the sports wires.

Evey may have been a nuisance in the control room, but he was more than that to Simmons. It was not unusual for Evey to hire a broadcaster without telling Simmons or to recruit inexperienced Hollywood friends for production positions. Nevertheless, Evey did offer the occasional good idea, such as superimposing the score in a corner of the screen while a game was in progress, a commonplace practice years later. But for Simmons, his positive contributions no longer outweighed his numerous foibles. Simmons considered Evey a "jock sniffer," someone drawn to the business because of the ample opportunities to hobnob with star athletes, an irksome quality that Simmons found no longer tolerable. Simmons was most perturbed, however, by Evey's notion that he could run a television network as well as Simmons could.

"One thing about Evey that came out very clearly as we went along was that no matter who was in charge of running this thing called ESPN, he felt he had a divine right to run it along with him," Simmons said. "He'd hire people without letting me know, friends from California who he wanted to see on the air. He was very, very difficult to work with, although on the other hand, he was very supportive financially through Getty. You took the good with the bad in this instance."

Simmons added, "He could charm the pants off you one time, and then the next day, you wanted to rip his heart out."

Simmons's relationship with ESPN soured because of Evey. He started hating going to the office, dreading what Evey would do next.

Just as Simmons began looking for graceful ways to make his exit from ESPN, officials from the United States Football League (USFL), which was forming as an alternative to the dominant NFL, made covert contact first with Evey and then Simmons, who they wanted as commissioner. What intrigued Simmons about the USFL was working from the other side. Instead of begging the sports leagues for programming, as he had been doing for the past three years as president of ESPN and for much of his career at NBC, he could be the seller. Increasingly, this new league looked as if it would be Simmons's escape hatch from Evey.

Simmons quietly negotiated with the USFL and by June had a handshake agreement with the upstart league. Simmons then called Evey in Los Angeles and they met at a restaurant near the Getty building. The conversation, heated at times, lasted five hours. Simmons complained about Evey's meddling. Evey implacably maintained that he had a right to make key decisions because he controlled the finances. Simmons knew it was time to leave after he noticed that Evey had never asked what it would take to keep him. They ended their marathon session with Simmons saying, "Stu, goodbye, I'm going to take the other job."

After the meeting with Evey, Simmons got in his car, drove fifteen minutes to the USFL headquarters, and later had his first press conference as commissioner of the new league. His last day at ESPN was June 14, 1982, and, coincidentally, three days later, ESPN announced an agreement with the USFL to televise thirty-four games a year for two years. ESPN paid $11 million for the rights. The press lauded the network again.

Evey moved quickly to find a replacement. Connal was elevated to executive vice president and chief operating officer, and Evey hired Bill Grimes, an executive at CBS radio, to run the network's finances. "I think, quite secretly, Stu was not unhappy to see me leave," Simmons said. "When Bill Grimes came in, Stu thought he had his next pigeon. He thought he would have more control over him than he did me."

Simmons never revealed to anyone, not even his close friend Connal, how difficult it was to leave the network he refined. ESPN staffers got their first hint when at a going-away party in Bristol, attended by almost everyone in the building, Simmons stepped under a huge banner signed by each ESPN employee to say goodbye. Instead, he broke down in tears.

Simmons was the most influential president in ESPN's history. He molded the network and laid the foundation for what it is today. Almost every significant event in ESPN's history can be traced, in some form, to the Simmons regime.

Although Grimes, more of a corporate man than Simmons, was no puppet, he endured Evey's meddling with more composure and less resistance. The Grimes reign would be remembered for one very significant achievement. In January 1983, the network began charging cable stations ten cents per month for each subscriber carrying the network, a cable-first. Until then, ESPN was a free station, but the network needed cash, and after painstaking analysis by Evey, it took the risk of charging for its service, changing the landscape of cable forever.

It was a bold, daring move, which showed that Evey, while at times an unrepentant showoff, still had strong business instincts. (The charges earned ESPN $10 million in revenue in 1984 and $35 million in 1985.) Few cable stations rejected ESPN's payment plan, and, just as Evey expected, the ones that did were inundated with phone calls from irate customers complaining about ESPN's disappearance from their cable package. After a Kansas affiliate refused the rates and whacked ESPN from its package, picketers protested outside the cable company's office. ESPN was back on within seventy-two hours.

The move demonstrated ESPN's clout in cable land. It had graduated from a network at the edge of a financial cliff to a force that once-indifferent cable operators could no longer live without. ESPN was here to stay.

• • •

It was a typical night of boxing for Marchiano and ESPN analyst Al Bernstein one hot evening in July of 1983. They were in another sweltering, claustrophobic gym, watching two up-and-coming fighters, and putting on a terrific broadcast for ESPN's series "Top Rank Boxing."

This fight was in West Warwick, Rhode Island, and hometown fighter Rafael Lopez, a lightweight from Pawtucket, was losing to Juan Veloz from New York. Bernstein told viewers several times he had Veloz ahead on his scorecard but cautioned that because Lopez was the hometown boxer, anything could happen.

Lopez won in a unanimous decision, which was popular with Rhode Island fans, but infuriated Veloz, his manager, Marchiano, and Bernstein. The referee failed to count four knockdowns scored by Veloz, ruling them slips instead. Replays clearly showed three of the big punches were knockdowns. Marchiano was indignant, browbeating the referee in a postfight interview, then telling the press later, "We know about hometown leanings, and you can argue about bad decisions only so much. But this was outrageous. And people don't realize how much television magnifies everything."

What happened in the aftermath showed ESPN's magnifying power. After the fight, the ESPN switchboard was jammed with thousands of callers denouncing the results and wanting to know what could be done about it. (The answer: Nothing.)

Because the boxing series was such a ratings success and the network was starved for new material, ESPN sometimes ran the same fight seven times in one week, including twice during prime time and several times over the weekend. As for Marchiano, he was showing the rest of the country what viewers in New York already knew, that besides his other broadcasting gifts, he was a blunt, honest reporter unafraid to express his opinion.

Marchiano enjoyed the network, but hated living in Bristol. He wasn't alone. Most ESPN employees, from the highest levels of management to the janitorial staff, despised the city. Many disdained Bristol's restaurants, which didn't serve beer after eleven o'clock or decent food after ten. Gayle Gardner groused ceaselessly about the nonexistent social life, and the few people of color who worked at the network tired of being stared at when they walked around town. Bristol jokes were as rampant in the newsroom as betting pools.

One more joke at Bristol's expense was added to the till. Marchiano was driving back to his hotel after broadcasting a fight in Texas when he heard a catchy Mac Davis song on his car radio. "Happiness is Lubbock in my rearview mirror" instantly resonated with Marchiano, who suddenly couldn't wait to return to Bristol to unleash his caustic adaptation of the song to the newsroom. Substituting Bristol for Lubbock, a group of anchors or producers leaving work for the day would chant in unison, "Happiness is Bristol in my rearview mirror." After a few verses, the phrase was shortened simply to "Happiness."

Although he had brought laughs to the newsroom, life was becoming more serious for Marchiano, who had been working without a contract for seven weeks. Although Connal was revered by the production staff, he never clicked with Marchiano, which led to an impasse on a new deal.

Marchiano decided to meet with Connal in Bristol to speed negotiations along, a move Marchiano later regretted.

"We start to talk, and he's talking to me like he's a prep school dean," Marchiano recalled. "So I said, 'Go fuck yourself.' I told him straight out. 'Go fuck yourself with that attitude. I'm not some fucking kid. Chet hired me. Is my salary too much, is that the point?' He said, 'Yeah. You make too much money.'"

Things escalated from there. Connal told Marchiano, "What do I need you for? I've got guys I pay $35,000 a year who do 'SportsCenter' who can do what you do. But I need you for boxing." Marchiano replied, "Damn right you do."

Seventeen years later, Marchiano says, "I learned my lesson. That was the last time I negotiated without an agent in the room. You can't tell your boss to go fuck himself."

The two strong-willed men agreed on one indisputable fact: Marchiano's boxing knowledge was too valuable for ESPN to lose. They also agreed that Marchiano would no longer anchor "SportsCenter" but focus solely on the Thursday night fights. Marchiano was ecstatic about his new deal because now he could work for other networks and, perhaps most important, never have to cross the Bristol border again.

That Sunday, Marchiano was anchoring his last "SportsCenter" with Ley in the ESPN studios. At the end of the show, Ley turned to Marchiano and said, "I guess there is just one more thing left to say." Marchiano looked into the camera and smirked, "Happiness is Bristol in my rearview mirror."

Ley had a surprised look on his face. The control room, where everyone was in on the joke, burst into laughter or stared speechlessly at the monitor. Greg Gumbel was watching from home and almost fell off his couch. Marchiano's irreverence notwithstanding, he merely echoed the attitude of many at the network.

Marchiano left the studio, got in his car, and once on Middle Street could see the studio in his rearview mirror. He thought to himself, "I'll never have to come back to this place ever again."

Not everyone was amused by Marchiano's antics. The next day, Connal wanted to take the deal off the table because of the quip. After weeks of unproductive talks between ESPN and the agent for Marchiano, Marchiano was fired on August 3. He immediately landed a job at a New York City station, and, although gone, his infamous catchphrase remained a permanent part of ESPN lore. For years, whenever someone left ESPN, he or she was toasted with what was called a "rearview mirror party."

Many times an actual rearview mirror was sneaked into the building for the gathering.

In 1983 there were other changes besides the departure of Marchiano. ESPN broadcast the flat and poorly produced "Business Times," a two-hour show of a discussion of the morning's financial news. After Simmons left, the production department asserted itself, and for a brief period, erroneously viewed "SportsCenter" as a minor player in the ESPN universe. Thus, all the "SportsCenter" segments were cut to only fifteen minutes in one of the worst decisions the network ever made. The reaction to the move was swift and loud. In addition to thousands of viewer complaints, the media ripped the move. George Grande, over breakfast with Grimes and Evey in Manhattan, pleaded for reinstating the thirty-minute time slot. Evey and Grimes agreed with Grande, and a month later, the show regained its normal time frame.

An incident at the 1982 World Series underscored to Grande the burgeoning presence of "SportsCenter." Grande was standing in line to get his press credential when the man in front of him lied to the clerk behind the window, "Hi, I'm George Grande from ESPN." Grande tapped the impostor on the shoulder and said, "Actually, I'm George Grande." "Sports-Center" was the focal point of ESPN, the unifying entity that made the network what it was. Grande believed that to deemphasize the show would be to diminish the network.

Still, technological limitations, a minuscule budget, and a small ragged staff continued to hamper ESPN. Its crew at Super Bowl XVIII consisted of Berman, analyst Paul Maguire, a producer, and a cameraman. Between shooting "SportsCenter" and feature stories, Berman made hurried trips to the airport to send tapes back to Bristol.

For every setback or weird, whimsical incident, there was a wonderful leap forward. Bornstein, whose job Evey had saved only a short time before, orchestrated ESPN's coverage of the America's Cup race in September of 1983. The network had planned on showing only an occasional update of the seventh and final race between Australia and the United States. Like the overwhelming viewer response to the boxing match decision in Rhode Island or to the decrease in airtime of "SportsCenter," racing fans, by the thousands, phoned in, requesting nonstop coverage. ESPN broke away from scheduled programming to show the last race in its entirety, which despite almost no promotion by the network, earned a 2.4 rating, meaning 547,000 households were watching.

It was a sign of ESPN's increasing power. Over all, the subscriber count was up to twenty-five million and as a way of providing additional regional programming feeds, Getty purchased time on the Galaxy I satellite, a souped-up version of the Satcom 1. ESPN was becoming a more attractive property: Turner still desired it, and now, ABC, which once thumbed its nose at ESPN, was taking a hard look at the future of the network. Indeed, two years earlier, Evey, with Ed Hookstratten's help, leaked word that ESPN was willing to discuss an association with a major network. After Evey deftly played Turner, CBS, and ABC against each other, jacking up the interest, ABC won. On August 9, 1982, the American Broadcasting Company bought ten percent of ESPN for $20 million, with an option to purchase thirty-nine percent at $2.2 million a point. By taking ten percent of ESPN for $20 million, a market value of $200 million was established for the network. The deal allowed ESPN to use ABC's programming leftovers. Because ABC owned the rights to the British Open but broadcast only the later rounds on Saturday and Sunday, ESPN sent announcer Jim Simpson and a producer overseas earlier in the week to air the initial matches on Thursday and Friday, using ABC's technical crews.

Despite the stodgy presence of one of the big three networks, cable retained many of its Old West qualities. Turner, the old sheriff in town, was furious about losing out to ABC. In 1983 he and Evey's rivalry crested, spilling over during a party at the Playboy Mansion owned by Hugh Hefner. Evey and Turner both attended, unaware of the other's presence. At the end of the night, they accidentally met while waiting for the valet to bring their cars. Evey was with his striking daughter, Christine, a five-foot ten-inch blonde, and Turner was with an equally beautiful woman, some ten years younger than him. At first, they looked like two gunfighters ready to square off, then each man calmed down and made uncomfortable small talk.

"By the way, Ted, this is my daughter, Christine," said Evey.

"Yeah, right," Turner responded, "and this is my daughter, Tina."

Evey cocked his arm back and prepared to punch Turner in the mouth, when the valet, who had arrived, grabbed Evey's arm.

By 1984 rumors were swirling that Getty faced a takeover by Texaco. As Getty became increasingly restless after losing $67 million on ESPN, Evey knew he had to make one more major play. At the Winter Olympics in Sarajevo, he coddled up to Fred Pierce, the president of ABC.

"Do you have any interest in buying the rest of ESPN?" Evey asked.

"What kind of deal do you think we could get?" Pierce said.

Evey said he was certain Getty would go for $175 million. The number was under the $200 million ESPN was valued, but Getty would have enshrined Evey in the oil Hall of Fame if he could get that price, considering its initial investment was a paltry ten million dollars.

Texaco did indeed purchase Getty in 1984 for an astounding ten billion dollars, and because it borrowed large sums of money to make the purchase, Texaco needed to sell off many of the nonoil parts of Getty, such as ESPN, to ease its debt load. The bidders for ESPN lined up quickly, the principals being ABC, NBC, and the ever present Turner.

In Bristol, city officials panicked, fearful they'd lose the city's fourth-largest taxpayer, which accounted for $5 million a year in tax revenues alone, not to mention the sales of homes, burgers, and alcohol and the brisk betting business. The *Bristol Press* commented in an editorial: "City officials must surely be frustrated to realize that there are limits to what they can do in an effort to keep any firm in Bristol. Those decisions are made elsewhere, in corporate headquarters, for reasons which range from idiosyncratic matters of personal preference to hard economic considerations."

Secretly, Bristol officials were hoping ABC would purchase ESPN because they thought ABC would be the least likely to make any major changes, such as uprooting the company and moving to Iowa. Bristol got its wish when ABC won by simply emptying its wallet. ABC purchased 85 percent of ESPN in June of 1984 for $188 million. ESPN's distribution hardware, mainly ESPN's satellite broadcasting facilities, were sold for $14 million. Other parts of the network were chopped up and sold as well, and in all, ABC paid more than $230 million for the sports network.

The sale was heavily criticized by some media and financial analysts as overpriced. Turner, perhaps due to sour grapes, asserted that ESPN's programming was unimpressive and its advertising sales force weak, said ESPN "has been unable to get major sporting events. And with the advent of regional sporting networks carrying major local games, you really wonder whether a twenty-four-hour sports network is viable anyway." Pat Robertson, president of the Christian Broadcast Network, said paying that much money for ESPN violated the tenets of good business.

Texaco had acquired ESPN's debt in the purchase of Getty and was relieved that ABC had taken the company off its hands, caring little about sports television. Evey's instincts about ESPN back in 1979 when he made his pitch to the Getty board while standing before that oblong conference table proved correct. Evey wrote a letter of culmination to the director of the company, Gordon P. Getty, thanking him for the support throughout the past four years, especially during those difficult times when ESPN seemed nothing more than a sinkhole.

> Dear Gordon:
> During a recent meeting with Mr. John McKinley, chairman of Texaco, he was most complimentary of his firm's evaluation of the assets of Getty's Diversified Operations, which have been identified for sale.

As you know, on April 30, it was announced that Texaco had reached an agreement with ABC for the sale of ESPN for the total amount of $237.5 million. Despite many articles in the press to the contrary, as a director of Getty, your judgment and encouragement in supporting ESPN management since the inception of this venture in 1979 has been vindicated by the magnitude of that sale and the fact that Texaco has realized a gain on the transaction of $67.5 million and repayment of the Getty debt.

After the sale, Evey resigned from Getty, the last of the pioneers to walk away from, or be forced out of, the creation called ESPN. Evey felt betrayed by the covert negotiating process employed by Getty because few people, including him, were in the loop. Afterward, Evey fell into a severe depression. His professional life, as well as his relationship with his family, plunged into shambles. In August of 1985, Evey entered the Betty Ford Center for treatment of alcohol abuse.

Evey was the most controversial of the early group, treating people harshly, even cruelly, at times. Yet Evey was as important to ESPN as Rasmussen, his son Scott, Simmons, or Connal. Evey recognized its potential when other money people did not.

Although made up of a volatile mix of men—Rasmussen still gets irked just at the mention of Evey's name—ESPN would never have materialized without the contributions of each of them. Rasmussen birthed the idea of a twenty-four-hour sports cable network, Scott slogged through the early legwork and supported his father, Simmons made ESPN a professional network, Connal, who later resigned, found key production talent and modernized ESPN's technology, and Evey not only rammed funding through the Getty conglomerate but held the oil company at bay when executives wanted to cap the well. Remove any one of them from this group, and ESPN might not have been formed at that time, or perhaps not until decades later.

Ironically, the group is more unified now than they were twenty-one years ago. Each feels that ESPN—in particular, Bornstein, who served as president of the network and is now a top entertainment executive—has tried to wipe the original group's contributions from history. Bornstein has taken credit for ideas the pioneers tested decades ago, they say.

"The guys running ESPN now are rewriting history in their own image," Grande said. "They take credit for things they know full well they did not originate."

Grande cited as an example the idea for multiple ESPN networks. In the biography information from ESPN's fifteenth-anniversary guide, Bornstein is credited with "the creation of new divisions and networks." Bornstein has further perpetuated this notion in the press.

Nineteen years ago, Simmons wanted to add to the main station three additional regional networks, an ESPN East, ESPN Central, and ESPN West. Simmons hoped that the original ESPN would eventually feature solely traditional sports—he firmly believed that one day ESPN would almost exclusively broadcast the NFL, major league baseball, and the NBA—while the other ESPN networks would show regional teams (for example, ESPN Central might show University of Michigan football games) and the alternative sports would slowly gravitate toward the satellite ESPN networks.

"I guess if you say it over a period of years—that you started everything—you begin to believe it," said Simmons. "The fact is Steve did not invent a lot of the things he takes credit for. And the lack of recognition by the network of the early pioneers is very cruel. It hurt me, and I tried to ignore it for a long time, but deep down inside I couldn't."

Simmons said Connal was more furious than he was about the rejection. Connal and Bornstein feuded often, and Bornstein held an eternal grudge against Connal, who once vetoed a scheduled promotion for Bornstein.

"Scotty took the pain of the network ignoring him to his grave," Simmons said. "We fought those early battles, and a part of us is still there now, even though the people there want to ignore us and forget about us. They have a tremendous amount of arrogance because they have become so big."

Simmons said Connal was upset by an incident prior to the network's ten-year anniversary celebration in Bristol in 1989. When neither Simmons nor Connal was invited to the event, *New York Post* columnist Phil Mushnick, a longtime friend of Simmons, asked Rosa Gatti from public relations about the snub. Fearing negative publicity, Gatti rushed Simmons an invitation several days before the anniversary, but Connal never received one, Simmons said. So Simmons declined to attend.

Evey became so enraged when a letter he wrote to Bornstein in December of 1994 went unanswered, he fired off another nine months later. "Steve, this letter sounds self-serving and perhaps [for] the most part it is," Evey wrote. "However, the Bill Rasmussens, Getty Oil, Chet Simmons, Scotty Connal, who preceded you, or worked with you, are deserving of your gratitude for providing the foundation you had to build upon. With great personal sacrifice, many of us contributed a great deal to making your career possible. It deserves your respect, and, quite frankly, your gratitude. One day you will join us and hopefully, your successor will recognize and appreciate your contributions." The second letter, Evey said, also went unanswered.

The unanswered letter was not surprising. Bornstein to this day has a reputation for being at times cold-hearted, even ruthless, in his treatment of some people. One person who worked with him closely said that "Steve is the kind of guy who would walk up to you, shoot you in the head, then go take his kids to church."

ESPN would grow, slowly and inexorably, for the rest of the 1980s. By the end of the decade, the network was the most profitable service on cable, easily surpassing CNN, and earning $100 million a year. In February of 1985, the network adopted a new logo and corporate name, ESPN, Inc., to go along with its new bottom line.

Tom Mees walked into the newsroom a few days after the announced sale, holding a stack of newspapers, the articles regarding ESPN circled with a ballpoint pen. A small group of anchors and others had gathered near his desk and were talking. Mees urgently broke in.

"We've taken our hits," Mees announced. "People laughed at us and said we were crap. But now we're on our way. We're not there yet, but we're close."

Some snickered at Mees's pie-in-the-sky prediction. Still, it was prophetic. ESPN would soon experience the kind of unexplainable, freakish growth television network executives dream about. But along with the explosive expansion came a series of crises, shrapnel that would almost cripple the ascending network.

PART 2

Heroes

9   "Men Are Acting Like Animals"

TV Guide writer Howard Polskin began a 1986 profile of Gayle Gardner by describing Bristol. "Don't be surprised if it feels like you've reached the middle of nowhere, because that's exactly where you are." In the article, Gardner groused about the city's effect on her social life. "It's very boring," she said.

This public censure of Bristol wounded its citizens and government officials. The mayor, John J. Leone, still smarting from the now public knowledge that ESPN employees only liked to see his city from their rearview mirrors, wrote the magazine to complain.

Fed up with Bristol and offered an anchor position at NBC, Gardner bolted the network two years later. Gardner was one of a significant number of producers, directors, and talent who had lost patience with the long hours and empty personal life.

Also around this time, social geographer Robert M. Pierce rated Bristol as the seventeenth worst city in the country, which became another source of jokes inside ESPN. Although Bristol bashing was in vogue, it was not the central reason for the exodus of personnel in the mid-1980s.

"People reached a certain stature and then just disappeared," Greg Gumbel said. Gumbel worked for three "SportsCenter" executive producers in five years and feared the network would never stabilize. When the Madison Square Garden network called, offering him the host's chair on its sports show and doubling his $155,000 salary, Gumbel could not resist. The loss of Gumbel's professionalism and immense skills is felt even today.

Chris Berman, his head on a swivel, watched the increasing number of faces walk out the door. Concerned, he approached Gumbel, who was only a few days away from leaving.

"Maybe I'm crazy for staying, Greg," Berman said, "Should I start looking for a way out?"

"You would be crazy to leave," Gumbel told him. "You are this network and they will always take care of you."

Berman was becoming a household name across the sports world, but he sometimes imagined stardom at a major network. Those thoughts usually faded away. When Marchiano, whom Berman admired, urged him to show patience, Berman heeded his advice. Besides, he was still charmed with ESPN, giving, in the vernacular of the sports he covered, all he had to the network.

After a Tampa Bay Buccaneers game in December of 1986, Berman finished shooting his stand-up and caught an eight o'clock flight to Hartford so the tape could be used on the eleven o'clock show. By the time he landed, close to ten o'clock that night, a snowstorm was burying the state, making roads nearly impassable. Nevertheless, Berman drove seventy miles per hour from the airport, racing to get the tape on the air. Following him in another car was a terrified Odjakjian who figured a Buccaneers highlight was not worth his life and slowed to under fifty, then to a crawl. Berman barreled on and the tape made the show.

Like other anchors, Berman had his share of disputes with the ever-rotating "SportsCenter" management production staff. By the middle of the decade, Berman had concocted nicknames for nearly one-third of all professional baseball players. Fans loved the Bermanisms, but they were a sore spot to management, who thought they'd become tedious and undermined the network's efforts to be taken seriously as a news source. Berman was ordered to stop using them. He obeyed but not without putting up a strong, at times verbal, fight. On the air, he protested by calling players by their full names (New York Mets outfielder Mookie Wilson became William).

The nickname cancellation was reported in *USA Today*, and ESPN received yet another indication of its growing prestige and the popularity of Berman. The network was besieged with thousands of phone calls and letters asking for the Bermanisms to return. By the time pitchers reported to 1986 spring training, the goofy monikers were back. Around the building, Berman heralded his victory as a triumph for democracy. It was more than that: For the first time at ESPN, an anchor had trumped the corporation, proving himself even more powerful than the network.

While Berman was making headlines, the programming department was adding to its scheduling trophies. College basketball remained the main course at ESPN. The network signed a three-year deal to televise Big

East hoops, leading an ecstatic Georgetown coach named John Thompson to call the agreement one of the biggest moments in the conference's history. The games, which aired on Monday nights, would often repeat four times within one day.

In March ESPN expanded its college basketball coverage to include more featured broadcasts of conference championship games and cut-ins to forty-five others. The raft of coverage was later called "Championship Week" and became the standard for all college basketball broadcasts. Because of Odjakjian, who deftly orchestrated the coverage from his producer's chair, ESPN defined college basketball and turned the month of March into a maddening national hoops obsession.

Dick Vitale's colorful personality, even if it was over the top at times, was another reason for the preeminence of ESPN's basketball coverage. In 1987, tiny Austin Peay College led heavily favored Illinois at halftime of their first-round NCAA Tournament matchup. Vitale was so confident Illinois would prevail, he said on the air he would stand on his head in the studio if they lost. The Illini were upset and Vitale kept his word. Ley helped Vitale balance himself as he stood on his head in front of millions of people.

Vitale's shtick was immoderate in every sense, too loud, too wordy, too full of superlatives. His on-air persona sometimes overpowered his smart analysis, a criticism that would stick with him. He had a keen intellect and was as knowledgeable of basketball as anyone. He was a former head coach at the University of Detroit and in the NBA for the Detroit Pistons, yet it was his histrionics that set him apart, earned him fame, and induced lucrative book deals. Vitale often complained to friends in the newsroom that his knowledge of the sport was overshadowed by his untempered style, yet he acknowledged that he had paradoxically created the problem himself.

Two years after Vitale stood on his head, the sixteenth-seeded Princeton Tigers led top-seeded Georgetown at halftime in another first-round NCAA tournament matchup. Before the game, Vitale, sporting a Princeton sweater, pledged he would walk the sixty miles from Bristol to Providence, Rhode Island, site of the game, and dance with the Princeton cheerleaders if the heavily favored Hoyas lost. The game went down to the final second with Georgetown winning, but at halftime the Hoyas had trailed by eight. Vitale and studio host John Saunders sat stunned, silent for the first few seconds as the cameras cut to them in the Bristol studios for the halftime break. Then Saunders interrupted the stillness: "I guess speechless would be the way to describe us here. The only thing I can say, Dick, is that the head of the Princeton cheerleading squad just called and wanted to know what size tutu you wear."

Vitale had created his own conundrum. If he restrained his frenzied alter ego, he would lose fans; if he indulged his counterpart personality, he would lose respect for himself. Vitale always walked a fine line between showman and serious analyst. When he first joined the network, he confounded, then annoyed, his broadcasting partners with his unbroken enthusiasm and tendency to dominate the broadcast. To help him mesh better with his partners, ESPN paired him with ultraprofessional Jim Simpson. Simpson was blunt. "If you talk too much," he told Vitale, "I'll have your microphone cut."

In their first game, Vitale, either ignoring or forgetting Simpson's warning, began the broadcast in usual fashion, talking more than he should have. At the first time-out, Simpson told the producer, "Cut Dick's microphone." Unplugged by the no-nonsense Simpson, Vitale sat there in a stupor as Simpson called the game himself. At another time-out, several minutes later, Simpson leaned to Vitale and asked, "Are you ready?" Vitale promised, "I'm ready." Vitale's microphone was reactivated, and for the rest of the game, he was more sparing in his words.

Despite Vitale's zaniness, no one ever questioned his work ethic. Before a 1996 show, Vitale developed a serious nosebleed, but instead of walking off the set, he stuffed cotton up his nose, removed it, and then went on the air.

The popularity of college basketball did not confound the network, but other viewer habits did. Australian-rules football failed to receive large ratings, but the numbers showed that viewers sampled it for several minutes, then changed the channel. Eventually, it developed a small cult following, and one year Johnny Carson mentioned Australian-rules football and ESPN in the same sentence in his monologue. Billiards and cheerleading shows sometimes posted better ratings than hockey. Auto racing drew large numbers of viewers and provided some of the best moments of levity, such as at the beginning of the Winston 500 race in May of 1986 when a thief stole the pace car. ESPN cameras caught the police stopping the vehicle and pulling the perpetrator by his hair out the front window.

By 1987 "SportsCenter" was increasing in popularity and thus the ratings grew, burying for good whatever misgivings the programming department may have had about it. The programming department grew right along with "SportsCenter." Layers of coordinating producers (one of the higher-ranking positions, with the responsibility for running a particular section of production or show), producers (a sort of supereditor), directors (keep the control room from turning chaotic), assignment editors (responsible for everything from scanning the wires to buying satellite time), and production assistants (the ultimate gophers) started to fill the building.

The profile of "SportsCenter" was also rising among the people it covered. Athletes began to tune in to see themselves on the extensive highlight packages or to watch their interviews. During a live interview, running back Eric Dickerson announced he was being traded from the Los Angeles Rams to the Colts.

The number of specialists and specialty programs were expanding along with ESPN's personality. Vitale keyed college basketball on Mondays and Tuesdays. Peter Gammons, a well-connected baseball writer, was splitting his time between the *Boston Globe* and ESPN. There was also "Golf's Leading Money Winners" on Fridays and "Monday Night Quarterback" during "SportsCenter."

ESPN still lacked a major sport; it's only professional sport property was hockey, which was a distant fourth in terms of popularity behind basketball, baseball, and the NFL. Grimes, Roger Werner, the network's new money man, and Bornstein, the programming whiz, who were called "The Three Musketeers" inside ESPN, were unified in their opinion that for ESPN to take the next step it needed to grab a piece of the NFL. This would remain a goal when Bornstein was later promoted to executive vice president in charge of programming and production and Werner replaced Grimes as president and chief executive officer of ESPN.

Finally, professional football decided to cautiously probe cable, even though network television maintained three times the viewers. Rozelle, Cleveland Browns' owner Art Modell, and Pinchbeck, after a series of talks with other cable operators like Turner, decided to split its product between Turner's TBS and ESPN.

"We made a mistake in doing that," remembered Modell. "ESPN deserved to have all sixteen games. But instead, we sold the first eight to Turner and the last eight to ESPN."

On March 15, 1987, two months before ESPN became the first cable network to reach forty million homes, the NFL awarded the network a three-year contract to televise eight regular-season Sunday night games, four preseason games, and the Pro Bowl. ESPN may have been miffed at the NFL for not having a shot to telecast every Sunday night game, but the complaints in Bristol were few, especially after the ratings came in. The December 6 telecast of Chicago at Minnesota was watched by 8.42 million people, a cable record. ESPN's NFL telecasts during that season were watched in an average of 5.9 million homes, and its overall twenty-four-hour ratings were up thirty-three percent.

"When we got the NFL," said Gardner, "there was a celebration that lasted a week. Everybody knew it was the biggest thing to happen to ESPN. It energized the place."

• • •

Karie Ross always said the sports television world held three strikes against her. She was female, blonde, and Southern. Ross grew up in Clinton, Oklahoma, population 8,000. Her father was an oil man who took her to University of Oklahoma football games when she was still in diapers. For as long as she could remember, wearing orange was forbidden by her father because that was the color of rival Oklahoma State.

Ross considered a career as a meteorologist until she discovered her allergy to chemistry. Instead, she went to Oklahoma on a partial scholarship and majored in print journalism. She was constantly told how pretty she was and that television would showcase her looks. None of that mattered to Ross, but she gravitated toward television because that's where the job offers were. She started doing sports at a small station in Oklahoma City before moving to Columbus, Ohio, where Bornstein, while visiting in-laws, saw her on CBS affiliate WBNS. He was impressed. Several months later, in late 1987, she was in Bristol.

Because Ross grew up around sports and locker rooms, she was only mildly disturbed by the men in the ESPN newsroom who talked about the lengths of their penises within earshot, sometimes just to get a reaction from her. When producers spoke to her chest instead of making eye contact, it was annoying, but not debilitating.

Ross enjoyed her early days at the network. She was not a sports geek, and unlike some of the men, couldn't say who won the 1963 World Series without looking it up. But she knew sports, especially football, and there was a time Ross felt ESPN could be her home for years.

After her first night on the air, that all changed. She was sitting in the newsroom, working on the script for the late "SportsCenter," her desk tucked snugly under a bank of large television monitors. The newsroom buzzed, as always before a show, and Ross blocked out the noise by concentrating on her work. But then the volume on the monitors became too loud to ignore. On the televisions, she distinctly heard the sounds of a man and woman having sex, followed by laughter from directly behind her. When Ross turned in her seat, a group of fifteen male producers and directors were standing in front of the monitors, alternating their stares between the screens and Ross. "They were looking at me, and then looking at the screens," Ross remembered. "So I looked up, and they had put on pornography, and two people were doin' it on the screen. The guys were standing around just to see how I would react."

Ross had just received her first indoctrination to life at ESPN. Her second came at an ESPN house party in Bristol. "I walk in and on the table are hamburgers, hot dogs, chips, and a bong," Ross said. "I said, 'What is that?' Somebody said, 'It's pot.' Then I said, 'I better leave because if the police come, my name will be in the paper.' I mean there were drugs everywhere and people were doing them all over the house. I got the hell out of there."

But the incident in the newsroom lingered with Ross. As the months rolled on, and Ross learned more about ESPN's culture, she began to realize that what happened to her that night was minor compared with the humiliations, discrimination, and harassment endured by lower-ranked female personnel almost daily.

Ross worked on several ESPN shows, including "College Football Gameday," and then later a number of "SportsCenters," with Berman, Mees, John Saunders, and a handsome, funny new face named Patrick. He had joined the network in March of 1989 and hosted the 2:30 A.M. "SportsCenter" with Berman. As had Gardner, he noticed just how nuclear Berman's voice is in the studio. Patrick also noticed just how popular Berman was throughout the building and the sports world. That year Berman had received an $800,000-a-year offer from NBC Sports, at least $600,000 more than his ESPN salary. Over the next six months, Berman and ESPN underwent intense, and secret, negotiations. Berman ended up staying for $600,000 a year, less than the NBC deal, but significantly more than he was making before his new deal. It was a landmark contract, showing that the network would step up to keep its own. It also began a close friendship between Berman and Bornstein.

In the fall of that same year, Olbermann substituted for "Up Close" host Roy Firestone, who had gained a reputation for cajoling his interview subjects to tearfully reveal their innermost secrets. Two years later, in December of 1991, Olbermann left KCBS-TV in Los Angeles to join ESPN radio, three years after rebuffing an earlier ESPN offer to host "SportsCenter." Olbermann had no regrets about leaving the station, where he once said his sports reports were perceived purely as an obstacle to getting more news about Madonna.

Unknown to Berman and the new anchors was the tempest that was consuming Ross. She had unintentionally become a sounding board for the complaints of dozens of women who were suffering from sexual harassment. They turned to her because she was one woman at ESPN who possessed even a shred of clout.

While Ross was busy holding therapy sessions, the network was entering a new era, one to be shaped by Olbermann and Patrick and the indomitable Bornstein, who had raised the bar for programming. Poised to become an integral part of American culture and the most dominant force in television sports, ESPN, in January of 1988, won three cable ACE awards for its America's Cup coverage from the previous year, and then a sports Emmy that same summer for its college basketball coverage, the first such award ever given to a cable network. When Bornstein was promoted to executive vice president of programming and production in May of that year, few questioned the decision. Bornstein had the quick intellect and forcefulness needed to guide the network as it expanded in size and stature.

Gearing up for this growth, ESPN's satellite dishes now numbered more than a dozen, forming an expansive garden outside the main building. The network purchased additional land from the city for production facilities. But as the network expanded its reach to its customers, in the Bristol offices at home, two to three associate producers shared a desk, and talent quarreled over a priceless commodity—parking spaces.

ESPN was like a child emerging from puberty, outgrowing old clothes and transforming into adulthood. The following memo, posted by Bornstein throughout the main building, illustrated the point:

> In order to facilitate our growing production demands and priorities, the remote production and studio production departments have been joined together to form one consolidated organization and retitled as ESPN's "production department."
>
> As coordinating producers, both Steve Anderson and Terry Lingner will maintain the dual responsibility of managing and leading the remote production section of our new production department.
>
> Kirk Varner assumes the position of news director and is responsible for all studio-originated production activities.
>
> Bob Scanlon, formerly director, network operations, has been named director, production and program operations. In this new position, he will assume responsibility for the production department's financial management, personnel scheduling, graphics and music areas. In addition, Bob will oversee the integration and formatting of our network programming.
>
> In their new functions, Steve, Terry, Kirk and Bob will report to me.
>
> Bill Fitts will assume the new position of executive producer, special programming and as such will be responsible for overseeing and coordinating the production, editorial and creative elements, and continuity associated with all packaged programming. In this new role, Bill will report to vice president, programming, Loren Matthews, who, in turn, continues to report to me.
>
> Dick King, formerly manager, network facilities, has been promoted to the position of director, network facilities. He will maintain responsibility

for ESPN's network facilities/traffic, broadcast operations control and commercial traffic areas. Dick will report to vice president, operations and engineering, Reggie Thomas, who, in turn, continues to report to me.

The dizzying organizational changes recalled the early days of the network. But now it was Bornstein who was at the helm, effectively rerouting every function of the network through his office. Bornstein's need to control swelled right along with ESPN's budget. This did not overshadow the fact that his moves were solid ones. Perhaps the best was elevating Anderson, the top people person in ESPN management, who was trusted by everyone.

Awards. Reorganization. Look-in games. ESPN was a forward-looking company—in all ways but one. Bornstein's missive contained no mention of women at the top. ESPN was for men, and the men were not uncomfortable making that clear to the few women at the network, who were coming to Ross with a variety of complaints, some minor annoyances, others cruelly degrading.

After playing softball games in Bristol, male producers would report to work still wearing tank tops and shorts, drinking beer on the "Sports-Center" set (Walsh, however, says the only beer drinking he knows of on the set happened not in Bristol but on a West Coast remote), and watching pornography on the monitors. That locker-room mentality permeated the main building.

Some stories Ross heard were more serious than women being forced to stare at posters of Hooters babes near their desks. Women confided in Ross about being fondled, threatened with losing their jobs if they did not sleep with supervisors, and constantly pursued for dates. One male producer was so aggressive in his pursuits that the women wagered on how long it would take him to ask out a new employee.

"The atmosphere was very tough on women, because in those days, it might have been a twenty-to-one, or thirty-to-one ratio," said Bill Wolff, a former producer. "The men are all single, the men are all horny, and they are in Bristol where there is nothing to do, and you work all the time. So the women were objects of desire for just being there." Wolff made a close female friend at ESPN because he was one of the few heterosexual men in the building who didn't ask her out on a date.

The experience of Alice Robinson* was typical. She began at the network as a production assistant, and her main responsibility was to scan the news wires for offbeat items that could air on "SportsCenter." Her supervisor worked for the weekend shows, a man in his fifties with grayish hair and a bushy, uncombed mustache. One day in March, Robinson missed an item about a racehorse that won at 350-1 odds. When the writer called her over to his desk, Robinson thought she was going to be chastised. Instead, he reached in his desk and pulled out floor plans to a house he had just purchased. "This is my bachelor pad," he said. Pointing to a room, he added, "This is where we could sleep together." Robinson was stunned. Before walking away, she said sarcastically, "Good luck with the house."

Robinson says after that encounter she tried to avoid him as much as possible, but he was her supervisor. Encounters were unavoidable. Several days later, the two were talking about an NBA story when he blurted, "It should be a sin to look as good as you do today. I hope somebody is fucking you the right way." Robinson told him she did not appreciate that kind of talk and walked away.

Later that week, when a group was heading to a local restaurant for dinner, Robinson made what she now admits was a major mistake. Because most of the cars heading to the restaurant were full, she was forced to ride alone with her boss. During the entire trip, he told Robinson how much he wanted to have sex with her.

"I once had a secretary say to me, 'How is it that you don't sleep with the guys you work with? There is so much pressure,'" said Robinson. "That was the mentality of some people. The men tried to make women feel like the only way they could get ahead was to sleep with management. The star women anchors did not have that pressure, because no one dared to try anything with them. They were too high profile. The men pursued the production assistants, the associate producers, the producers. I have worked in a number of news organizations since ESPN, and I have never seen anything like it."

So why didn't more women sue the network? Robinson echoed dozens of others interviewed, including a number of harassment victims, who said, "One of the biggest things was the intimidation factor. Management, and sometimes the harassers, made it clear to you, without question, to keep quiet, and if you did not, you would hate the repercussions," Robinson said. "The television networks were losing luster, and ESPN was gaining in power. It was the place to be, the place to go, and you didn't want to get on their bad side."

"Sometimes you blamed yourself," Robinson added. "You said to yourself, 'Maybe it's me. Is my skirt too short? Did I say something wrong?' Today I know how silly that is. I did nothing wrong."

Ross felt the most egregious examples of sexual harassment stemmed from the allocation of time in the editing bays. When a story is put together, it is meticulously edited in cramped booths. There were only a handful of the units, so producers often bartered times. If one producer was on a deadline and needed a slot immediately, usually another producer traded their time. The traffic was often coordinated by the highlight supervisors or the "high supes."

Ross was alarmed when a young, attractive woman associate producer came to her in a panic one afternoon. She needed an editing bay immediately for a football piece and had asked a high-ranking producer to switch times with her. The producer said he would, but only if she first went on a date with him and then slept with him. Ross had previously heard such complaints about the producer, as well as others.

On behalf of nearly a dozen women, Ross had discussed these complaints with management several times, but saw few results. By now, she was becoming irate. Ross wrote an anonymous letter to *USA Today* detailing the problems. Because the letter was unsigned, it was never published.

"There were no women in management when I was there," Ross remembered, "so I think most of the men didn't care. The atmosphere was truly bad for women. Not for someone like me who was a high-ranking woman, but for an entry-level woman or a low-ranking producer. I haven't experienced anything like it. You have to understand that ESPN still had a start-up mentality. There were few rules, and people were rarely punished for what they did. Women were also afraid to complain because they would get fired and feared ESPN would ruin their name in the television business."

"There was rampant sexism at the network," recalled Julie Anderson, a former producer at ESPN. "A guy would take your highlight package and rewrite it, and you knew it was only because you were a woman. You were up against people's ideals. I worked with this guy who had the IQ of a squirrel, but because he knew more about the Boston Bruins than I did, he thought he was a genius and I was stupid."

Some time later, Anderson would produce an award-winning ESPN show examining racial issues in sports. Anderson eventually became the director of documentaries for HBO.

Ross had reached her boiling point by the beginning of 1989. Outside Bristol, the media, clueless about the struggles of women at the network, continued to report, and swoon over, ESPN's skyrocketing growth in size and influence. In January the network reached 50,132,000 homes, making it the first cable station to surpass fifty percent penetration of U.S. households. That month ESPN also signed a four-year, $400 million contract with major league baseball to televise 175 games a season. The deal would eventually lose tens of millions of dollars, but ESPN benefited from the prestige of owning baseball.

In October "SportsCenter" provided the first live pictures from the San Francisco–Oakland World Series after a destructive earthquake registering 7.0 on the Richter scale had rocked the city. For a short period, ESPN's generator-powered satellite dish provided the only national coverage from the area. Berman and Ley were hosting the coverage when Berman received a tip from a major league baseball source that the games would begin again in exactly ten days. Berman, who has a number of sources in almost every sport, breaks news, he just does it differently. That day on the air, Berman said, "If I were to take a guess, I would say the World Series will begin again in ten days." It did.

These milestones were impressive, but they did not stymie Ross's desire to achieve another kind of breakthrough. ESPN was about to experience its own seismic eruptions.

• • •

On a crisp March day, more than a hundred employees gathered in the ESPN cafeteria, sitting through the usual mundane topics—overtime, vacation schedules. When the employees were asked if there were any additional questions, Ross stood up, and, shaking, turned the meeting into anything but mundane.

"Most of what I have said about this subject has been ignored by management, so I thought this might be the best way to address things, and just get some topics on the table," Ross began, still shaking. "I want sexual harassment at this network to stop. It's wrong. Trading time in the editing bays for sex is wrong. Men are acting like animals. When a women walks into the building, it's like, 'fresh meat.' It is so unprofessional, and it is criminal. The people who are doing these things know who they are. This network needs to do something about it and stop ignoring the problem. I'm tired of women coming to me upset because they can't do their jobs without some jerk trying to sleep with them."

Ross spoke some five minutes, each word a dagger. What she said surprised no one in the room. What was surprising, however, was that someone had finally addressed the problems publicly. When she was done, her audience shifted uncomfortably, discharging no sound until Ross was thanked for her comments and the meeting broke up.

"Karie got up and really let people have it," Anderson said. "It was incredible. She really spoke up for all of the women. I remember I was cringing when she was talking. I was scared, but I was glad she was doing it. After the meeting, the bosses would all say, 'We didn't know.' But they knew. You would have to be completely dumb not to at least hear about the harassment that was going on."

After her lecture, Ross received dozens of letters in her company mailbox from ESPN women who shared their harassment stories and supported her speech in the cafeteria. One was written by Robinson, who said in her note that Ross was "unbelievably gutsy." Ross's words will never be recorded by ESPN in any official history, but they were pivotal. She had given women their first voice.

The problems that incited Ross's verbal spanking grew in part from a stifling work environment. There remained strikingly long days, just as in the early days when badminton tournaments and other arcane programming dominated ESPN's airtime and the parking lot was a mantle of mud. Now the network was successful, growing significantly in stature, but not in employees. While the workload doubled between 1985 and 1990, the size of the staff increased only slightly. A typical day for a producer in Bristol started at 5:30 A.M. and ended around 10:00 at night, broken only by a quick lunch in the cafeteria and then a Caesar salad from the White Birch for dinner. In between there was an NFL show or "SportsCenter" to produce and sometimes up to five management meetings to attend. Even if there had been something to do in Bristol, no one had the time to do it.

More than one producer was hospitalized with exhaustion. Odjakjian had worked eighteen-hour days since 1980, now they stretched into twenty. Instead of returning fifteen calls a day from coaches and athletic directors, as in ESPN's prehistoric days, there were 150 calls in any forty-eight-hour period. Eventually Odjakjian was forced to take a one-month leave of absence because of stress.

"Brilliant work comes out of every pore of that building," said Mark Mason, who ran ESPN radio, "but it is a repressive, depressing, sad place to work sometimes."

Producer Loren Matthews, who came up with "Big Monday" as a phrase for the all-night college hoops smorgasbord at the beginning of the week, received a promotion and bonus. It came with a price, however. The workload was a primary cause for a heart attack that almost killed him.

If it was miserable for the high-ranking manager, it was worse for the lowly production assistant, whose job was anything and everything. They made $18,000 a year, with overtime, and most worked from 6:00 in the evening until 3 A.M., obviously prime hours socially. They did research, scanned for highlights, and if they were lucky, took one day off a week. For many of the nontalent at ESPN, life was, and continues to be, an obsessive, all-consuming, and at times depressing existence.

Wolff's girlfriend lived in New York and his time off was sometimes less than a day, so to see her, he was forced to leave ESPN late Saturday night, make the two-hour drive to the West Village, sleep in the next day, then leave Monday morning at 4 A.M. to get back to Bristol in time to start work.

"I was this twenty-five-year-old guy who was lonely, with no social life, and my life was all sports, all the time," said Wolff. "I felt isolated from the rest of the world. It was such a rigorous and consuming life. I was totally burned out, as were at least ninety percent of the other production assistants and almost everyone at ESPN."

For much of ESPN's history, women were grossly underrepresented in the most crucial part of the network, the production department. Now they were slowly trickling through the front door. Still, as the 1990s approached, production was ninety-seven percent male. The harshness of the work schedule brought the producers closer together, but it also led to irresponsible, even criminal behavior. And much of the aberrant behavior was aimed at women, who were never fully accepted into the brotherhood of the abused. Instead, the few women in production served as a source of odd amusement for the overworked and undersexed male production workers, many of whom felt women didn't belong at ESPN in the first place because they knew nothing about sports. "At ESPN," Scott Ackerson said, "we weren't even close to being politically correct."

The hopelessness the women felt about their situation was worsened by a human resources department woefully inept at handling the increasing number of harassment cases. The department was understaffed and poorly trained, forcing the women in the newsroom to distrust anyone but themselves and a few men at the network.

"Women and men never talked about issues that offended women," Ackerson remembered. "It was woman to woman. The biggest problem women felt was that they had nowhere to go."

The hostility toward women inside ESPN did not abate after Ross's courageous speech. The problem was too systemic for one speech to provide the cure. In fact, after Ross left the network in late 1989, and as ESPN grew, it only got worse.

But for now the network had to address Ross's explosion in the cafeteria, which sent ESPN management into a panic, the tremors of which were felt all the way in New York at Capital Cities/ABC. There was a strong desire to correct the problems Ross spoke of and equally intense impulses to cover both companies from damaging lawsuits. If women had banded together and filed a class action case, there is a chance it could have hurt the network's finances and pristine image in the press. In many of the harassment cases, ESPN was in clear violation of state and federal laws.

ESPN initiated a series of sexual harassment seminars, both for victims and incoming employees. They were viewed as a joke by both the men and women. Many of the men thought the women were too sensitive. The women felt the meetings were designed more to protect ESPN than to effect change.

Groups of fifteen to twenty people, men and women, crowded into the offices of human resources soon after the blistering speech in the cafeteria. They were shown films on what constituted sexual harassment and how to handle it. Several dozen women met separately with department officials and, while sitting around a small table, were asked if they had any problems with harassment or discrimination. Many said they did and then were asked to fill out one-page questionnaires, listing the incidents. Some women had endured so many problems, they added five pages of handwritten notes to the questionnaires. They wrote about having their breasts grabbed in the newsroom, computer messages asking for sexual favors, and being physically shoved into a corner and fondled. One of the most common complaints focused on high-ranking producers or assignment editors, who offered the plum jobs or stories to women in exchange for dates or sex. There were even complaints that sexism and harassment interfered with the flow of getting information on the air. ESPN cameramen at college games sometimes shot as much tape of women cheerleaders as they did of what happened on the field or court. Back in Bristol, editors had to wade through countless scenes of scantily clad women to get to the highlights, which caused unnecessary delays.

If ESPN managers did not know they had an epidemic on their hands before those meetings, they did now.

Capital Cities/ABC distributed a memo in June of 1988 to ESPN employees regarding its sexual harassment policy, which was followed by ESPN's posting two months later. The latter read:

> As stated in ESPN's "Equal Opportunity and Treatment Policy Statement," it is contrary to federal and state law and to ESPN policy for any employee to harass any other employee with regard to sex, race, ethnicity, religion or minority/affirmative action status. Any employee determined by management to be guilty of such forbidden behavior will be subject to discipline, up to and including firing.
>
> In general, such prohibited harassment consists of verbal, physical or mental abuse of an employee by another with regard to his or her personal

characteristics, which are legally prohibited from being the basis for individual discrimination. In other words, a person may not be harassed because of or with respect to his or her race, creed, color, national origin or sex.

While what constitutes racial, ethnic or the other types of harassment should be self-evident (use of insulting names, etc.), sexual harassment is an area of concern and a detailed explanation of it is in order. Sexual harassment involves unwelcome sexual conduct directed at an employee by any person which affects his or her employment or working conditions by being: (1) a condition of employment, (2) a factor in his or her career advancement, or (3) the cause of an intimidating, hostile or offensive work environment or a substantial interference with his or her ability to do the job. Such conduct includes but is not limited to the following:

– Sexually-oriented teasing, joking, hazing, abusing or insulting.
– Explicit or implied demands for sexual favors or activity, or other unwanted sexual advances.
– Touching or physical advances including pinches, pats and caresses, and blocking or impeding movement or interference with normal work or movement.
– Visual harassment such as display of lewd or suggestive posters, photographs or drawings.

The memo continued to note that any woman who was the subject of harassment should report the incident or incidences to human resources immediately.

Ross had done her part to begin initiating change at ESPN. As she started to walk out of the cafeteria, still shaking nervously, she was approached by a man who had frantically scribbled notes throughout the meeting. He had shocking white hair and a white beard, and to Ross he looked like Santa Claus. John Walsh shook her hand and asked her opinion on how to eradicate harassment at the network. They spoke for several minutes, and Ross was impressed with his intelligence and sincerity. After serving as an adviser for ESPN, beginning in 1987, Walsh began working full-time as the network's general of journalism on January 11, 1988. His job was to tighten up "SportsCenter" and make the newsroom a place of business rather than a fraternity house. Only Chet Simmons would have more of an impact on ESPN than Walsh. He would hire its best reporters, turn "SportsCenter" into the most significant sports media vehicle in history, and inject a sorely lacking professionalism into ESPN's institutional demeanor.

10   The Genius and His Army

As an adviser, John Walsh had spent months studying ESPN, brick by brick. Most of his attention focused on "SportsCenter." Lurking in the back of the room during editorial meetings or in the rear portions of the studio while a show aired, frenetically taking down notes on his omnipresent notepad, Walsh was a mystery to most of ESPN's employees. His odd appearance and manner added to the intrigue. Walsh's wispy, snow-white hair stood out from the full, darker manes of the younger staff, and some were slightly put off by how he rarely looked them in the eyes, not knowing he was legally blind.

Bornstein wasn't bothered by Walsh's disarming stare; he was too entranced by his expansive mind. Walsh had many ideas for improving ESPN, most centering on a plan to beef up "SportsCenter" and to make it the cornerstone of the network. Bornstein was quite impressed. Walsh, he concluded, was the right person to strengthen ESPN's journalism, as well as to supervise ESPN's potential advance into radio.

Too many focused on Walsh's eccentricities instead of his uncanny abilities. Walsh had a journalistic sixth sense that allowed him to discern trends and issues that escaped ESPN producers and executives, who were used to soft news and the highlight-oriented world of television sports. Walsh had started the smart *Inside Sports* magazine and once headed *Rolling Stone;* consequently, he was firmly plugged into the network of premier journalists and editors.

When Walsh came to Connecticut in January 1988 for a final round of interviews, he was staying at a local hotel. Since Walsh cannot drive because of his poor eyesight, mail-room clerk Mike McQuade was conscripted to meet Walsh in the hotel lobby and taxi him to the network station. McQuade asked his supervisor how he would know it was Walsh. "You will know," he was told. "He's an albino."

When McQuade arrived at the hotel, he could not believe his eyes. The lobby was teeming with men and women in town for a convention—one for albinos.

Walsh finally got his ride to the newsroom and his job as executive editor. With the strong backing of Bornstein and others, he started to turn ESPN upside down, beginning with its culture. Some of his massive changes were agreeable to the rank and file, others infuriated them. In the end, most of Walsh's early decisions, some difficult, others obvious, were the correct ones. Walsh disputes this, but others say one of the first things he did was move the beer drinking on the "SportsCenter" set to the parking lot and then to eliminate it all together. He also ordered that the Hooters posters come down. Walsh also instilled a dress code: Producers could no longer report to work in Bermuda shorts and T-shirts; they instead had to wear slacks and shirts with collars. Managers were told to wear jackets and ties, and on the air, reporters were reminded to do the same. The crushing hours remained brutal, especially for the production assistants, and would indeed become worse, but Walsh at least showed more flexibility.

"I would be at the station by 7 A.M. and leave by midnight," Julie Anderson remembered. "I realized that after working about a year, I had never had a weekend off. I went to John and said, 'John, I'm a single woman, I have no life, I need a weekend or two off.' I never worked back-to-back weekends again. John was like that. He took care of you."

Walsh's lieutenants were like him—print editors who did not know a camera lens from a studio light but had a strong journalistic background. Bob Eaton, Jim Cohen, and later Vince Doria became Walsh's trusted partners. Doria was one of Walsh's most impressive management hires. He helped to build the *Boston Globe* sports section into one of the best in the country, basing it on superb editing as well as strong writing and reporting from the likes of Bob Ryan, Ron Borges, Will McDonough, and Leigh Montville.

Walsh also boosted the research department, which had consisted of one man, the tireless Howie Schwab, who suddenly had a dozen companions. Walsh hired additional producers and reporters, increasing the number of reporters on the scene instead of just picking up feeds and bolstering ESPN's stable of specific sport experts, almost all of them print reporters. After Walsh, shows like "NFL Primetime," which had used fifteen to eighteen minutes of video a show, were now running more than thirty minutes, and the ratings increased dramatically. ESPN even began showing boxing weigh-ins at which the fighters would step on the scale in their underwear in a crowded room filled with media members and fight officials, would make sure they had made their weights, and then would do a live interview on "SportsCenter."

Walsh left footprints everywhere. Producers often kept tapes of games or old interviews lying around their desks because there was no filing system. One night a custodian, incensed at the clutter, collected the tapes and hid them in a back room as retribution. In response, Walsh implemented a tape storage and retrieval system.

As he had promised Bornstein, Walsh's greatest changes were reserved for "SportsCenter," whose budget was nearly doubled. Odjakjian discovered just how much revamping of the show Walsh was considering when the two went to the White Birch restaurant for lunch. Walsh introduced himself and his vision. He felt fans could not get enough statistics and inside information about the major sports, so he proposed creating extensive separate shows for each of the sports. He also wanted to overhaul the graphics for "SportsCenter," making them punchier and more contemporary. When Walsh was hired, ESPN was the only network that went directly from one show to the next without commercial interruption—a strategy from its early days aimed at preventing viewers from switching channels. Walsh took the idea a step farther on "SportsCenter," pushing commercials even later into the show to stuff more meaty news into the early portions of the broadcast.

Walsh was always thinking about news—how to find it, how to increase it in weight and volume, and how to deliver it better. These thoughts consumed him. Even casual conversation revealed he was always grasping for ways of enhancing the network's reputation as a news source.

Jean McCormick, the Harvard-educated former "Nightline" researcher, was interviewing with Walsh to become the first woman studio producer on the same October day the celebrated Triple Crown-winner Secretariat died. Walsh asked what her thoughts had been on the ride to Bristol, and McCormick mentioned Secretariat's front-page obituary in the *New York Times* and the stallion's importance to sports history. Walsh sprung from his chair—"You're making me insecure about our coverage," he said, and he charged into the newsroom to ensure that ESPN had devoted enough airtime to the horse's death. When Walsh returned, he finished the interview by asking McCormick, as he had with others, to watch ESPN for one week and write an analysis.

Many of his suggestions to reporters and producers reflected his print background, where thirty sources for a story were not uncommon. In television, with stories lasting several minutes, at best, speaking to that many sources was excessive, but Walsh was accustomed to directing reporters writing forty-inch magazine pieces. His overzealousness aside, Walsh's instincts about news, reporting, and writing were respected throughout the company.

"When I had a story and I wasn't sure where to go, my first phone call was to John, and it is still that way," said reporter Jimmy Roberts. "I'm not blowing smoke. He is a very eccentric individual, and I don't always agree with some things he does, but this is the truth, he was, when I first started, and still is, the smartest man in television."

Walsh was desperately needed in the newsroom. "When I first got there, I was amazed at the lack of news judgment," producer Scott Ackerson said. "The way they approached things before John was not journalistically sound. A game was more important than an issue or news story. The only thing that mattered was, 'Who won the game?'"

Chris Mortensen had reported on professional football for the *Atlanta Journal-Constitution* before joining ESPN, and recalled the "major credibility problem in the sports-news department. I thought they could get a lot better. I didn't understand the way they reported news when it pertained to the NFL. The reporting was sloppy and a lot of times wrong."

Producers joke that ESPN's history falls into two categories, B.W. and A.W.—Before Walsh and After Walsh. Before Walsh, a "SportsCenter" broadcast might start with the big baseball game of the day, followed by all the other scores and highlights from the same league, followed by the other league's scores. If a coach suffered a heart attack or a high-profile receiver ranted about wanting the ball more, viewers had to wait until all of the scores were read first. After Walsh, depending on the gravity of the story, the order might be reversed.

Reshaping "SportsCenter" into an electronic version of a newspaper's sports section was a simple step, but an important one. Walsh reorganized the news delivery format. No one had to wait fifteen minutes to watch stories of substance.

"Even local news had learned how to sort things out according to their news value," Ackerson said. "That is what John changed at ESPN. He basically set up a newsroom. Editors, fact-checking stories, teaching people how to look at the long-term and the big picture. He increased the staff. There were more meetings, more of a formatted show, and most of all, John instilled structure."

Walsh had his detractors. The exit door was always open, and anyone who stonewalled Walsh was asked to use it. Accordingly, several producers said, creativity was stifled. All the directives came from Walsh and his new management team, heading down the line like a speeding train. Few dared to stand in the way.

The network was changing in another way. Young producers with degrees from UConn were being replaced by graduates of Harvard, Brown, and Yale. The new ESPN Ivy League appealed to Walsh.

A natural division developed between the B.W. and A.W. crowds. ESPN had taken a dramatic left turn from the days when management hung out with talent, producers, and even the production assistants. Walsh was all business and he did not want management socializing needlessly with the help. In later years, when the talented Steve Anderson left "SportsCenter" first for remote and then ABC, only to return a short time later, the divide had widened. Anderson had the people skills Walsh lacked, and he evolved into a translator for him. Walsh would bustle by a desk, bark an order, then scurry along to perform the next chore on his list, earning Walsh the nickname "drive-by" among some producers. It was not unusual for Anderson to later receive a phone call asking for clarification of a Walsh request.

Walsh's hires were sometimes treated disdainfully by the B.W. clique. Charley Steiner had worked almost his entire career in radio. He knew how to write a crisp news lead and could smell a potential story long before it matured into one. Steiner was working in New York for the RKO Radio Network when an organizational restructuring put him out of a job. Because he had nine months left on his contract, Steiner decided to go to his weekend home in Woodstock and play tennis for as long as his backhand could hold out.

One Friday afternoon in May of 1988, Bornstein walked into a convenience store in Norwalk and after striking up a conversation with the clerk, told him he worked for ESPN. "That's funny you're in the media, too," the clerk said, "because my favorite broadcaster on the radio just got fired." Bornstein asked who it was. "Charley Steiner, of course."

After returning to Bristol, Bornstein mentioned Steiner's name to Walsh, who already knew Steiner, and called him in Woodstock.

"We want to make 'SportsCenter' more journalistic and less jockish," Walsh told Steiner, "so come try out for us."

Steiner was confused. "For what?"

"As an anchor, Charley, an anchor."

Steiner did, and he was terrible. "Red light over the camera means what?" Steiner joked. "I was hideous. But when you go into it having no expectations, you leave feeling fine." He didn't expect to hear from ESPN again, and he had received an offer from shock-jock Don Imus to join his new show at WFAN radio in New York when Walsh called back and told Steiner he was hired.

"For what?" Steiner said.

"As an anchor, Charley, an anchor."

Steiner, thirty-nine at the time, with a scruffy beard and wire rim glasses, did not fit the stereotypical profile of a television anchor. He was another controversial Walsh hire and to some of the B.W.'s, Steiner's solid news judgment and dryly humorous writing was not enough to appease them. Before one of Steiner's first days on the air, one of the other "Sports-Center" staff members, whom he would not identify, approached him in the newsroom.

"You're the new guy, huh?" he asked Steiner.

"Yeah," Steiner replied.

"This fucking place is going to shit," the person said before walking away.

Steiner quickly adapted to the sparse writing of television and he was perfect for the expanded "SportsCenter," which now included guests in the studio and live interviews. One of his first assignments was an interview with the legendary polysyllabic sportscaster Howard Cosell, who had a rocky public image.

"Howard," Steiner asked, "the perception is you've become a bitter old man."

"Bitter? I'm not bitter," Cosell replied. "It's the sportswriters."

"It's the sportswriters" became another running punch line around the newsroom, almost equaling in stature "Happiness is Bristol in your rear-view mirror."

Steiner, whose solid boxing analysis continued the ESPN tradition started by Marchiano, proved Walsh right. He was an exceptional addition to the network, an anchor who was at complete ease writing and reporting news. Walsh made other hires, none more important than three reporters recruited at the same time as Steiner. These were the best reporters in the network's history, people so skilled they gave ESPN the immense credibility that Bornstein would later use to market the network around the world.

• • •

Walsh's tentacles stretched into almost every nook of the journalism world. Whereas he spent weeks on the telephone, recruiting his kind of people to the network, it was just as common for someone to call him and

ESPN's buildings were once located on a mud-caked lot. Now the network has a sprawling complex with over thirty satellite dishes.

ESPN founders Scott Rasmussen and father Bill, circa 1979.

From left, Scotty Connal, Sal Marchiano, and Stuart Evey, promoting an ESPN boxing event, circa 1980. Connal provided the network's technical backbone; Marchiano was its skilled boxing expert; and Evey pushed financially, backing ESPN through Getty's chain of command.

CANDACE BARBOT/*Miami Herald*

The immensely brave Karie Ross, a one-time ESPN anchor, here interviewing former tennis great Bjorn Borg in 1992. Ross was considered a hero by women at ESPN in the late 1980s for standing up to sexual harassment at the network.

One of the most respected media members in the business, Christine Brennan interviews CNN anchor Wolf Blitzer. Brennan, a former *Washington Post* reporter who now writes a column for *USA Today*, is one of many current and former print journalists ESPN uses in its coverage. Brennan reports on the Olympics for the network.

The first ESPN logo. Bill Rasmussen initially called his dream "ESP-TV," then added the word "network" to make it sound more impressive. Connecticut printer Guy Wilson decided the elliptical circle added a flair that would distinguish ESPN from other stations.

The tireless Andrea Kremer, left, the best reporter in ESPN's history, and former producer Sam Marchiano outside the Chicago Bears training camp, circa 1994. National Football League executives, coaches, and players say Kremer is the person they respect and trust the most. Marchiano, daughter of Sal Marchiano, is now a solid reporter at Fox Sports.

Anchor Bob Ley, former producer Jean McCormick, and producers Heather Faulkner and Bob Rauscher accept an Emmy Award in 1996 for their work on *Outside the Lines*. ESPN has won twenty-nine sports Emmy Awards.

Steve Bornstein outside the ESPN studios in 1993. Chris Berman calls him "the smartest man in television. All the money ESPN is making? It's Steve." Considered brilliant and egotistical, when Bornstein was head of ESPN, he helped turn the network into a global entity.

MARILYNNE YEE/NYT Pictures

ESPN has some of the best talent in sports radio. Keith Olbermann called former host Tony Bruno "truly the most brilliant talent at ESPN." Tony Kornheiser's afternoon show is one of the most substantive on radio. Above, Nancy Donnellan, known as "The Fabulous Sports Babe," discusses the latest sports news in this photo from 1997; she left the network in 1999.

CHUCK SOLOMON/Sports Illustrated

The extremely intelligent—and extremely eccentric—John Walsh, the gatekeeper for ESPN's journalism, in the network's newsroom in 1992. Walsh changed "SportsCenter" from a fluffy show of highlights to the most respected television sports news information vehicle ever. While Walsh made the network more professional, he also mishandled several incidents involving sexual harassment and ESPN employees, and some say in recent years he has become more corporate man than journalist.

Keith Olbermann, applying makeup before a "SportsCenter" broadcast in 1992. Olbermann is the best talent in the two-decade history of "SportsCenter." He constantly fought with management—and sometimes with his fellow anchors.

Anchors Dan Patrick, left, and Mike Tirico, writing their scripts before "SportsCenter" in 1992. Patrick paired with Olbermann to create their well-written, well-reported, and humorous show. "ESPN took off the seat belts, and sometimes we abused that power, but rarely," said Patrick. "They trusted us and we gave them a great show." Tirico has been called "the Michael Jordan of ESPN" because his ability is so strong he makes everyone around him better. However, Tirico was suspended for three months after sexually harassing women at the network.

Dan Patrick, watching a highlight tape before a "SportsCenter" broadcast. Patrick is respected by almost everyone, from the athletes he covers to the producers of the show.

ABC's critically acclaimed show "Sports Night" takes a behind-the-scenes look at a fast-paced nightly cable sports show. Olbermann ripped the show as "unrealistic" because a woman and a black man run the fictional network, something Olbermann says would never happen at ESPN.

make a recommendation. That is how ESPN and Jimmy Roberts became the unlikeliest of companions.

Roberts began his television career as a gopher for ABC News, getting coffee for the talent and making airport runs to deliver executives to their flights. ABC officials noticed a latent talent in Roberts, giving him an opportunity at something more substantial. He slowly moved up the chain of command to assignment editor, writing and producing for the news and sports divisions. At the assignment desk, Roberts honed his skills, and by the time he was focusing solely on sports, working with Cosell, he was a trusted part of the ABC Sports machine. Working for Cosell was mayhem. Cosell was up and down, mean-spirited one day, amiable the next, unpredictable always. Cosell often called Roberts at home at seven in the morning on Sundays, startling the young Roberts. "Jimmy, I'm sending the limo for you," Cosell would stutter into the phone. "We're going to Churchill Downs for the races. Be there in fifteen minutes."

Roberts learned an underappreciated skill from Cosell. Cosell could ask a tough question without the subject getting angry or aborting the interview. Roberts, a wise apprentice, developed Cosell's sublime combination of fearlessness and tact. Roberts was soon ready to leave the protective net of ABC, tiring of being a spare part in a behemoth. But the sports world was not ready for him. Roberts applied to dozens of small stations around the country but was rejected each time in letters he still keeps at home. Then Walsh called on the recommendation of his former partner at *Inside Sports*. Walsh and Roberts both had an inkling a special relationship was about to begin.

Roberts started at ESPN the first week of June 1988. Initially, he was quietly concerned about his status in the media food chain. "Oh, my God, I'm on cable," he fretted. In his mind, ESPN was not a single step down from ABC but several flights.

He focused on the job instead of his status, earning Walsh's immediate respect. He covered mostly New York, living in a moderate apartment building on E. Fortieth Street in Manhattan, driving to a Giants, Rangers, or Knicks game, shooting his stand-up in the parking lot, then racing to the Port Authority bus terminal to ship the tapes to Bristol. There were still rough moments, such as the time Roberts took several dozen takes to finish a thirty-second stand-up, but those were few. He was a bona fide talent.

So was Andrea Kremer, and Walsh could spot talent, which was why he and Anderson were having lunch with her in January of 1989 while Kremer was covering Super Bowl XXIII for NFL Films. Walsh was again projecting, as he had with Roberts, and could discern that the athletic, 5-foot 2-inch, ninety-five pound Kremer had substance and fire. This time, however, Walsh quickly discovered he had competition.

Kremer was already considering two job offers. One was from HBO's "Inside the NFL," as their field reporter. The other was more appealing. NBC wanted Kremer to do NFL play-by-play, a job no woman had ever held on a regular basis. Kremer had struck up a friendship with NBC announcer and broadcast coach Marty Glickman, who had followed her work at NFL Films, as all hardcore football fans had. Glickman had always told her, as NFL Films founder Steve Sabol had, that the networks would one day come calling. Both men were right.

Kremer was intrigued by the NBC offer but unsure of the timing. She knew emphatically she could do the job. Kremer had watched hundreds of hours of raw football film and practice footage while working for Sabol. As a result, she could break down the counter-trey running play of the Washington Redskins better than some coaches. Her hesitation had its roots in history. A woman pioneer in sports media faced countless perils. Even after she had met with NBC officials, did a brilliant demo tape, and was offered a package of six games, Kremer remained wary. "I thought I would be seen as a novelty," Kremer remembered. "It just wasn't the right time." Kremer's decision became easy after a shift in management at NBC Sports. Now, in addition to the pressure of being a first, the uncertainty of working for a new regime loomed. ESPN was suddenly the best option.

She called Glickman, who had hoped Kremer would pick NBC. But because of the change at NBC, Glickman knew the right place for his friend was ESPN. "Kid," he told her, "you made the right choice."

Kremer's first piece for the network was on the Chicago Bears preparations for the draft. It sparkled with the kind of reporting details and insight rarely seen on the network in the B.W. days. She analyzed the Bears' scouting process, interviewed almost every coach on the team, and offered predictions on whom Chicago might select. She handled her premier live event for ESPN with equal grace, hanging out on the day of the draft with Florida State two-sport star Deion Sanders at the home of his then agent. Sanders sported gold glasses and a gold necklace shaped as a dollar bill. "I can see you are wearing your signing bonus already," Kremer joked.

Kremer was well prepared for what would become an impressive reporting career in sports television history. The daughter of a Philadelphia judge, who had emphasized to her the twin virtues of toughness and education, she was equally content performing classical ballet or watching an NFL game on television. Between breaks during dance rehearsal in high school, she would slip on a radio headset to get an update on the Eagles game.

Kremer attended the University of Pennsylvania because it was close to home. She had three minors (English, sociology, and anthropology)—but no life. There were ballet classes five days a week, a brief stint in law school, and eventually a scholarship to the American Ballet Theater. Kremer loved to dance but knew ballet was not for her when she overheard one dancer complain to another, "I ate an apple today. I feel so fat."

Writing was always a hidden passion, so when she heard the largest weekly newspaper in Pennsylvania was looking for freelancers to write dance and theater reviews, she jumped at the chance. Her writing was so impressive that when the sports editor stepped down, Kremer was asked to take control. Over the next several years, she turned a four-page, mostly high school-oriented sports section into an expanded must-read that oozed with professional sports. The advertising reps kept pictures of Kremer on their walls—they adored her and the money she was hauling into the paper.

When Kremer was working on a cover story on the economic impact of a Super Bowl on a city, the reporting trail led her to NFL Films, because they had produced a promotional film for the city of Philadelphia. She peppered one of the company's executives with dozens of questions. Instead of being annoyed, he wanted to hire her. Kremer liked their work and a few months later returned for an interview, which consisted of a written and verbal test. One question was to define a trap play. Kremer's answer was lengthy and exact, needing extra space, filling a full page. She noted that the Pittsburgh Steelers probably ran a trap play better than anyone. NFL Films was so impressed that they stored Kremer's test answers for future reference and offered her the job seven days later.

Kremer produced, directed, edited, wrote, and even scored music for NFL Films, learning every facet of television. Sabol admired Kremer's ideas and work ethic and wanted to put her on the air. She was nervous until a close friend gave her a piece of advice. "When you're before the camera," Kremer was told, "all you need to do is be friendly, fuckable, and informative." The words were crude, but Kremer understood the point.

Kremer's first on-air pieces showed savvy, creativity, and, as usual, deep research. She was able to coax athletes and coaches into doing things few others at NFL Films, or anywhere else, could. When Kremer crafted a story on the cerebral Oakland Raiders tight end Todd Christensen, she sat in a chair, dressed as a therapist, wearing glasses, a conservative suit, and bow tie, while Christensen reclined on a couch and talked about the burden of being an intelligent football player. For another story, Kremer asked

Eagles coach Buddy Ryan if she could borrow his defense, and after a puzzled look, he complied. Kremer then produced a piece on what players really discussed in an NFL huddle.

With each story Kremer tackled, she was becoming a stronger reporter, gaining a deeper understanding of television production and growing the additional three and four layers of skin a woman needed to survive in sports journalism. When ESPN hired Kremer in May of 1989 to open the Chicago bureau, she brought that thick hide with her to the network. It was needed almost immediately. She was the first female reporter ESPN had hired, and producers weren't used to women in that position, let alone one like Kremer—highly intelligent, knowledgeable of all sports, and a tireless perfectionist. Kremer had more production experience than the first three producers at ESPN she was paired with, giving them ideas and correcting their mistakes. Kremer took no guff, irritating some of the men, who might not have complained if Kremer had been a male.

Soon after joining the network, Kremer flew from Chicago to Bristol for a meeting with top executives Eaton and the likable Cohen, who were, and remain, two of Kremer's strongest supporters. After discussing story ideas in the office, all three went to lunch in Bristol. The conversation turned serious when Cohen and Eaton explained they needed to speak to her as friends. They gently relayed complaints from producers who claimed Kremer was too tough on them and difficult to work with. Kremer's heart was pounding; she was furious. Still Kremer kept a calm demeanor.

They concluded by asking for Kremer's thoughts. She stayed cool, then responded simply, "I have a question more than a response," Kremer said. "Would we be having this conversation if I was a man?"

Cohen and Eaton looked at each, and Cohen offered the only honest answer he could. "Probably not," he said.

11

Radio Daze

Television was the place Kremer always suspected she might softly land. To Chris Mortensen, television was still the enemy.

After covering baseball and then the Falcons for the *Atlanta Journal-Constitution,* Mortensen was considered one of the best football reporters in the country. When the short-lived daily sports newspaper the *National* asked Mortensen to join its star-studded staff, it underscored Mortensen's solid reputation. Once at the paper, Mortensen made a swift impact, breaking the story that University of Florida running back Emmitt Smith was leaving school his junior year to enter the NFL draft.

A slew of other scoops followed, and they all caught the eye of Walsh, who dispatched producer Bob Rauscher to begin the process of recruiting him to ESPN. Mortensen met with Rauscher and producer Fred Gaudelli for lunch in New York, where a proposal was put forward. They wanted Mortensen to join the network in a smaller role as an analyst for the NFL draft, then in an expanded one once Mortensen demonstrated he could survive in television. They had hoped Mortensen's connections would give them a harder news edge both on "SportsCenter" and on their growing number of professional football shows. Mortensen was intrigued, and any lack of respect he had for ESPN's football reporting was tempered by the reality of his financial situation. The *National* was running out of money, and strong rumors were swirling about its impending doom.

But there was a caveat. "I had been in the print business for twenty years at that point," Mortensen said. "The step into television was not an easy one. To print guys, television was still kind of the enemy. It was almost like treason. We considered television people to be frauds."

Mortensen overcame his bias and joined the network. Walsh and Rauscher saw immediately just how many connections he had in the NFL world, which of all major sports is the toughest to infiltrate as a journalist. NFL executives and coaches, who tend to be controlling by nature, trust few people implicitly, and it can take years to build relationships. Mortensen had reached that point and beyond. His sources were strong in every part of the league, from players like Dallas quarterback Troy Aikman to top general managers like George Young from the New York Giants. Reclusive Oakland Raiders owner Al Davis even returned his calls.

There was only the annoying matter of presentation. Makeup wasn't mandatory to work the phones at the *Journal,* smiling wasn't a requirement to sit in a football press box. On television, however, looks counted. And Mortensen needed work. He began spending time with consultant Andrea Kirby, who helped turn print frogs into television princes. Getting Mortensen to just sit down and listen was difficult because he was always in pursuit of news.

"I know we have to spend time on this," he would tell Kirby, "but right now, I have to go chase this story."

When Kirby was given time with Mortensen, she furnished several tips, in John Madden, chalkboardlike sessions, to make the adjustment to television a less tortuous one. She started by instructing him to make two columns on a piece of paper, one for the things he liked about himself, another for the ones he did not, then focus on the positives and project those images. It sounded a little strange to Mortensen, but he did it anyway.

The night before his first "NFL Countdown" show, Mortensen was bluntly reminded he was no longer in the print business. Rauscher had been studying Mortensen's audition tapes almost daily and decided that Mortensen looked mean wearing his thick mustache. He was asked to cut it off and did. He also started using hair spray, which to print reporters was the ultimate act of humiliation. After seeing Mortensen's new clean-cut look on ESPN, one of Mortensen's former editors was startled and called his old friend. "What the hell have you done to yourself?" he asked.

Despite the tips from Kirby, Mortensen still felt uncomfortable, sometimes feeling like Alice falling down a rabbit hole into a strange world. On the air, Mortensen rarely smiled or laughed, which had been noticed by many in the building. He was asked to put on a smile even if it was a phony one. Mortensen began practicing his smile before a mirror at home and on the road. He soon felt it was time to unveil it.

In a tradition that continues today, Mortensen provided a fresh story or slant almost every show, the result of cultivating years of contacts and a work ethic that fit snugly into the frenetic and exhausting ESPN milieu. Mortensen usually arrived three hours before the show to work the phones, often times gathering more fleshy information than ESPN had time to use on the air. Walsh was ecstatic; he wrote Mortensen a letter telling him he was "a great addition to the network."

One "NFL Countdown" show in the middle of the 1989 season was no different. With one exception. While breaking another important story, Mortensen focused his mind not on the story but on the complaints and suggestions from everyone—his presentation. After spilling his scoop, the network went to a commercial break, and Ackerson, then the coordinating producer, barked into Mortensen's ear, "Mort, why were you smiling?"

"Everyone has been telling me to smile, so I smiled," Mortensen replied, incredulously.

"But, Mort," Ackerson said, "you just talked about a coach getting fired."

• • •

For someone nearly blind, Walsh had great vision. Roberts, Kremer, and Mortensen would set the standards for all other ESPN reporters who followed. Somehow, Walsh perceived skills in the trio others had missed, and although the common denominator among the three was splendid reporting instincts, they each brought a different talent to the network. Roberts had thorough interviewing skills and a strong moral compass, Kremer plucked every detail she could from a story and her sources trusted her with the most intimate details of their lives, and Mortensen, nicknamed "tid-Mort" because of the football nuggets he was constantly breaking on air, was the most connected man in the increasingly important NFL.

Walsh had almost everything in place: hard news–hewned reporters, improved technology, and sports-starved fans. Most important, he'd elevated the status of "SportsCenter," eliminating its reputation as a journalistic punch line. It was edging closer to Walsh's exacting standards.

There was just one more thing. Walsh wanted anchors who could handle "SportsCenter" like a pilot: with steadiness, with boldness, when needed, and with some color and style. He liked reporter Bob Ley, and looked for ways of elevating his presence at the network, as well as that of others. But Walsh had another idea he had been toying with for months, one that would lift ESPN to unprecedented popularity. Implementing the idea, as well as dealing with another embarrassing incident involving an ESPN employee, would occupy much of his time.

• • •

Alice Robinson thought the harassment problems were behind her. The supervisor who embarrassed and angered her with his overt lustings lasted one year at ESPN and was gone. Robinson never found out the whole truth, but there were rumors he was shown the door after other women had complained about his advances. But those were only rumors. Male producers still gawked at her, and the occasional married manager asked her out to dinner, yet she was certain the most hellish of times had to be over.

Throughout the first few months of 1990, the network bounced between elation, due to the February announcement that ESPN had signed a four-year agreement to televise thirteen NFL games, and envious grief, with the news that the NCAA's first-round games would be shown on another network for the next seven years. CBS was carrying the NCAA ball now. ESPN staffers threw a party in the conference room that resembled more of a memorial service, complete with champagne and tears.

Robinson was about to suffer her own highs and lows. The latest bizarre and unsettling chapter of her ESPN life started with a harmless computer message from Mike Bogad, who worked in the production department. "I just wanted to say you look nice today," he wrote her.

More such messages followed. Looking back, Robinson says she should have foreseen what followed. At the time, Bogad seemed harmless. He stood about five feet five inches tall, weighed more than two hundred pounds, was balding, and looked like an overgrown teddy bear. He had played a significant part in bringing more women to ESPN, especially behind the camera. Bogad was intelligent, charming, and friendly.

Because Bogad held a position of power and was well liked by Walsh, Robinson trusted him and a friendship developed. Not only that, Robinson got to know Bogad's wife, a researcher at ESPN renowned for her deep knowledge of sports, extremely nice personality, and astonishingly neat handwriting.

Robinson felt comfortable with Bogad and his wife, and when the couple traveled, they asked Robinson to house-sit in their large condo in Southington, Connecticut, a short trip from the ESPN complex. She considered it a way of earning extra money, something a PA could always use, and a painless good deed.

After returning from a trip, Bogad and his wife expressed their thanks to Robinson for looking after their place. Then his wife went into the kitchen and as Robinson was about to leave, Bogad whispered something in her ear.

"Did you sleep with somebody in my bed?" she said he asked her. "I hope you didn't leave any stains."

Robinson remembered, "I was obviously shocked. It was disgusting. Not only because of what he said, but because his wife was in the other room. Suddenly, he was not the nice guy I thought he was."

Robinson decided she would avoid Bogad at all costs. She made another vow: She was no longer going to be passive. She had learned a lesson from watching Ross, deemed a hero by many ESPN women. Reasoning with each individual man was ineffectual—sexism was too ingrained in the network. Robinson knew what she had to do. If there was another episode, she would take action.

• • •

In April 1990, the network aired an opening day triple-header to debut its new baseball package. Eight weeks later, ESPN showed two no-hitters live in one night, the man-giant Dave Stewart of Oakland against Toronto and Fernando Valenzuela, the chubby Los Angeles Dodgers pitcher who blanked St. Louis. In the ESPN offices, Dan Patrick was in sports heaven.

His ESPN odyssey actually began years earlier, in 1979, when Leonard and Grande were making their debut and Patrick was a senior at the University of Dayton. He and his roommates shared a house with no heat to afford cable, and Patrick was one of the several thousand watching ESPN's debut. He had considered a career in broadcasting, and now, watching ESPN cemented his intention.

He turned to one of his roommates, pointed at the TV, and said, "That is where I'm going to be."

Patrick wrote to Ley a few years later, enclosing a demo tape of himself. "You're a talent," Ley wrote back, "but get local experience." So Patrick did, eventually landing a job at CNN, where he was hired in 1983. He left five years later after his request for a $5,000 raise was rejected. Then on March 4, 1989, his dream transmuted into reality as Walsh hired him as an anchor. He bantered on the two-thirty "SportsCenter" with Berman and noticed, as everyone else, that Berman had a voice like a megaphone.

Patrick fit into the ESPN culture easily—viewed as a good guy because he attended the ESPN offsite house parties and respected because he had talent, albeit unpolished. He also readily adopted ESPN's stubborn inferiority complex. It was always ESPN against the rest of the world, despite its increasing success. Patrick had come from CNN Sports, where it was always CNN against the rest of the world. After a few years, he came to treasure ESPN, caring for the network as few others on the Bristol campus.

"I've always been in it for the long haul," Patrick said. "I worked at CNN where it was us against them. I kept that mentality at ESPN."

Patrick's delivery on "SportsCenter" was effortless. Producers enjoyed working with him because he wasn't just hair and face. He was a solid writer who did his homework and kept his ego in check.

Patrick also succeeded in earning the trust of those around him without appearing too political. As Olbermann would later, Patrick went to management on behalf of a producer who deserved a pay raise, or quietly supported some women in their struggles. Olbermann used a bullhorn to get what he wanted; Patrick used a handshake in a back room.

Months after Patrick joined ESPN, Roger Werner resigned as president and chief executive officer to pursue private interests. Bornstein, the heavy favorite to succeed Werner and the man whose thumbprint could be found on every operation of the network, was officially named president and CEO in early September of 1989. Bornstein's added power meant more power for Walsh as well, because Bornstein approved of his work with the newsroom.

Walsh kept a steady eye on Patrick, impressed with what he saw. At the same time, he continued his steadfast search for new anchor talent. On January 13, 1988, Walsh's forty-second birthday, he and Steve Anderson locked themselves in a room to review videotapes of talent from around the country. On the very first tape was Keith Olbermann, a Los Angeles sportscaster from KCBS-TV whose performance dazzled them both. Walsh sensed that he may have found the other half to a "SportsCenter" anchor tandem with intriguing potential.

• • •

The computer had become Robinson's worst enemy.

While working in the newsroom at her usual laborious job as a PA, scrolling down the wires, fighting to stay awake on only four hours of sleep, she had managed to mostly avoid Bogad. They had had one confrontation. Robinson called in sick one day, but Bogad saw her at a softball game and then told supervisors. Robinson was suspended for a short period. Robinson's act was not unusual among the PAs—they sometimes had to call in sick just to get a day off. But if Robinson already hated Bogad, that episode intensified her dislike of him even more.

Whether the incident colored Robinson's judgment became irrelevant because Bogad continued sending Robinson e-mails, which changed in intensity from irritating but benign to more direct and uncomfortable. One in particular infuriated Robinson, not because it was racier than others, but because she had lost patience.

"Why don't you unbutton your blouse another button," she says he wrote, "you would look better."

Robinson walked across the room and stood several inches from Bogad's face. "Why don't you leave me alone?" Robinson says she told him.

One problem for women at ESPN was the lack of unity. Only a handful of them discussed the issue openly; others kept the problems to themselves or, worse, resigned. Robinson was unsure if she was the only subject of Bogad's increasingly lewd interest. She decided to start her own investigation. She went to a film festival in Hartford with Julie Anderson and during a quiet moment, asked Anderson if she knew about her pursuer. Anderson's face, mimicking someone about to vomit, provided the answer. Anderson explained how he regularly asked the women PA's and producers out for dates or made sexually inappropriate comments. Robinson was dumbfounded at the pervasiveness of the problem. A few days later, she would discover another layer.

One workday afternoon in Bristol, Robinson was approached by two women who said they needed to speak to her in private. The three went to a corner of the tape library, which was unoccupied. The two women asked Robinson if she had problems with Bogad. Robinson said yes and described her experiences: the messages on the computer and the comment at the house. The two women shared similar tales pertaining to inappropriate electronic notes. Then their voices dropped to a whisper. Bogad, they said quietly to Robinson, had gone further, touching them inappropriately and asking them out on dates. The women were especially disgusted, Robinson remembered, because they, as Robinson, knew and liked Bogad's wife.

"All these women were going through, some worse, some the same, what I was going through," Robinson said. "That's when I decided I had to do something. I didn't care if I lost my job or not."

Robinson and a small group of other women filed complaints against Bogad with human resources, a move that ignited a chain reaction that would rock the network. The women were asked to fill out questionnaires detailing every episode involving Bogad or anyone else. At first some balked, fearing severe reprisals, but one woman called a meeting, and Robinson, as well as others, spoke up. "If we don't do this," Robinson said, "the men will continue to act this way and nothing will change."

Almost everyone in the group then complied. They wrote down details of what happened, not just fingering Bogad but other ESPN employees, mostly in the production department. Again the accusations ranged from the crassly juvenile to the serious. One man shouted repeatedly across the room to a woman PA that she had "nice tomatoes" and asked if she was wearing a bra. Another was asked what sexual position she liked. During a small staff meeting prior to a "SportsCenter" show, a researcher quoted a David Letterman line just to irritate a woman producer, saying, "And that's what America needs, a good sucking." There were complaints about sexually explicit interoffice handwritten notes, phone calls, and e-mail messages. Some women provided evidence such as diary entries and copies of the computer traffic.

Eventually women, some in small groups, others individually, met with Walsh, one other executive, and a human resource person. Some conversations focused on Bogad because he was one of the highest-ranking employees accused of improprieties, and most of the women were assured his situation would be handled properly by the company. They were also emphatically told something else: There would be serious consequences for mentioning any of this conversation to anyone outside ESPN.

Bogad was never seriously disciplined, only receiving a stern lecture from management. Several years later, another group of women would again file complaints against him, alarmingly similar to the initial ones. This time human resources director Ricardo Correia handled the investigation. He found the women's accusations, numbering some half dozen, credible.

One woman, who reported to Bogad, told a story typical of his tactics. He sent her a number of e-mail messages, and one message, discussing routine work issues, suddenly veered off course when he wished her a happy birthday, asking: Is a "birthday kiss allowed?" When the woman said no, he wrote back, "I knew that answer, but I had to ask you!!!" After receiving similar messages several months before, the woman claims she had told him to stop. He ignored her request. The messages were not particularly vulgar, or threatening, but they violated the network's sexual harassment policy because they were clearly unwelcome, and they were constant.

The conclusion to the second series of investigations differed from the first. Bogad was given two options. He could resign with no consequences, meaning ESPN would erase this from his employment record, concealing it from future employers. The second option: He could be fired.

Bogad protested both options, hinting he might sue the company. ESPN called his bluff: If you sue, the harassment complaints will be used against you, the network threatened. Four years after the initial complaint, Bogad finally left ESPN, taking a job in Chicago for a company who knew nothing about his dark history.

On November 17, 1993, six months after Walsh had appointed Bogad and Norby Williamson to the positions of coordinating producers for "SportsNight" on ESPN2—despite all the problems that had swirled around Bogad—Walsh posted a terse memo to the entire production staff:

> I regret to announce that Mike Bogad is resigning from ESPN in order to pursue other interests and to spend more time with (his family).
>
> In over five years, Mike has made many contributions to the news and information programming at ESPN.

Bogad left ESPN but found himself accused of more improprieties a short time later while working for a sports network in Chicago. Bogad was accused by a woman anchor there of inappropriate computer messages and personal remarks. The woman went to management with her problems, and Bogad was asked to leave the station before he was fired.

The woman, who now works for a major television network, asked that her name not be used and said through her agent that Bogad's actions were "horrendous," but she has put the episode behind her. She did not go into further detail.

Bogad remains in the television business and says he cannot discuss what happened at ESPN because of a confidentiality clause signed with the network when he departed. He also denies the sexual harassment allegations leveled against him at the Chicago network.

It was fitting that as the entire distressing episode unfolded with Bogad, a group of women crowded around a television in the newsroom in October 1991 to watch live coverage of Anita Hill's testimony before a Senate Judiciary Committee, regarding alleged sexual harassment by Supreme Court nominee Clarence Thomas. "I felt I had to tell the truth," Hill said. "I could not keep silent."

Robinson, who later left ESPN, understood what Hill meant. "I think that moment, when she was testifying, was the most quiet the newsroom has ever been," remembered Robinson, "and it was one of the most emotional moments of my life."

• • •

In the spring of 1991, ESPN won seven Emmys, a sure sign that Bornstein's programming decisions and Walsh's crusade to upgrade "SportsCenter" and the reporting staff were having the desired effect. Later that year, Bornstein axed the network's morning news business program, "Nation's Business Today," and replaced it with rebroadcasts of the previous night's "SportsCenter." Some producers felt it was a strange move. Why would anyone want to watch the same "SportsCenter" again? What they failed to grasp, and what Bornstein did, was that "SportsCenter" was more than a news broadcast. It was a habit, an impossible one to break. Viewers would watch it the way "Star Trek" fans tune into the Sci-Fi channel to watch the same episodes of Captain Kirk fighting the same aliens over and over.

Steiner could sense ESPN was ready for another one of those bursts forward. He wondered when ESPN would begin marketing its logo on hats and shirts the way other networks did, a question Steiner asked Bornstein one morning in the newsroom. Bornstein was not surprised by the question. He had spent months pondering it.

"Now is probably not the right time," Bornstein told Steiner. "At some point soon this place is really going to take off. That's when we'll do it."

Walsh was doing his own thinking about the future. He called Patrick to his office, and when Patrick walked in, Walsh and several other members of management stared solemnly at him. Patrick thought he was in trouble.

"Dan, we're thinking of hiring Keith Olbermann," Walsh said.

Patrick was surprised, but pleasantly so. He knew Olbermann fairly well and always thought he was talented. "Do it right away," Patrick said. "Hire him. He would be a great addition."

With Patrick's blessing, Walsh went forward. Olbermann announced he was leaving KCBS to join ESPN on December 16, 1991.

• • •

In a mostly positive March 1990 article about Berman, *Sports Illustrated* writer Franz Lidz dropped in this grenade.

> SportsCenter makes few journalistic demands, because journalism is not really its game. On this night in New Orleans, the big story is a report by a Washington, D.C., TV station that over the last ten years three top NFL quarterbacks had tested positive for cocaine but had received no counseling or treatment. Berman was with San Francisco 49er quarterback Joe Montana earlier in the day when Montana was asked if he had ever flunked a drug test.
>
> Now Berman is prowling the studio, his face creased in disgust. "Who cares?" he says. "Who cares? Who cares? Who cares?"
>
> Who cares about what?
>
> "I never thought the press would ask Joe this crap. I mean, this is serious crap."
>
> He plops down in front of an IBM Selectric and taps out a few lines. "How's this for an opening?" he says. "As Gary (U.S.) Bonds sang, 'Way down the Mississippi down in New Orleans . . .'"
>
> What does that have to do with the allegations about the quarterbacks?
>
> "Nothing, really," says Berman. "But since I'm in New Orleans, I

thought I'd slip in some lyrics about the city. I firmly believe you do this stuff for yourself. If anybody else gets a kick out of it, it's a bonus."

But what about the drug controversy?

Berman mops his brow with his schmutz rag and says, "Just listen to what comes next: 'They call New Orleans the city that care forgot. Well, today the city forgot a lot more than care.'"

What do you mean by that?

"Huh?"

The stuff about the city forgetting.

"Hey, I'm an impulse guy," he says. "I've got a pretty good idea of what I'm doing, but I don't want to totally understand it because that would mean it's all premeditated. This may not be Pulitzer Prize material, but it's a way to get into the story."

So what did the city forget about?

"Uh, journalism," he says. "It forgot about journalism."

The city forgot about journalism?

"Listen, the issue to me is not whether any quarterbacks did drugs. The issue is—I think journalism and human nature took a beating today. I mean, the TV report was an obvious grandstand play. That was premeditated. The whole thing reminds me of Amadeus. I mean, why is it that when somebody reaches the pinnacle of his profession, we have to chisel away at his monument? They even took shots at the guy who went to the North Pole. They said he didn't do it. I mean, why? Can't we just enjoy something that's beautiful, like a flower? Do we have to pull the petal off?"

• • •

Chris Berman, as any high profile media figure, certainly has his critics. Many can be found in print journalism. Like Lidz, they find Berman's style at times superficial, even sycophantic. What his critics have to admit, however, which is sometimes easily lost in Berman's outsized personality, is that he is matchlessly connected throughout the sports world. He can call just about any professional sports franchise and get the scoop long before his print or other TV rivals. Whether it is team president Carmen Policy from the Cleveland Browns, St. Louis baseball manager Tony LaRussa, Indianapolis Colts general manager Bill Polian, or Buffalo Bills owner Ralph Wilson, Berman's deep well of sources always makes him even money to break the big story.

Moreover, unlike many of his peers in television, Berman is endeared for his genuinely friendly demeanor and kindness. Involved in numerous private charities, Berman will say hello to anyone, whether it is Ken Griffey Jr. or the janitor at the ESPN studios in Bristol.

Still, the criticism in SI distressed executives back on the ESPN campus, who had been working assiduously to change the image of the network and of "SportsCenter" from a fluffy sports station of highlights to one of substance. It was clear Berman had failed to discern the real significance of the story, which was that the NFL's drug-testing program may be discriminatory, protecting its white stars while disproportionately punishing its black players. That Berman missed this, or simply ignored it, reinforced perceptions about him—and ESPN.

There was something else at work, however. More than ten years had passed since a bright-eyed Berman first walked across that slop-filled parking lot to apply for a job at ESPN. During this time, Berman's stature and power within the network grew exponentially. So popular with fans was Berman that his name had almost achieved the same branding power as ESPN's. Thus, to lose Berman would mean to lose some of the value of the ESPN name. So the network gave him a little longer leash, indulging his occasional soft journalistic ethics. And Berman took advantage of this, as manifested by the SI article.

He had forged a close relationship with the Bills and 49ers because of his extensive coverage of both teams as they dominated their respective conferences in the late 1980s and into the 1990s. The relationship, in several cases, may have crossed the line; Berman once accepted a Super Bowl ring from the 49ers franchise. Berman's overtly cozy relationship with the Bills and 49ers threatened to violate the foremost journalistic commandment: Thou shalt not get too close to the subject.

That was not a concern about Olbermann, who was a writer and journalist first. Olbermann may not have been above throwing a temper tantrum or two, or three, but he respected the news-gathering process and was aware of the line that anchors and reporters should not cross with their sources or the subjects they covered.

After leaving Channel Two in Los Angeles, Olbermann planned on taking three months off, vacationing languidly in Hawaii. Two days into 1992, Walsh called Olbermann's agent in a panic, explaining that ESPN was launching a radio network soon and was in desperate need of a third host. Walsh hoped that Olbermann, who had radio experience, could help fill this position. Olbermann had been hired to anchor the eleven o'clock "SportsCenter," which was what he expected to do after his vacation. He agreed, however, to help out. What were a few vacation days compared with beginning his new job on a good note?

In just a short time, Olbermann and Walsh became aware of their profound differences. Olbermann, the straight-laced Chuck Wilson, and Tony Bruno, whom Olbermann considers one of the most talented persons who ever worked at ESPN, helped launch the ESPN radio network, which featured sixteen hours a week of sports news and analysis. Olbermann was not shy about expressing his opinions: He disliked how host Nanci Donnellan was promoted by the network while Wilson and Bruno were not. Olbermann protested by writing a three-page memo to Walsh.

Walsh was soon on the phone again to Olbermann's agent, this time complaining about the note. "He's got to understand that he's not running the radio network or ESPN or anything else," Walsh said.

There was a pause, and then Walsh, always an admirer of good prose, added, "But, boy, is this a well-written memo!"

• • •

The early days of the radio network mirrored the humble beginnings of ESPN television. There was a general manager, two producers, two associate producers, an update man, several board operators, two tape editors, a technical supervisor, a researcher, one secretary, and three hosts: Wilson, Bruno, and Olbermann. The three men, and later Mark Mason, the general manager, helped build ESPN radio from dust, turning it into a prosperous, shrewd addition to the franchise.

The price of success, as on the television side, was again eighteen-hour days and no personal life. A typical radio shift lasts four or five hours, but ESPN radio shifts went seven. Most of the programming was outstanding, and a fortunate portent occurred on the first weekend when Olbermann broke the story of Danny Tartabull signing with the New York Yankees.

Mason's day usually began at three in the afternoon and did not end until well after one in the morning. Bruno's schedule was horrific but illustrated his dedication to the job. A morning radio host on WIP radio in Philadelphia during the week, Bruno would leave on Friday afternoon for the five-hour drive to Bristol, where he taped several interviews for ESPN Radio, then began a seven-hour shift at six on Saturday evening and another the next day at the same time. He would sign off the air at one on Monday morning, just in time to make the five-hour drive back to Philadelphia to be on the air by six.

Walsh expected ESPN radio to uphold the standards, at least the ones he was trying to establish, of ESPN television. A stickler for attaching some fact to a score, just as on "SportsCenter," Walsh declared that ESPN radio updates could not simply report a game's results; they needed to add additional facts about the game, for instance, how many times Joe Montana was sacked.

Sometimes Mason would go home feeling he had put on a great show only to get a phone call from Walsh, who tuned in consistently. Walsh would admonish Mason for missing some obscure score from a game in the West.

"As you might imagine," Mason said, "when Walsh did those type of things, they made us better, but they drove everyone nuts."

Mason tried to make life at the network at least tolerable by cutting side deals with the staff. He often found himself in the uncomfortable position of asking producers to come in on their only days off or to skip family reunions. So he bargained—work today and you'll get an extra day off later. When management discovered Mason's humane policy, he was ordered to stop it.

Bruno kept spirits high with his continual tongue-in-cheek lampoons of the Dallas Cowboys in the cramped ESPN radio newsroom. Some staff members were cracking up after one Bruno jokefest when Walsh happened to walk into the room. He pulled Mason aside. "You have to calm these guys down," Walsh chided him. From then on, moments of levity became known as "TMF." Whenever Bruno or Olbermann would incite laughter among the group, which was often, someone would interject, "Uh, oh, it's a TMF moment—Too Much Fun." Most of the frolicking was eventually relegated to Bruno's hotel room at the Radisson several stoplights up the street from ESPN. In his decidedly plain hotel room, Bruno and his ESPN radio cohorts would gather on weekends to watch sports, laugh at each other's jokes, and just act silly—all at a safe distance from Walsh.

Nanci Donnellan would go on to become one of the most popular sports radio hosts in the country, calling herself "The Fabulous Sports Babe." (Later, *Washington Post* columnist Tony Kornheiser joined ESPN radio. Critics have unabashedly praised his show for its humor and intelligence.) Donnellan, as Olbermann, had her clashes with Walsh.

During the 1994 baseball strike, Donnellan was interviewing union executive Gene Orza when she began a question by saying she had read *USA Today*. Orza, who exhibited shades of elitism and could be brusque, interrupted her to suggest that if she was getting her information from that newspaper, she was in trouble. Donnellan was incensed, convinced that Orza would have never treated a male radio host so rudely. She immediately hung up on him.

Donnellan had clearly lost her cool, but Walsh would commit perhaps an even bigger mistake. Orza, a friend of Walsh, called him and demanded an apology, threatening to freeze out ESPN from any strike-related information. Walsh fecklessly drafted a letter of apology for Donnellan to sign; she refused.

The episode demonstrated what was, at times, Walsh's hypersensitivity to good manners and decorum. Walsh hoped to make ESPN more businesslike, which started with politeness toward coworkers and toward every business contact. This was another crusade of Walsh's, probably a good one—the newsroom could indeed use a generous dose of good manners. Some in the radio division, like Olbermann, however, believed Walsh was insincere, that his manners police was just another way for ESPN to control its people. Then an incident happened that Olbermann says changed his opinion of Walsh forever and caused his loss of trust in his boss.

Olbermann was in the radio newsroom late one week in early January of 1992 when Walsh introduced someone to him. "Keith," Walsh said, "this is a friend from my ink-stained wretch days." Olbermann shook hands with the man, a former newspaper grunt named Larry Schwartz whom Walsh had brought to ESPN radio as a researcher and consultant.

Like some other middle-aged men at ESPN, Schwartz became enamored of a young woman more than ten years his junior. His obsession was associate producer Kelly Sullivan*. Sullivan had always been a magnet for the clumsy predators and the new hire fit the bill. He began calling Sullivan at home for nonwork-related reasons, even trying to reach Sullivan at her parents' home. Sullivan, who was producing for ESPN radio, let Schwartz know in no uncertain terms that she was not interested and that she wanted the calls to stop.

Olbermann and others assert Schwartz became verbally abusive to Sullivan, directing epithets at her in front of a small group. Sullivan, her nerves frayed, filed a sexual harassment claim with the human resources department against Schwartz. It was surprising that Sullivan waited as long as she did before complaining; Olbermann and Bruno had become used to seeing her arrive at staff dinners in tears, shaken over another incident.

Walsh, Gatti, and others urged Sullivan to drop her complaint. She refused. Her case was a slam dunk, in part because of Olbermann, who in the case of prickly workplace issues never hesitated to provide assistance. Olbermann volunteered to share with human resources what he witnessed Sullivan endure, as did several others in the department. "Keith did the right thing," said one executive who was at ESPN radio during that traumatic period. "He helped her when he didn't have to."

Schwartz presented a more complex picture of his relationship with Sullivan. "I never asked her out," he said. "We were friends at the beginning. Over the phone, she used to cry on my shoulder. She told me about all of her bad relationships with men." Schwartz maintains Sullivan once called him in his hotel room to go out for a drink.

What changed the relationship from friendly to hostile? Schwartz says he does not know. Schwartz did say that Sullivan filed sexual harassment charges against him for berating her in front of a number of ESPN employees, but his subsequent suspension was for "conduct unbecoming," not harassment.

Then, Schwartz says, several years went by until another incident in which he made inappropriate remarks to Sullivan, and she responded by calling him "a fucking asshole." Sullivan again complained, and at that point, an official with human resources told Schwartz he had to leave ESPN. Schwartz says he received a salary bonus when he departed "and ESPN would not have done that for someone who was harassing people constantly."

The situation with Schwartz remained a divisive and troubling one within the department for years and was typical of sexual harassment claims at ESPN and other companies. The woman who files the claim makes one set of allegations while the accused tells a drastically different story. Management is left to sort out the mess.

Schwartz's problem with Sullivan did not prevent Walsh from hiring him again. According to Walsh, Schwartz was a consultant for the SportsCentury project that aired in 1999. Walsh said Schwartz is an "arm's length distance from the network."

About Schwartz, Walsh said, "I remember the Schwartz one. I was not in on that one. . . . I was not participating in the discussion of it because I knew Schwartz, and I did not want to get involved in it. I heard about it." Walsh's statement directly contradicts the versions of others—including two top former executives—who maintain Walsh was intimately involved in the episode because Schwartz was his friend.

Toward the end of the ugly episode, at a regular Saturday production meeting, Walsh addressed the staff. His topic was the recently dismissed Schwartz. "I know a lot of things have happened and a lot of things have been said," Walsh explained. "I just want you to understand that he is not a friend of mine and I didn't bring him here."

Olbermann, standing in the back of the room, was dumbfounded. Others at the meeting were equally appalled. Not only had Walsh expressed to many of them that the researcher was a friend, Walsh had made it clear that he was instrumental in bringing him to the network.

"I never trusted Walsh after that," Olbermann said, "not for a minute."

After Schwartz departed, Mason felt the entire sad incident was behind everyone. An incident soon after, however, suggested that maybe he was wrong. In reviewing Sullivan's work, which he always considered excellent, he rated it as such. A few days later, Walsh asked Mason to come to his office. He held a copy of Mason's review of Sullivan in his hands.

"There are no excellents," Walsh exclaimed. "Excellent is the standard. You grade excellent as the standard."

12

Crisis

Walsh may have bungled the handling of Sullivan's complaint, but he continued to make astute hirings and to shuffle the personnel into place like a master chess strategist. Chris Myers was brought on as the Jimmy Roberts of the West Coast. He reported on Pete Rose's ban from baseball, on the tragic death of college basketball star Hank Gathers, and, making a trip to Dallas, on the sale of the Cowboys to Arkansas oil man Jerry Jones.

Myers wanted to gain more anchor experience at ESPN, and the network agreed, moving him to Bristol for the 2 A.M. "SportsCenter." Myers coanchored with Mike Tirico, a Syracuse University graduate and instant favorite of Walsh. It took just several months for Tirico to earn the tag "the golden tongue" among some producers. Myers and Tirico had chemistry on the set and were close friends off the set, with Myers inviting Tirico to his house for dinner several times.

Myers created the "Did You Know?" segment, which runs at the end of "SportsCenter," after Tirico started tossing out facts at the conclusion of the show as a way of filling time. Myers's phrases like "three-ball in the corner pocket" for a three-pointer were clever but drew a caution from management, who thought he sometimes got too cutesy.

Walsh was stockpiling anchors as if he were expecting some sort of talent drought. A persuasive sales pitch brought Robin Roberts to ESPN from Atlanta. A tall, stately daughter of a Mississippi educator and an Air Force officer who was a member of the first black flying group, the Tuskegee Airmen, she was an anomaly in the sports television business, a woman who happened to be black. Roberts was as bright and talented as anyone at ESPN, but she struggled making the transition from a culturally diverse city like Atlanta to a mostly white one like Bristol. During one of her first afternoons in ESPN's hometown, she was shopping at a local mall and saw another black person she did not know. They waved to each other.

Among the dozens to greet Roberts on her first day was Julie Paradis, the notorious schedule keeper, known for her outrageous schedule demands. "Nice to meet you," Roberts said to her. Paradis replied, "You won't be saying that soon." Roberts quickly began pulling double dips, anchoring the seven and eleven o'clock "SportsCenters."

Roberts was flawless as an anchor and even more impressive working on the "NFL Primetime" set with Berman and analyst Tom Jackson, the former Denver Broncos linebacker. She kept up with the quick banter and occasionally took over the show, tempering the testosterone-soaked atmosphere with reasoned, calm insights. ESPN quickly discovered that Roberts had a strong personality and was unafraid to take chances. When John Saunders stepped down from the "NFL Gameday" show, the morning setup of the day's games and one of ESPN's most important programming slots, Roberts went to Walsh and lobbied to replace Saunders. A week later, Walsh gave Roberts her answer. "Let's do it," he said.

Roberts was the first to anchor the Sunday morning "SportsCenter," which Walsh wanted to mimic a fat weekend newspaper. The two-hour show brimmed with features, highlights, live interviews, and in-depth issue-oriented stories. Roberts played the perfect airwaves traffic controller, slickly maneuvering from one item to the next.

Roberts was not reluctant to show emotion on the air, whether a hearty laugh or even a few tears, the latter a cardinal sin for women in the business. When her close friend, tennis star Arthur Ashe, died from an AIDS-related illness, Roberts's voice cracked and her eyes moistened as she read details about his life and death. She concluded "SportsCenter" by introducing a photo tribute to Ashe, saying, "We appreciate your being here and letting us mourn with you. Now, with some thoughts and some memories of the late, great Arthur Ashe. God bless."

After the cameras were off, Roberts wiped her face, and thought, "Oh, boy, I've ruined my credibility. Women aren't supposed to cry on TV."

Roberts had established such trust with viewers that her emotion was accepted as humane, instead of being degraded as a weakness. Viewers, male and female, flooded the network with thousands of letters of support for Roberts.

Roberts never experienced the harassment endured by other women at ESPN. A former collegiate basketball player and one of the top scorers in Southeastern Louisiana University history, Roberts had a physical and emotional presence that was almost intimidating.

Her only gender-related annoyance came at the premiere of the ESPYs (the ESPN-sponsored Academy Awards of sports) when an ESPN executive chastised her for wearing a dress deemed too risque.

Overall, like Berman and others, she treasured ESPN. As the child of an Air Force pilot, Roberts was used to moving from city to city. As an adult, however, she shunned the nomadic existence, choosing to stay at ESPN even when opportunities arose at other networks.

"I didn't want to be the answer to a trivia question," Roberts said. "I wanted people to remember that I was at ESPN. Women in television come and go. We're judged by harsher standards. Men who dump their wives and have twenty-somethings on their arms are looked at as virile and sexy. Men grow old and they are distinguished. When women grow old, it's, 'Let's bring in the next blonde-haired, blue-eyed woman.'"

Roberts's presence pervaded ESPN, as did Charley Steiner's, whose boxing coverage was transforming him into a popular face at the network. Despite Tyson's penchant for eating prison food, the sport of boxing still had plenty of stars. Fighters enjoyed their conversations with Steiner and trusted him. When Steiner covered championship fights in Las Vegas, celebrities as much as boxers clamored for a moment of his time—another exhibit of ESPN's growing stature.

"Here's a Jewish guy from Long Island going to Vegas and I was like the mayor," Steiner remembered. "You could usually pick me out from a crowd at those fights because I was the only guy not wearing fake gold medallions around my neck."

Eventually Steiner, Roberts, and Ley, who was beginning work on the "Outside the Lines" investigative reporting series, were brought together on the six-thirty "SportsCenter." The trio formed a heavy-hitting lineup, which later developed a rivalry with the late-night edition of the show hosted by Patrick and Olbermann, who made their debut on April 5, 1992, three months after ESPN started a new-look "Big Monday" basketball show with Big East, Big Eight, and Big West triple headers, and five months before the network and the NHL agreed on a five-year contract.

Olbermann and Patrick's maiden show did not contain any singularly revealing moment that heralded the greatness to come. Instead, there was more of a gut feeling, a premonition that something special was afoot. As for Walsh, he believed—no, he knew—that pairing them would pay huge dividends.

After the initial Olbermann and Patrick "SportsCenter," Patrick was spooked at the coordination between the two anchors. Olbermann was so confident of the duo's future that he nicknamed their eleven o'clock broadcast "The Big Show," tweaking the thirty-minute CNN late-night sports program, which ran a half-hour shorter than Olbermann and Patrick's broadcast. Some of the anchors from the six-thirty crew, mainly Ley, chafed at the nickname, considering it demeaning to them.

Patrick and Olbermann's broadcast may have been the franchise, but Steiner, Ley, and Roberts felt their show was just as good. In many ways, it was.

"It's pretty fair to say that Dan and Keith took the network to another level," Steiner said. "They had a pretty big playground to play in, and they played really well, but we were just as good. That's not sour grapes. Robin is as talented a broadcaster as there is. She had great credibility and so did Bob."

One disadvantage plaguing Steiner, Ley, and Roberts was management still hovering around the office as they prepared their broadcast and went on the air. The bosses obsessively tinkered with the show, and their presence diminished the trio's willingness to take risks. When Patrick and Olbermann were on the air, most of the top executives were home in their robes and slippers, allowing a freedom that the duo exploited nimbly.

Patrick never really compared shows. Patrick, however, knew that Olbermann and he were special. "We were onto something," he remembered, speaking of their early shows. "We could tell. I thought, 'This guy is different. This guy is fun. We're completely opposite, but that's good.' You would never pair us together in high school or college. It was basically the right time and the right place."

• • •

Despite Walsh's compulsive efforts to turn workers into monks, the notorious ESPN house parties continued unabated into the 90s. Bristol still had little to offer and ESPN employees still needed a release from the relentless work hours. It was not unusual for anchor Gary Miller, after more than a few beers, to shave his rear end at a party to loosen everyone up or for an entire houseful of revelers to guzzle well into the night, despite having to report to work early the next morning.

One house party in the fall of 1992 was relatively tame, with only a handful of drunks. Most people were sitting in the living room watching a football game. Karen Brooks*, who recently began as a production assistant and was considered an up-and-coming talent, was standing near a group of friends when anchor Mike Tirico approached her. A current ESPN producer watched and heard what happened between Tirico and Brooks and offered his account in an interview. Other current and former ESPN officials confirmed the story.

Tirico did not introduce himself to Brooks, he simply began talking to her. "You're the most beautiful woman in here," Tirico told her. Brooks ignored Tirico and started to move away from him. He followed, as did several friends of Brooks, staying within earshot just in case Brooks needed rescuing.

Tirico trailed Brooks around the party for several minutes until Brooks finally snapped. "Why don't you fuck off," she said. "Get away from me." Tirico simply stood there, and Brooks turned and left the party. Brooks's friends walked out with her, informing her along the way that the man was Tirico.

Brooks got in her car, her friends theirs. They were all headed to a local restaurant for a late dinner. Unknown to Brooks, Tirico had followed the group outside. Brooks began pulling out of the driveway when Tirico stepped in front of Brooks's car, putting his hand up, signaling her to stop. She hit the brakes, and Tirico walked to the driver's side of the car. Brooks reluctantly rolled her window down. "Get out of the way," she told him, "I don't want to hit you with my car."

"You're the most beautiful person I've ever seen and I think I'm in love with you," he said.

"Listen, fool, I've never talked to you before," she replied, "and someone told me you're married anyway so what the hell are you doing?"

"No, I'm engaged," Tirico said, "but I didn't think I'd come here and fall in love with anyone."

Brooks had heard enough and was ready to leave. By now, her friends saw Tirico standing next to her car and began backing up their car, wondering what was happening.

Brooks started to roll her window up but before she could, Tirico reached into the car and attempted to put one of his hands between her thighs. Brooks grabbed Tirico's arm. "Get the fuck away from me!" she screamed. Her friends were now out of the car and hurrying toward Brooks when Tirico quickly headed back into the party.

Brooks told several close friends of the strange episode, as well as an encounter she had with Tirico when they accidentally met the following day in the ESPN parking lot. Tirico approached her, and Brooks thought he was going to apologize for his behavior. Instead, Tirico said, "All I did all day was think about you."

This convinced Brooks that what had happened at the party was no drunken fluke. She responded, "What you did the other night was so inappropriate. If you don't discontinue this behavior, I'll get someone who will." Tirico said merely, "OK" and walked away.

Several months passed before every detail of what happened at the party and then in the parking lot had circulated throughout the gossipy newsroom. Some were astonished at Tirico's behavior. Others were not. One of the latter was the fiery Susan Glass*. She came to ESPN from the Sports News Network to produce the graveyard shift "SportsCenter." Karen Ross, whom she knew well, had warned Glass before she came to Bristol: "A different type of woman has to work there. It is a very bad place for us. Just brace yourself." Glass wondered, "How bad could it be?" Her answer came soon enough.

Glass became friends with Tirico and his fiancée, dining with them numerous times. Then one day she received a startling e-mail from Tirico in which he confided that he wanted to sleep with her. Several similar messages followed. Glass decided to minimize contact with him, a difficult strategy because Glass produced the two-thirty "SportsCenter" and worked closely with both Myers and Tirico, who were friends.

In March, late one night after the network's extensive coverage of the NCAA college basketball tournament draw, the hoops staff went to unwind at a bar in Bristol. Glass was walking to the bar when Tirico intercepted her. Glass said Tirico remarked, "I wish I was single. If I was, I would throw you on the table right here and fuck your brains out."

Glass first thought Tirico had too much to drink. "I kept trying to give him the benefit of the doubt, making excuses for him," Glass recalled. "I was thinking, 'Maybe he's had too many beers. I should just walk back to my seat.'"

Glass said she told him to go away and leave her alone.

"I know you want to screw me," Glass maintains he said, "so let's leave."

Glass told him again to stop but Tirico persisted. When a small group of the college basketball staff decided to leave and go to Denny's, Glass left as well. She followed analyst Jim Valvano and his close friend Saunders in her car and then sat between them at the restaurant, saying little to anyone. After only a few minutes, Glass decided to leave, climbed in her car and, driving over sixty miles per hour, made her way down Interstate-84 toward her home near Hartford.

Suddenly Glass noticed a car pulling up along on her left. She peered indifferently at its driver, then froze, realizing it was Tirico. Tirico was waving his hand in a motion that she interpreted to mean he wanted her to pull over. Instead, she continued driving, increasing her speed significantly. Tirico increased his speed as well, staying alongside her.

Glass decided to hit her brakes suddenly, veering toward the exit a short distance from the two racing cars. The move, she says, caught Tirico by surprise, and he continued on the highway.

"To say that episode was bizarre is an understatement," Glass said. "It was terrifying. But the next day, the fear was gone. By then, I was really, really angry."

• • •

The following evening, the early morning "SportsCenter" with Myers and Tirico may have been the most awkward in the network's history.

Glass, still seething over her unnerving encounter at the bar and high-speed incident on the highway, approached Myers and told him what happened. Myers himself had a reputation as an aggressive flirt around the office, but he had never been accused of such bizarre behavior. Myers was appalled and shocked. The circuits in his brain started misfiring: This was not the Tirico he knew. Was she talking about an impostor? Was this the Mike Tirico he and his wife had taken to dinner once a week? His friend?

Myers may have doubted the story from anyone else but Glass. A senior producer, Glass commanded respect throughout the building and possessed an impeachable character. She had been an outspoken critic of ESPN's boys club atmosphere before the Tirico incident, maybe even bitter about it, but Myers and others held her in high esteem.

Myers sympathized with the plight of women at ESPN. He noticed that Glass, like other ESPN women, was worn-out by the double standards prevalent at the network. When she was interviewed by producer Bob Rauscher to produce the "College Gameday" show, Glass says Rauscher warned her, "If you get the job, you won't be able to spend as much time with your boyfriend."

"First of all, I didn't have a boyfriend," Glass remembered. "Second of all, why is something like that even brought up? They don't say that sort of stuff to men." She eventually got the job.

For now, Glass was mainly concerned with what Myers felt she should do about Tirico. She asked his advice, which Myers did not hesitate to give. "Just tell him to never do anything like that again," he said. "Do you want me to say something?"

"No, not right now," she said. "Let me talk to him first."

Tirico took a different tack with Glass than he did with Brooks. Just minutes before the show aired, Glass said Tirico approached her near the set and began to apologize for his conduct. Glass cut him off, saying, "If you ever do that again, I'll kick your ass." Glass never doubted she could back up her threat, because she was more athletic than the fairly diminutive anchor. Tirico said nothing and walked onto the set. He put on a spotless performance, with Glass in the control room producing and Myers working next to him, wondering if there was a hidden side to his friend. Meanwhile, hundreds of thousands of viewers watched, oblivious to the drama that had just unfolded.

• • •

As word about Tirico's indiscretions filtered throughout the newsroom, and even outside ESPN, Glass, a leader among some of the women producers and production assistants, asserts other women came to her with their own horror stories about Tirico. They complained that Tirico made references to their physical features, touched them inappropriately, or expressed his desire to have sex with them. The allegations sounded disturbingly familiar to Glass.

Like Ross and Robinson before her, Glass decided to take stock of other women in the company, but her personal investigation focused on Tirico and his behavior. In fewer than three weeks, Glass discovered she was not alone in her problems with Tirico. Five women told her they had been harassed by Tirico. One of them was Brooks, whom Glass approached while both were working the 1992 NCAA Final Four Basketball Tournament.

"I've got to talk to you," Glass said. "It's about someone in the building."

Glass told Brooks about her incident at the bar and then later on I-84, and Brooks recounted every detail of her experience at the house party. After these revelations, Glass felt compelled to take action, but not before seeking advice from others at ESPN whom she respected besides Myers. She needed assurance that she was not being irrational. One of those she turned to was college football host Chris Fowler.

"No matter what happens," he told Glass, "you'll have my support."

• • •

"I was never faced with that type of situation before," Glass said. "There were no women in management to go to. Women were alone at ESPN. If you ever ran into trouble, you had no help. I thought I could help change that, and I didn't care how much trouble I got in, and I knew I would get into deep trouble because I was turning in one of John's favorite people. I went forward anyway."

In an indication of her character, Glass decided to tell Tirico what her plan was, including exactly what she was going to say to Walsh. She pulled Tirico aside before the late "SportsCenter" to tell him she had spoken to five other women who claimed he had sexually harassed them.

"I'm going to turn you in to John for what you've done to me and those other women," Glass told Tirico. "I just wanted to be straight-up with you so you didn't hear it as part of any gossip."

Tirico had a worried look on his face. "Well, if that's what you're going to do, then do it, but I'd hoped you wouldn't," Glass recalled Tirico saying.

Later that day, Glass met with Walsh for more than half an hour. She somberly enumerated the charges against Tirico. Glass says Walsh asked few questions and offered no sympathy. "You are going to have to go on the record," he told Glass, "and the other girls are going to have to go on the record."

Glass said they all were willing.

Many of the past harassment problems had involved producers or managers, people anonymous to the public. Keeping those incidences silent and out of the media was simple. The Tirico matter, however, was a different animal. Tirico occupied a highly visible position, and as one of the network's top talents and a favorite of Walsh, his problem would require a more cunning approach.

• • •

Tirico grew up in Queens, New York, listening to every syllable uttered by Marv Albert as he broadcast the New York Knicks and Rangers. Like Albert, he attended Syracuse University. More than a year before he earned his degree, Tirico was working at a local TV affiliate, handling sports on the 6:00 and 11:00 broadcasts. His work ethic was unrivaled, his dedication unwavering. One of the proudest moments of his life was the day he graduated from Syracuse University: Finishing up with commencement in the morning and a brunch in the afternoon, Tirico soldiered off to work his two shifts later that evening.

In 1991, at the age of twenty-four, Tirico landed a job at ESPN, where management, bullish on his abilities and typically understaffed, tested him early with a range of assignments. Tirico handled them all fearlessly and proficiently. No ESPN anchor had ever been so impressive at such a young age. His work ethic and skills were not his only impressive qualities.

"He is one of the most nurturing talents I've ever worked with," said a producer who has worked often with Tirico, "very willing to share his expertise. He never tried to be smarter than you, like a lot of talent try to do. In a professional setting, he goes out of his way to help people."

When Tirico arrived at ESPN, sexual harassment problems were at their peak. Opinions differ on what led Tirico to act the way he did. Some maintain Tirico was an impressionable young kid who made mistakes by following the examples of those around him. A sweep around the newsroom would have revealed to him high-ranking male producers, as well as talent, engaging in gross misconduct and in certain cases doing so with impunity. One former high-ranking ESPN executive even wondered if Tirico, who is black, would have been punished if he were white. At the time of Tirico's troubles, a popular producer and a football analyst, among others, were guilty of violating the network's sexual harassment policy but escaped discipline, the former executive said. Both men are white.

Ricardo Correia campaigned earnestly for women at ESPN during his tenure, and although he does not defend what Tirico did—far from it—Correia thought he smelled a double standard at work with the Tirico situation. "Of course I don't condone what he did," Correia said about Tirico. "But treat people consistently. And there was inconsistent treatment. Always inconsistent treatment. If I could sum up my tenure there, it was inconsistency, inequality, in terms of [punishment for sexual harassment], and level of importance. If you were in this kind of position, you got to do these kinds of things and it was OK. If you weren't, then you couldn't do it."

Others at ESPN concur with Correia's general sentiments but doubt Tirico was in any way a victim. Hidden beneath his affable personality, they assert, was a dark and disturbing one, offering a textbook explanation for his behavior: a man abusing his power, nothing more, nothing less.

What was not in dispute was that the allegations against Tirico disarmed management. In 1992 there were more than eight hundred employees at ESPN, some two hundred in production, and many of those production staffers were talking about Tirico. Talent and producers gossiped equally about the situation, speculating on what action the company would take. "What a lot of people were saying," remembered Glass, "was that ESPN would sweep it under the rug."

It was in this atmosphere yet another incident of sexual harassment emerged, this time, however, not involving Tirico but three production assistants. Two of them, both men, were discussing the third, a flamboyant woman who offended some of the other women because she wore tight shorts and cowboy boots to work and spoke openly about her sex life. The ESPN computer was again a conduit for trouble.

It was after two in the morning and the three had been working more than twelve hours straight. Lack of sleep and a long day turned the mood from professional to silly and beyond.

"What if we both did her?" one male PA wrote to Patrick King,* speaking of their female counterpart. King and the other male PA had been writing to each other for the past several minutes, using the computer's "topline message" format. It allowed two people to communicate solely with each other.

"She couldn't handle our seventeen-inch dicks," King wrote back.

The other production assistant thought the last message was funny and showed it to the woman production assistant, who was standing nearby. She failed to see the humor and promptly reported the incident to Rauscher, the producer on duty, who then met with King. He apologized to the woman PA, who in the end was not terribly upset by the incident. But King had chosen the wrong time to cross the line, even if it had been only a brief, single foray.

• • •

A week after the computer message ordeal, management continued evaluating the Tirico matter while also focusing attention on King. He was asked one morning to report to the human resources building, located near the parking lot. He thought to himself: I must have forgotten to sign some benefits form. When he arrived, King was summoned to the office of Michael Schnipper, a labor lawyer by training who headed human resources. Also in the room were Rauscher and Steve Anderson. King immediately realized this wasn't about any forgotten signature. For twenty minutes, the three men quizzed him about the week-old incident.

"This is a big deal," Schnipper concluded. "John Walsh called in from an airport to ask what happened," which was not as grave as it sounded, because everyone routinely checked in with the office, whether they were on assignment or simply at the pizza parlor up the street.

Then came the kicker from Schnipper. "If you're not careful," he said, "you're going to see Bristol in your rearview mirror."

The message was unmistakable—he was about to be fired. "I could have killed myself that night," King said. "I could have stopped my car on the Tappen Zee Bridge and taken the Nestea plunge."

Schnipper told King they would get back to him, and a week later, after reporting to work around five in the evening for his nine-hour shift, a page went out over the building's loudspeaker, requesting King phone Walsh's office. King did and was told to report immediately. Only seconds after anxiously settling in across from Walsh, King was given the news he feared. He had been fired, ending his thirteen-month relationship with the network. "This is the hardest thing I have ever had to do," Walsh said.

"John Walsh told me to leave the premises at that point," King said. "I left the meeting, I put on my coat, and I walked out the door. I started my car, I drove off. I did not pass go, I did not collect two hundred dollars. I did not say goodbye to anybody, I did not tell anybody what happened." Later, King did tell Chris Myers, who had befriended him and reacted to the news with indignation.

King used most of his two days' severance pay to buy a train ticket home. Only later, with the help of senior producer Barry Sacks, whom King considers one of the most decent people at ESPN, was he able to negotiate a written resignation. "The way PAs are treated," King added, "we were like interchangeable parts, just a bunch of jackasses right out of college. They don't think of you as having any personal worth."

King is both right and wrong. He is correct that ESPN views PAs, and many of its personnel, including anchors, as nothing more than, "meat puppets," as Olbermann says. Management was indifferent to the individual needs of its employees because it could be. In 1992 the network was receiving thirty thousand resumes a year. To distinguish themselves from the mass of others, some etched resumes on footballs or boxing gloves. One man once followed recruiter Al Jaffe into a bathroom and handed Jaffe a resume at a urinal. There were college graduates who would have given up their little sisters to work at ESPN, even be abused by ESPN.

The network knew it could squeeze the lifeblood out of its assistants, and if any buckled, thousands waited in line to replace them on the PA conveyor belt.

King erred in not realizing his new-found worth to the network. The male production assistant on the other end of that raunchy e-mail was suspended for two weeks without pay. As for King, an ex-indentured servant, he was now more valuable to ESPN than he had been as an ESPN employee. King was suddenly a cautionary tale—his worth now measured in terms of his value as a scapegoat.

Several days after King was fired, on a Tuesday afternoon, ESPN held a company meeting in the cafeteria. Almost everyone from production attended, including talent, which accounted for some two hundred workers. Employees who had the day off were also asked to report. Aside from the annual company Christmas party, it was the largest gathering of ESPN employees that year.

Several ESPN executives were present, including Walsh, and the meeting began with them reading a list of harassment incidents and then warning that this type of behavior would not be tolerated. It was the first time the network had addressed the issue of sexual harassment with the entire staff. Some staffers felt it was a sincere attempt to put everyone on notice. Others thought it was transparently self-serving—the company covering itself in case someone filed a lawsuit.

"They were doing it to cover their asses legally," said Olbermann, who was at the meeting. "That's the only reason, not because it was the right thing to do. Each top management person stood up and said, 'Sexual harassment will not be tolerated. . . . Sexual harassment will not be tolerated.' Then one man stood up and said, 'Sexual harassment will be tolerated.' He accidentally left out the word 'not.' Some of us just kind of looked at each other and said, 'This is a joke.'"

Olbermann says he and several other anchors were told before the meeting that a sexual harassment lawsuit from an unidentified woman was pending, which influenced his interpretation of the meeting. Although Olbermann may have been critical of ESPN's motives for the meeting, he agreed it was needed. Olbermann asserts that the atmosphere for women at the network was terrible.

"The only women in management who were allowed to succeed were either physically unattractive or docile," said Olbermann. "If you were pretty, you were hit on, and then a threat. If you were strong, you were a threat. Management wanted women who were nonthreatening."

Olbermann continued: "I think that [1992] was a crisis period for the network. I think management did try to nip it in the bud. I used to think there was a small group of people committing seventy percent of the problems. But I think it was worse than that."

"What really bothered me," Olbermann added, "was during the time when all the harassment was going on that year, the company started, I feel, to use Robin Roberts more. You have to understand that Robin is a great talent. Great. She keeps getting better and better, which is unusual in this business because she has not leveled off. But you saw Robin everywhere during that period, every promotional campaign, everywhere. It was like the network was saying, 'We can't be sexist or racist because we have a black woman.'"

Significantly, no names had been mentioned at the company meeting in connection with the incidents—except one: King. Executives revealed the entire incident, including King's dismissal. King says he was afforded no chance to respond or be represented.

King's mistake was that he lied when first asked about what happened, initially denying sending the message. King admits that was wrong and he deserved to be punished. Yet King was hardly the most pernicious of ESPN's sexual harassers. He did not exhibit a pattern of abuse, instead misstepping just once. But King was dispensable, and therefore a handy symbol of ESPN's intolerance of sexual harassment.

In the weeks following that afternoon, the network posted fliers throughout the building, warning that sexual harassment was a crime and would not be tolerated, another ostensible sign that ESPN was serious about reform.

For every step forward ESPN took in abolishing sexual harassment and sexism, an awkward moment, or series of them, sent the network crashing backward. Instead of being anonymously interviewed by management, Tirico's accusers—the network will not disclose the numbers, but several of the women involved, a former executive and current producers, claim it was six women total—were paged over the building's public address system and asked to report to Walsh's office. Some in the newsroom were incredulous, feeling the women were violated twice, first by Tirico and then by ESPN, because the women's names were not kept confidential.

Such a spectacle seemed to be a form of intimidation. A future complainer who wanted anonymity would think twice before filing a grievance if their names were going to be broadcast over the loudspeakers.

Nonetheless, in the end, the women's statements proved extremely damaging to Tirico. He was suspended for three months and ordered to seek counseling, according to Glass, ESPN producers, and executives. With the exception of part-timers or those like Berman with irregular schedules, a blank schedule box almost always indicated punitive action by management; a signal well understood by the entire staff. For much of his three-month suspension, Tirico's schedule boxes were indeed left blank.

Because Tirico was only suspended and King fired for a far less egregious transgression, many at the network were outraged. Glass was additionally angry when several days into Tirico's suspension, she got a phone call at home from the woman who is now Tirico's wife. There was a time when Tirico, his wife, and Glass were friendly. Those days were a hazy memory.

"I want to know why you're hanging out with Mike," she asked Glass.

"Talk to your husband and ask him to tell you the truth," Glass replied, "and don't ever call me again." She never did.

The newsroom was unified in its relief that the stinging Tirico episode was over. A traumatic event in the cable company's history, the repercussions were dramatic. The close friendship between Myers and Tirico ruptured permanently (though Tirico maintains the two were never that close to begin with). Walsh irreversibly lost some of his luster among several women producers for his protection of Tirico but his discharge of King.

In discussing Tirico, Walsh cozied up to the Connecticut privacy laws, which, he said, prevented him from speaking specifically about what happened to his star anchor. Walsh implied that Tirico's mistakes were a result of his youth and he has become a different person. "Michael was twenty-four years old then," Walsh said. "He has [since] been beyond perfect. He goes out of his way in terms of friendship. He goes out of his way in terms of being good to people. And in fact, he has relationships with many women in the workplace."

"There are some of these incidents that I would not characterize as egregious," said Walsh, "in terms of the perspective of it."

But if they weren't egregious, Walsh was asked, why was Tirico suspended for three months? Walsh again said he could not discuss the specifics. Walsh then addressed the general atmosphere at ESPN: "There was a period of time that we went through, that all companies went through, in the late 1980s and early 1990s, where the culture of the workplace changed significantly. We had to react to it. And there were a number of things that happened that we had to react to with varying and different degrees. I think we were as proactive as we could be."

There was one more piece of fallout from Tirico's suspension. The company decided it needed a strong leader in human resources, which is the reason Bornstein hired Correia near the end of 1992 to direct the department. Correia, a bluntly honest man, was the first to openly address ESPN's problems with sexual harassment.

When he first met with Bornstein, Correia told him, "I am not a yesman. I take things that aren't working right and I fix them." Bornstein replied, "No one will stand in your way."

"When I got to ESPN, what was mainly happening were two things," said Correia. "The company was taking a nonaggressive stance against sexual harassment. Second, women victims were being paid not to say anything, asked to sign waivers that they would not sue, and then asked to leave the company. No one was trying to make the culture better. It did not take me long to see that if you were a woman, especially an attractive woman, you had to put up with being constantly hit on," Correia added. "If you were a woman and you went on the road for company business, many times you faced compromising positions. You were groped or forced to hear sexually related comments or jokes. For some women, they became one of two things: They either became invisible or they became one of the guys. But any women who put up resistance were put in a very tough spot."

One of Correia's first moves was to replace the sexual harassment video ESPN used to educate its employees. The old one, called "The Power Pinch," was ineffective for two reasons. First, it focused on a more traditional corporate environment in which employees worked nine to five. Eight-hour workdays were a rarity at ESPN, especially in production. Second, the older video always showed a boss in a compromising position with a subordinate. ESPN had a variety of harassment situations, including subordinate to subordinate.

There were still sexual harassment workshops for both incoming and existing employees. A portion of a written introduction to the course read: "There are five taped vignettes which might very well touch some sore spots and spark disagreements. Situations depicted in the vignettes persist because many people believe that harassment in the workplace is an inescapable by-product of relationships at work. Informed, open discussions following these vignettes will prove that the assumptions underlying such beliefs are false and that sexual harassment need not be tolerated."

Correia said his conversations with workers accused of harassment usually opened with him flatly saying, "Whatever you're going to deny, don't do it again." It was this kind of directness that earned Correia respect.

Few outside of ESPN knew of Tirico's suspension. One person who did know was intrepid New York Post television critic Phil Mushnick, a bulldog of a reporter never bashful about criticizing the network. After learning of the suspension, Mushnick mined a little deeper, coming close to discovering the facts. But he needed better sources, so he called Olbermann and Patrick for confirmation. Both tried to talk Mushnick out of writing the story—or at least into postponing it.

Olbermann said he told Mushnick, "'He's going to be gone for three months, see how he is when he comes back. If the same behavior is still there, you have your answer.' Then Phil called me back and said, 'I have to run something. My bosses are calling me a pussy.' I told him, 'Then charge them with sexual harassment.'"

Mushnick ran the piece without mentioning Tirico's name. (Mushnick, however, confirmed in an interview he was writing about Tirico.) Incensed, officials at ESPN became obsessed with identifying the source who had leaked the information. With Orwellian determination, the network launched its investigation using a computer program to trace all calls made from and to ESPN during the relevant period. The results were inconclusive. (Mushnick said he is aware of several instances in which ESPN has used this technique to track down leaks.)

When Tirico returned to work from his suspension, his career picked up right where it had left off—on an ascending course with limitless possibilities. Tirico would go on to get one of ESPN's plum NFL jobs and later host the network's golf coverage. One of his first postsuspension assignments was a "Sunday Conversation" with Duke University basketball star Bobby Hurley. The producer for the show was Brooks. Some at the network were rankled that such a thing could happen. Brooks was advised by close friends not to accept the assignment.

Only a handful at the network knew that the pairing of Brooks and Tirico had been no accident. Management feared that Brooks might take legal action against ESPN; by teaming her with Tirico as soon as possible, the network in a small but inspired way was protecting itself. ESPN might later argue that had the issues between Brooks and Tirico been that severe, how could they later work together without incident? The move was shrewd—though darkly cunning.

Brooks accepted the assignment. Though uncomfortable, both Tirico and Brooks handled themselves and the situation professionally. For Brooks, her bravery had brought her full circle.

• • •

Few people in television are more charming than Tirico. He has a kind, reassuring smile and a professional demeanor that betrays his youth. Spend only a few minutes with him and Tirico can make you feel like his best friend. He typifies the answer to a mother's prayer for her daughter. Unquestionably, some day Tirico will be hosting a morning television or network evening news show if he so chooses.

In October of 1999, Tirico agreed to a brief interview, which occurred in the conference room on the thirty-seventh floor of a towering Manhattan office building. Tirico, with Walsh sitting by his side, at times offered a sincere, intelligent, and passionate defense.

"I shouldn't say this, I don't want to say this, but I'll sleep better if I say this. . . . If I've been there just under half of the life of the network—I am now in my ninth year and ESPN is in its twenty-first—if you count the people that I've worked with that I have professionally and personally made their time at ESPN more enjoyable, remembering I just don't work on "SportsCenter," or just on the NFL, or just radio, or just the Internet, or just the remote side of college football and for college basketball. Or the people I've worked with at ABC for three years. I could say there are a thousand people out there who I've worked with, who would say that their experience overall has been better because they worked with me."

"Just to say that my contributions to the place, to the people at the place, and how much I bend over backwards to be a good coworker with these people, to say that doesn't override a couple of bumps in the road [eight years] ago?" Tirico said. "It makes me sick. It really does. I've given a lot of my life to that place, a lot of my hard work and compassion as a person has gone to the people there. To say that nine years of hard work and thousands of people that I've touched is not important enough to be in a book about ESPN, and the [sexual harassment allegations] are?"

Tirico added: "And I'm not looking for anybody to say, 'Mike Tirico is a great guy.' I don't live for that. Ask producers who I work with. I don't live to see my face on TV. I'm not about that. I'm about doing a good job for the viewer at home. When you know that the things people are trying to bring up are going to in some way hurt your family; forget about me. I don't want my wife, my family, and my future child to have to go through this."

In many ways, Tirico is right. Few say anything negative about him. Coworkers enjoy him as a colleague, find him easy to talk to, and almost universally praise his work.

Yet during the interview with Tirico, one emotion was always missing: compassion for the women he harassed. The episodes continue to haunt some of his victims. One said she still has flashbacks of his vulgar, obscenity-filled phone calls or his pursuit of her in the newsroom. Glass said that on occasion she still relives the terrifying car drive home on a dark Connecticut highway.

Tirico also refused to admit he did anything wrong. He even disputed that the Phil Mushnick article in the *New York Post* describing the suspension of an anonymous ESPN anchor for sexual harassment referred to him. Tirico called his harassment of the women "misunderstandings that happened when I was immature, twenty-four, and brand-new, in my first real experience in the world. . . ." Tirico's behavior, however, went beyond "misunderstandings." While he does not deserve to be branded forever, Tirico still, years later, has not taken responsibility for his actions.

Tirico, as ESPN was on the subject of harassment, was at times deceptive in his responses. If he did not want to answer a question, he called it vague. Often, he was evasive. "I'm not going to sit and get involved in conversations about the private lives of other people . . . ," he said in response to a question. Yet, as one of Tirico's victims pointed out, harassment in the ESPN workplace had nothing to do with her private life.

In other instances, Tirico disputed the accounts of a significant number of ESPN employees. Several said they have been told directly by Tirico that he feels he made mistakes because he saw others at the network acting in similar ways. Tirico has additionally told several coworkers that others who had violated the company's sexual harassment policy were either not punished or not disciplined as harshly as they should have been. The latter sentiment was echoed by Correia, who said punishment for harassment was often administered unevenly.

Tirico denies making these comments to coworkers. He was asked whether he witnessed other examples of sexual harassment at ESPN. "We're talking [eight] years ago now," he said. "It's really hard to go through specifics and say, 'Well, this may fit that and this may fit that.' Those things are very hard to characterize. To be very honest, it's not my position, or [any]one else's position, to make those observations for other people."

When asked for his recollection of the first time he encountered a problem or accusation involving sexual harassment, Tirico said, "I don't really understand how to specifically respond to that. I don't have any frame of reference for what you're trying to get at. If you're trying to ask me a general question, that's fine. I'm not going to sit here and go through a variety of individual stories that people may have."

Were you suspended for violating the company's sexual harassment policy, Tirico was asked? "That's up to the company to answer. I took a leave of absence from work . . . to try to get several things in my personal life in order," he said. "Which I did. I'm not trying to be difficult with you. I took a leave of absence from work. There were a lot of issues that I needed to settle in my own personal life, regardless of what was going on at ESPN. And I took a leave of absence."

At times management has suspended on-air personalities but allowed the suspended person to publicly call the discipline whatever he or she wanted to save the person and the network embarrassment in the media. Tirico was asked if his leave of absence could be described as such. "I'm not going to sit here and say ESPN should do this, should say this," said Tirico. "I'm telling you what I did as a professional. I took a leave of absence from work."

"My personnel matters are not your business or anyone else's business," Tirico added. "That's pretty common in every business. And I'm choosing to tell you as I did then that I took a leave of absence from work. I had some things I needed to get straightened out in my life."

The conversation with Tirico was at times disturbing in several ways. By calling his suspension a leave of absence, he was simply not telling the truth. Tirico, Walsh, and ESPN had formed a neat circle. Tirico could term his suspension whatever he wanted and then say ESPN's terminology was the company's business. Conversely, ESPN will not officially discuss Tirico's suspension in detail, claiming they are prevented by state privacy laws. Those laws, however, do not restrict the company from disclosing Tirico's suspension.

The most troubling aspect of this issue is that ESPN and Tirico insist ESPN's personnel matters are no one's business. Yet the network has investigated and reported often on the personnel matters of other corporations and the private lives of individuals.

Reporter Andrea Kremer obtained probably the best interview in the history of the network when in 1997 Minnesota Vikings wide receiver Cris Carter first admitted publicly that he had battled an addiction to cocaine and alcohol. The network chronicled the sordid details of broadcaster Marv Albert's journey through the justice system after he was accused of attacking a female acquaintance, and also raised questions on the sexuality of Olympic gold medalist Carl Lewis.

Tirico himself has reported on a number of controversial issues. At the NFL draft in April of 1999, Tirico forcefully questioned Dallas Cowboys owner Jerry Jones on the drug suspension of one of his players, Leon Lett. Furthermore, Tirico has publicly discussed the very personal problems of golfer John Daly, who has battled alcoholism.

After the interview, Tirico indicated he would later respond to several specific allegations. He never did. Instead, Tirico issued a statement through his agent: "In 1991, at age twenty-four, I joined ESPN and became friends with a group of coworkers who regularly got together after shows. Shortly thereafter it was brought to my attention that some of my actions were misunderstood and made others feel uncomfortable. I was disappointed for not seeing their point of view and sorry for making anyone else feel uncomfortable."

"Over the past eight years," the statement continued, "I've had the pleasure of working with hundreds of colleagues on a wide variety of projects and am proud of the many friendships that have grown out of these assignments."

Tirico has not faced any accusations since those troublesome days. Moreover, he has a number of close women friends at the network, including Suzy Kolber. He has moved on with his life, like the women victims, and is noted as one of the most selfless, courteous, and talented people in television.

"However wrong the things he may have done, they were done innocently," said a person close to the star. "It was a mistake. He does not deserve a scarlet letter."

●　●　●

By late 1992, Tirico's suspension was becoming history. Mortensen, now officially an ESPN football guru, was still making his twenty phone calls a day, breaking a meaty NFL story once a week. Jimmy Roberts was covering the Winter Olympics in Albertville. He did live-to-tape stories for thirty consecutive days, underscoring not only his skills as a reporter but his neverending battery.

Professional sports teams continued to allow ESPN unprecedented access. The network asked and was granted permission by Jerry Jones, the NFL's top showman, to place cameras in the team's office on the day of the draft, as they did with several other teams. Showing the raw reactions of the executives and coaches as they plotted their moves live on TV made for great theater. In Dallas, the cameras had an unintended consequence. Jones, always sniffing for ways to grab a little publicity to prove to a skeptical public that he was an astute football guy, approached head coach Jimmy Johnson, who ran all football operations, shortly before the draft was scheduled to begin.

"Jimmy, I have a favor to ask," Jones said. "Before you make the pick, since we'll have these ESPN cameras in the room, I want you to lean over to me and act like you're whispering something in my ear. I want to look like I'm doing something."

"What?" the Dallas coach said. "Fuck that. If it's about you looking good, then you pick the motherfucking players." Johnson stormed away angrily, returning less than an hour before the draft. ESPN had played an unintentional part in the beginning of the end of one of the most volatile football relationships in NFL history.

Then there was Kremer, who regularly produces a half-dozen great stories a year. She was one of several reporters who worked on a groundbreaking episode of *Outside the Lines* called "Men & Women—Sex & Sports Show." Kremer is a pack rat. For several years, she had collected newspaper clippings pertaining to athletes and their sexual promiscuity and sexual assaults. The clippings became the basis for the show, which took three months to produce and aired in the spring of 1992.

For her segment, Kremer traveled to the Oklahoma State Reformatory in Granite, Oklahoma, for an interview with convicted rapist Nigel Clay, a former Oklahoma offensive lineman. (Before she arrived for the interview, a penitentiary official warned her to wear pants to avoid exciting the prisoners.) Her spot was the most detailed and gripping of the special.

The *Outside the Lines* series, the brainchild of Walsh, was a smashing success. An early episode, "The Autograph Game," aired in late 1990. It spotlighted the lucrative world of sports memorabilia and won an Emmy. Over the next ten years, the show examined a rich mix of topics, including athletes and steroids, the relationship between politics and sports, race and sports, gambling and sports, the demise of sportsmanship, and the effect of AIDS on the sporting landscape.

Ley said in media reports about the athletes and sex show that it had been difficult getting athletes to speak openly on the subject, either on the air or anonymously. Anderson, the managing editor who oversaw the piece, told the press, "We feel it's time to examine male athletes' lifestyles in relation to women and sex because incidents ranging from sexual promiscuity to sexual assault have dominated the headlines over the past year."

Anderson's quote, in some ways, could have described the atmosphere at ESPN. If documentary film producers had trained a camera on the network during 1992, they might have produced an interesting *Outside the Lines* themselves.

Glass found the athletes and sex special deliciously ironic. She was one of just several heroes who had tried to improve life for women at the network. One more woman would arrive at ESPN three years after Glass, bringing even more awareness to a slowly improving situation, but Glass had taken the kind of brave steps few women would make again.

One afternoon Glass was talking to Pam Oliver, who was considering leaving an affiliate in Houston for ESPN. "We were on the phone and Pam asked me what it was like in Bristol," Glass remembered. "I told her, 'For a woman, not great. For a black woman, terrible.'" Oliver joined ESPN but asked to remain in the Southwest.

Glass's actions during the past year did not come without a price. Glass claims Walsh began to isolate her as a form of punishment for tarnishing his star Tirico. Shortly before one of the "SportsCenter" broadcasts she was producing, Glass was chatting with Myers and several other friends on the set. They were deciding on where to eat after the show when Myers explained he had other plans. "Fuck you," she joked to Myers, "you're always making plans."

Walsh, who had been standing nearby, returned to his office. Fifteen minutes before airtime, he called Glass, ordering her to his office. Miffed, she hurried through the covered walkway that connected the studios with the main building and entered Walsh's office.

Glass reports Walsh told her, "It is language like that that promotes sexual harassment." Glass replied tersely, "If it is OK with you, I have a show to do." She hustled back over the bridge and made the show just in time.

"I saw where things were headed," Glass said. "Walsh would take digs at me when he could. He did not look at it as Mike's actions got him into trouble, but that I got him into trouble. Steve Anderson was one of the good guys there, great people, and often said to me when I was going through all that stuff, 'You didn't do anything wrong.'"

Glass resigned from ESPN two weeks before she was scheduled to produce her first "College Gameday" telecast. She currently works for another sports network, saying even now, eight years later, that Walsh harbors resentment toward her. If she and Walsh are standing with a group of people at a convention or sporting event, she said, Walsh will say hello to everyone except her.

She left behind a proud legacy at ESPN, helping to improve conditions for women at the network. But work still needs to be done.

"Things are better now, but one of my bosses still stares only at my chest when he talks to me," said a woman ESPN producer. "And I mean only my chest. He's looked at my chest for a few years now. It has not grown. It has stayed the same. When that stuff happens, you feel like a PA again."

13   **SportsCenter**

Olbermann and Patrick's "SportsCenter" had all the qualities of chocolate cake: rich, filling ingredients of news and highlights thickly frosted with humor. Sometimes the humor, which often pulsated with irreverence, masked the finer points of the show. Patrick and especially Olbermann were wordsmiths who entertained the viewer with engaging writing and informed reporting.

The show required long, arduous hours to put together, even if it appeared at times that Olbermann and Patrick freelanced their way through it. ESPN's sweatshop culture extended to all the anchors, and for Olbermann and Patrick, that meant twelve-hour days.

They were usually in the building several hours before the 3:30 ideas meeting. At the meeting, Olbermann and Patrick reviewed the pretaped pieces that would run and discussed the sequence of the highlights, among other things. Often, the lead story was easy to call. If Nolan Ryan threw a no-hitter or Jerry Rice set another pass-receiving record, it received top billing. Sometimes the choices were not so clear.

On August 13, 1995, New York Yankee great Mickey Mantle died. After reporting to work, Olbermann and Patrick learned that management wanted to open the show with reactions from baseball figures on Mantle's death, then go to leaguewide baseball highlights, back to an eight-minute obituary, more highlights, and then a replay of several Roy Firestone interviews with Mantle for the "Sunday Conversation."

The Mantle coverage did not jibe with the baseball historian in Olbermann and the reporter in Patrick. They argued that because Mantle was such an influential figure, whose importance transcended sports, flipping back and forth between pedestrian highlights from that night's games and Mantle's extraordinary life would be inappropriate. They wanted the bulk of the Mantle coverage before the first set of commercials, which befitted Mantle's stature.

Because of Olbermann and Patrick and a cadre of producers, directors, and production assistants, the Mantle "SportsCenter" was probably the most emotional and well crafted of the two men's regime. The memorial coverage revealed the sincere affection each anchor had, from afar, for the Yankee Hall of Famer. Olbermann, who grew up in New York, adored Mantle, as did Patrick's father. During commercial breaks, Olbermann and Patrick usually chatted with one another. That night there was no idle conversation. When the show was over, "SportsCenter" had managed to gracefully honor the deceased Mantle and incisively explain his significance.

• • •

By four o'clock each day, Olbermann and Patrick were usually writing the show. Unlike many local sports broadcasters, ESPN anchors did not have writers, a policy that could be traced to the early days of the network. By 1993 "SportsCenter" anchors, including Olbermann and Patrick, still believed writing their own copy gave the show more soul. Plus, it reduced the chance of an embarrassing mishap when a TelePrompTer crashed. If the automatic cue cards stopped rolling, they could read from their own notes.

This part of the job, however, could be taxing. Soon both Olbermann and Patrick were writing not only for "SportsCenter" but for ESPN's Internet service and the radio network. In all, each was composing at least ten thousand words a week. Olbermann says he and Patrick decided they needed help with the writing and requested a meeting with Bornstein to discuss the idea.

"We wanted to get a writer, one writer," Olbermann said. "Not to write a lot of stuff, but to be the person in charge of finding out what the video on the bump going out of a section was. To structure the page in the computer with the roll cues. To find out what Mark McGwire said in an interview so we wouldn't have to make eight phone calls trying to track that information down."

"Bornstein would not even meet with us," Olbermann claimed. "'Talent is not my department.' Or as he related to us, 'Fucking talent is not my department.' My understanding of his dream is a network with no talent at all. Nobody on the air. Nobody on camera. Just people off-camera narrating highlights."

Olbermann and Patrick often spent the early evening before the show working the phones. The humor and wisecracks hooked viewers, creating an intense fan following perhaps unprecedented in television sports journalism, yet it was the reporting, fishing for details, that gave the show its backbone.

The humor was both natural and to some degree necessary. The show needed to distinguish itself because it was competing against the likes of "Nightline," Jay Leno, and David Letterman. Olbermann and Patrick walked an extremely delicate line between being funny, journalistically sound, and spontaneous. They walked it like skilled tightrope acrobats, rarely tumbling to the ground.

They searched feverishly for news, or sources called them, providing a tip or the latest gossip. If it was not a general manager, it was a player or a league executive. They had become so influential that during the baseball strike, an assistant player representative from the Houston Astros called Olbermann to ask if he had any ideas for settling the dispute.

Olbermann recalled a reliable source phoning with information on a major league baseball manager who had just been fired. When asked how he could be certain, the source reported that the manager's belongings were packed and he had already informed the team he was leaving.

On "SportsCenter," Olbermann and Patrick reported that the Los Angeles Kings had decided to fire Coach Tom Webster. During a meeting to finalize the decision, Kings officials noticed smoke near their office and realized they were in the middle of the Rodney King riots. Management decided to postpone its announcement until things cooled down in Los Angeles, both figuratively and literally. But "SportsCenter" had already reported the news.

So in addition to the phoned-in scoops from the likes of Fowler, Vitale, Kremer, Mortensen, hockey analyst Al Morganti, and Gammons, Olbermann and Patrick provided their own breaking stories.

"A lot of fans and critics got caught up in the schtick," said Patrick. "We laughed at that. We got defensive. 'So if you think it's schtick, we're going to prove you wrong.' We prided ourselves in writing and breaking news."

Whatever the reason for its popularity, the "Big Show" attracted an ardent following. Olbermann remembers a conversation he had with Bill Belichick, the former coach of the Cleveland Browns. "When I'm on the road, I watch the eleven o'clock show," Belichick told him. "Then I get up, I watch the six o'clock show on the treadmill. I watch it while I'm eating breakfast again at seven."

Olbermann interrupted, "It's the same damn show, Bill."

"I know it's the same show," Belichick responded. "So I get into work at nine o'clock, have a meeting with my coordinators. We all watch the show. So then at eleven o'clock or so, we bring in all the coaches and the personnel guys and we all watch the show. Then we have a team meeting over lunch at noon and everybody on the team watches the show."

Olbermann told him, "Bill, you've watched the same show six times."

"I know," Belichick said. "I know all the punch lines by then. I get to do the jokes."

Players were even bigger fans, none more ardent than Chicago Bulls superstar Michael Jordan. When Patrick began covering the NBA Finals in the early 1990s, just as Michael and the Jordannaires commenced their championship runs, he and Jordan became close. After the Bulls won their third straight championship, Jordan approached Patrick and said, "When you show up, I win titles."

Jordan enjoyed his relationship with Patrick and the network, which may have been due, in part, to Patrick's velvet treatment of Jordan. He rarely asked a question Jordan did not like, unlike Kremer, who might query Jordan about his failed experiment as a baseball player.

Jordan's first media stop after a big game was usually to the ESPN booth for an interview with Patrick. Here Jordan's legendary competitiveness would continue well after the game. On the air, he would try to match Patrick's wit crack for crack, and he was often successful. Off camera, their competition was even more drastic. After Patrick completed an interview with Jordan following yet another title, and both men were preparing to leave the arena, Jordan blurted out, "If we were playing, how would you guard me?"

"I can't guard you," said a surprised Patrick, flashing his trademark smirk.

"No, no, stand up," Jordan said. "How would you guard me?"

Patrick has always been a good athlete, standing about 6-feet 3-inches and weighing a sturdy 200 pounds. He was once an Ohio all-state basketball player and a good enough pitcher to attract the Cincinnati Reds, which offered him a position on one of their farm clubs. And he was almost as competitive as the Bulls player himself. But Patrick wasn't crazy. This was Jordan, after all. Still Patrick played along, standing up, putting his right forearm into Jordan's back as if he were guarding him while Jordan pretended he was about to make a move.

"I would put my arm like this, first of all," Patrick said.

Jordan cut him off. "Oh, yeah, you and twenty-eight other motherfuckers who guard me like that," Jordan said. They both broke up laughing.

Some players spoke to Patrick and Olbermann as much as they did to their coaches. Detroit running back Barry Sanders was a fan of the show and close to Patrick, who once left a message on Sanders's machine, "You had one hundred and fifty-six yards in the game last night, but you fumbled on the two." They had that kind of relationship with the players. They could joke with them but also be taken seriously.

Although Olbermann would later engage management in a series of bloody skirmishes and even tear apart some of his coworkers like Kolber, he and Patrick always had a respectful, at times close relationship. Patrick's calm demeanor seemed to soothe Olbermann, and Olbermann's creativity and writing talent elevated Patrick. Olbermann learned from Patrick how to narrate highlights with a restrained flair and Patrick learned from Olbermann how to craft a phrase with more bite.

Patrick also learned fearlessness from Olbermann. "Keith was able to give you the sense before you went on the air that was like, 'We're going to get away with murder tonight,'" Patrick recalled. "He was always willing to push the envelope. Not that I wasn't, but I needed a partner in crime. Overall, we always thought, 'Let's make good TV.'"

"ESPN took off the seat belts," Patrick continued, "and sometimes we abused the power, but rarely. They trusted us and we gave them a great show. Keith may have felt like we did not have freedom, but we did. On the air, we had more freedom than two grown men should have. I would look up at the clock during the show sometimes and I never told Keith this, but I looked up at the clock and saw there were fifteen minutes left, and I'd get sad because the show had gone by so quickly."

In some ways, Olbermann and Patrick were extremely close. Patrick is a Winston Churchill buff and Olbermann used to tape PBS specials on Churchill and bring them to Patrick in the studio, in addition to books on Shakespeare, another Patrick favorite. Baseball memorabilia, a passion of Olbermann's, became an interest of Patrick's.

Yet there were few social moments outside the newsroom, and some at ESPN characterized the relationship as a love/hate one. Loud, bitter arguments between the two occasionally reverberated throughout the newsroom, oftentimes involving trivial matters, such as whether a player should be in the Hall of Fame. Patrick always felt that the two should keep a professional distance away from ESPN. "I didn't think we should spend a lot of time together outside the show, because I didn't want to clutter the relationship," said Patrick. "Staying friends but somewhat distant prolonged the relationship."

By five in the evening, Olbermann and Patrick dived into the computer to check a preliminary list of the show's highlights and stories. One hour later, the two bolted for dinner, usually something picked up from the restaurant next to the main building. At 7:30, they settled in front of a single TV to channel surf, catching as many games as they could, and to begin writing the evening's copy. Sixty minutes later, they would narrate the tease, or the opening section of the show, as well as record any narrations for special features. At ten, they applied their own makeup, which would become the subject one of the more famous ESPN commercials shot by the Portland-based advertising company Weiden & Kennedy.

The firm was hired by the network in April of 1993 and spent months on the ESPN complex, studying the puzzling creatures who worked at the network. The "This Is 'SportsCenter'" series was created by writer Hank Perlman and art director Rick McQuiston, both of Weiden and Kennedy, the same company that created the "Just Do It" campaign for Nike and "Where Do You Want to Go Today?" for Microsoft. One facet of ESPN seemed to present intriguing advertising possibilities: Every night, the talent paraded into the bathroom to put on their own makeup. The tradition continued until the summer of 1995, when ESPN finally relented and paid for a makeup specialist. The advertiser produced a whimsical spot in which Olbermann and Patrick carry on in front of a bathroom mirror about the masculinity of hockey fighting, all the while applying makeup. "You need some more rouge," Olbermann says to Patrick. "Thanks," replies Patrick. "You know, your foundation has looked great recently."

Fifteen minutes before the show, the two men put the finishing touches on their scripts, making additions if, for example, a huge upset occurred or a breaking story crossed the wire. Five minutes later, they made the three-minute walk to the studio. Afterward, Olbermann and Patrick spent from five to ninety additional minutes in the studio correcting glitches for the re-airs.

Olbermann and Patrick never rehearsed the humor. Instead, they opted for improvisation during the flow of events. The spontaneity of one anchor produced an equally impulsive reaction on the part of the other, who freely responded with an approving smile or laugh. Sometimes the more mundane the reference, or inane the joke, the heartier the laugh. They once rolled with laughter when Patrick stumbled on the word "mound," as in pitching mound. When a camera panned during that same show to a heavy fan sitting in the stands, Olbermann said, "Lots of jokes come to mind here, but I want to keep my job." Patrick responded, "There's your darn mound."

A bubble surrounded the show and anyone who stepped into the charged and creative atmosphere was infected. When Steve Levy substituted for Patrick on a weekday show, Levy mistakenly said on the air that

New England Patriots defensive back Maurice Hurst had a "bulging dick" in his neck instead of a "bulging disc," Olbermann, and just about everyone on the set, lost it.

The news and humor were spiced with what became one of the show's trademarks: Clever catchphrases that kept the hardcore fan glued to the show while convincing the channel surfer to stop and watch. Instead of simply saying that Wayne Gretzky scored a goal, they'd say he put the "biscuit in the basket." A player who was on a hot streak was not on fire but "en fuego." A jump shot made from thirty feet was "from way downtown . . . bang!" An error in a baseball game or a player missing a crucial shot was not a choke but "Gggggggg!"

Many phrases were inspired by people or events at ESPN. Eaton answered his office telephone with an exaggerated "helloooo," and that became as popular around the newsroom as "Bristol in your rearview mirror" and "it's the sportswriters." Olbermann and Patrick appropriated the elongated "hello," which became a favorite among viewers.

The combination of charisma, outstanding reporting, sharp writing, and a biting sense of humor added up to the show's reputation as the best place to get sports information in the business.

"They did something that was pretty special," said Gumbel, who was a dedicated viewer. "They were brilliant. They were special."

Olbermann and Patrick were so influential, they spawned a generation of wanna-be's, the same way the coverage of the Watergate scandal led to a host of Woodward and Bernstein clones. Of course few came close to reproducing the charm of "SportsCenter." An anchor in Tucson badly fumbled a "that will happen" during his broadcast. A sportscaster in Dallas started slipping in a "premature jocularity," but it seemed contrived.

Even some colleagues at ESPN tried to imitate Olbermann and Patrick—often with dismal results. "What happened with Keith and Dan is the same as what happens in the NFL," said Gumbel. "Something works, then all of a sudden everybody wants to copy it. Dan and Keith were outstanding. Other people try to be them and fail miserably. I don't find it very entertaining or very fun to watch what appears to be an audition for bad comedy. And there are people who I think not only want to be funny but feel like they have to be funny. And the worst part of it is they aren't funny."

"You watch sometimes on 'SportsCenter' how long the buildup is to show a highlight," Gumbel continued. "I realize people are trying to make their mark and I realize the trend is, especially in sports, to be noisy, to be spectacular, to be loud, to be boisterous, to be outrageous. I have always suspected that is a cover-up for a lack of knowledge. There are a lot of sportscasters who make a lot of noise and you know what? They wouldn't know a weakside pick if it sat on their face."

Walsh never really appreciated the emphasis on the show's offbeat character (though Walsh strongly denies this). Exaggerating that aspect of "SportsCenter" would belie his opinion that the strength of the show rested primarily on its format not its personalities. One producer, in an attempt to explain Walsh's thinking, gave the analogy of a souped-up car and its driver. Walsh believed what truly mattered was the automobile, not the person behind the wheel. If the car was provided enough horsepower, Walsh figured, a four-year-old could drive it. That philosophy would later account for the parade of twenty-something, straitlaced, cookie-cutter anchors that would follow Olbermann and Patrick. Walsh wasn't always a Scrooge. He approached Olbermann in the newsroom after a show to tell him how much he enjoyed his reference to Chicago Cubs pitcher Tanyon Sturtze as Kaiser Soze, the mythical character from the film *The Usual Suspects*. For the most part, though, Walsh watched the show and winced, bristling at the mocking of an upcoming PGA Tour stop or Formula One race while reading a promo.

The newsroom could see that the duo—especially Olbermann—was on a collision course with Walsh, one as inevitable as snow in a Minnesota winter. Walsh was the *Christian Science Monitor;* Olbermann and Patrick were the *Village Voice*—complete opposites. This minor crack in the foundation would soon expand to the size of a riverbed.

As always, however, the network continued to grind forward, growing at a booming rate. In 1993, ESPN seemed to announce a new deal or promotion or contract agreement every week. In early March, the network televised its first ESPY show, billed as an annual celebration of athletic excellence. They packed as many high-profile athletes and entertainers into one room as possible and dished out awards in over two dozen categories. The show became a must-watch because of the many movie and television stars who attended, and lots did, like David Letterman, Dennis Hopper, and Samuel L. Jackson. The ESPYs allowed ESPN to promote itself as much as to promote the athletes.

Also that month, Jim Valvano, with the help of ESPN, announced the formation of the V Foundation, a charitable organization dedicated to raising funds for cancer research ($10 million has been raised so far). Tragically, Valvano, the former North Carolina State coach, would succumb to the disease a short time later, deeply saddening many at the network, especially Saunders. Before his death, the ever demonstrative Valvano delivered an unforgettable speech at the ESPYs on March 4, 1993, almost demanding his audience to never give up, even when the odds seemed insurmountable.

"To me there are three things we all should do every day," Valvano said. "Number one is laugh. Number two is think. And number three you should have your emotions moved to tears."

Other significant events took place that year. Bornstein, ESPN's president and CEO, was given the additional title of corporate vice president of Capital Cities/ABC; ESPN and the NFL signed a four-year agreement to again broadcast Sunday night games; ESPN provided the entire Stanley Cup final to Russian State Television, which served seventy million people. It was ESPN's first deal with the former Soviet Union.

And ESPN reached a contract agreement with Berman, still its brightest star, extending his deal to the year 2001. Berman became the first network television anchor, news or sports, to be signed into the next century, something that no doubt tickled the record-minded Berman. Unlike the first negotiation, which took half a year, this deal was hashed out in two hours. Berman was once making television minimum wage, but with his annual ESPN paycheck, appearance fees, and product endorsements, he was pulling in a seven-figure salary in 1993.

Bodies continued to shift in and out of the newsroom. A significant loss was producer Scott Ackerson to rival Fox, which in the summer of 1994 was beginning to expand its sports empire with the hopes of one day seriously challenging ESPN. In July, Ackerson met with Fox officials in New York and liked what he heard. He felt that Fox, which in a bold move had just acquired the rights to the NFL, was the only network with the cash to give ESPN a fight. He sincerely believed one day Fox would not only rival ESPN but surpass it. When Ackerson returned to Bristol, he met with Anderson, informing him he had an offer from Fox and needed twenty-four hours to decide. The next day, Ackerson resigned.

Ackerson's departure signaled the beginning of an exodus of talent from ESPN to competitor Fox. When a person leaves ESPN and discovers his career doesn't disintegrate, as many had been persuaded to believe, word spreads. Fox would later steal other key members from ESPN, which would develop a siege mentality, with paranoia rising to absurd levels.

Most ESPN executives, including Anderson, were out of town attending a funeral for a relative of Bornstein's when Ackerson made his decision. Ackerson gave his two-week notice to Sacks, who phoned Anderson to relay the message. ESPN was furious at Ackerson for jumping ship and ordered Sacks to make sure Ackerson packed his things and left the building immediately.

"Look, this is not my decision," apologized Sacks, "but you have to leave the building in one hour. They want you gone." Forty-five minutes later, Ackerson was escorted from ESPN by security.

Booting out a departing employee before the ink on the resignation letter dries—especially when that person is leaving for a competitor—is not an unusual practice in television. But this seemed a bit extreme.

"My first reaction when that happened was not anger or anything else," Ackerson said. "It was, 'At least tonight I don't have to work until three in the morning.'"

• • •

These changes all paled in comparison to one change that few thought would ever occur: Launching a second network. Yet ESPN had an impressive war chest and enough staff, numbering some one thousand people, to duplicate itself. The time was also right. Television was watched increasingly by young viewers—the Generation X crowd—and Bornstein felt ESPN should more effectively exploit this market. The handle often used in strategy meetings to refer to the second ESPN was "the MTV of sports."

Things moved quickly. Under Bornstein's supervision, John Lack, a solid-ideas man and smart producer, put the framework in place. Doria, the former *Boston Globe* sports editor, was chosen as the new network's managing editor and operating head. The motif was decidedly young and trendy. Quick, darting cameras. Mordant writing and strong opinions from the likes of radio personality and columnist Tony Kornheiser, sports novelist John Feinstein, and columnist Mitch Albom from the *Detroit Free Press.* The color-saturated, urban-hip set was housed in a garage-style building behind the ESPN complex. The suits sported by ESPN anchors would be shed on the second network. Anchors would wear ties and shirts with no jackets or jackets with no ties. Torn blue jeans were de rigueur.

Programmers wanted to avoid the basic sports food groups, leaving them for the main network. The new ESPN diet would consist of college basketball, beach volleyball, and roller hockey. Fitness shows, go-kart and hydroplane racing, and rodeo were also scheduled. Ironically, it was some of the original fare ESPN aired on September 7, 1979.

Madison Avenue coddled men and women ages 18 to 34, and the second network, like the main ESPN, would attempt to attract that audience. Advertising executives initially wondered if ESPN would be spreading itself too thin. There were doubts that some cable-operating systems would sign on.

But this was not the ESPN of Rasmussen's days. By now, ESPN had clout, based on a track record of nearly unchecked success. Thus, three of the top five cable operators in the country jumped on the second system as on a hot stock. Advertisers, initially cautious, eventually trusted the ESPN name, opening their wallets.

ESPN wanted its second network to be livelier and snappier. A series of meetings—at ESPN, there are always meetings—determined the name of the new network: ESPN2. What it lacked in originality, it made up for in understated clarity.

Executives decided ESPN2 needed a signature information show, something like "SportsCenter," only cooler. ESPN2's "SportsNight" wanted anchors with attitude. To many ESPN executives, Olbermann's sardonic style fit perfectly. They envisioned "SportsNight" as Olbermann's showcase. Bornstein, in one of his few conversations with Olbermann, told him, "We want you to be the Berman of this network. I mean it in all senses of the word. I want you to throw your weight around when you think it's not being done right."

For coanchor, ESPN hired Suzy Kolber from a small station in Florida, a true professional whose warm smile and constrained approach could offset Olbermann's cutting humor. Olbermann might rant for two minutes about the designated hitter rule in baseball, while Kolber, a good athlete, could delve into alternative, or extreme, sports. The match seemed almost as inspired as Olbermann's paring with Patrick.

Everything surrounding the launch of ESPN2 and "SportsNight" felt right. So confident was the network that on June 7, 1993, ESPN2 was introduced at the National Cable Television Association show in San Francisco. The network first said ESPN2 would debut on November 2 of that year. On June 14, just seven days after the initial announcement, ESPN announced the third-largest cable operator, Continental Cablevision, would carry ESPN2. (Soon after, two more of the top five would commit.) Buoyed by that piece of good news and the early completion of groundwork, the launch was moved forward from November to October 1.

As promised, on the first day in October, ESPN2 launched to ten million households, a solid number for a new cable channel and five times more homes than for the 1979 launch of the parent network.

All signs pointed to ESPN2 and its signature show as a potential hit. The new network had a popular anchor and big name in Olbermann and a bright personality in Kolber. Doria was a smart manager, money was ample, and the viewers were there.

Then why did almost everything about "SportsNight" go so terribly wrong?

• • •

Whereas ESPN2 had a name within a name—a muscular advertising campaign had viewers and employees both calling the second network "the deuce"—Kolber had a nickname as well. She was called "Miss Launch" and for good reason. In the late 1980s, she started "Dallas Cowboys Television," the first in-house NFL production company.

Her first anchor position was in 1991 at a CBS affiliate in West Palm Beach where she mostly worked the weekends. Kolber blended physical attraction, intelligence, and an expansive sports knowledge into an effortless presentation. By the summer of 1993, she was a sought-after anchor. Kolber sifted through dozens of feelers, narrowing them to three choices, an NBC affiliate in Atlanta, CNN, and ESPN.

The first time Kolber had heard of ESPN2 was during her meetings in Bristol with Walsh, Doria, and Al Jaffe, the network's main recruiter. She was a fan of ESPN, especially Robin Roberts, but worried about falling into a mile-deep pit of anonymity if she went to the deuce. She asked Walsh during her interview, "Am I going to fall off the face of the earth doing this?" Conversely, her interviews with CNN executives had gone better than those at ESPN, and after a gut-wrenching dinner with her boyfriend, she decided Ted Turner's station was the place to go.

Unaware of Kolber's decision, Jaffe called several days later to set up an audition. Kolber explained that she had already made up her mind to go to CNN. Jaffe was shocked. "Don't sign anything," he said. "I'll call back tonight." He did, around eight. "Forget the audition," he told Kolber. "The job is yours. We'll give you $100,000 a year." That was basically three times her salary in Florida. "This is getting interesting," she thought.

Kolber's choice became clear when the West Palm Beach station refused to release Kolber, one of its best talents, from her contract. CNN sensed a nasty fight and backed out of the Kolber derby. ESPN was unfazed and eventually bought out her deal with the Florida station.

Kolber began in August of 1993 and was put to work immediately—there was no grace period. She had no idea how up and down the next cycle of her life would become.

• • •

Kolber got a feel for the chaos immediately. The ESPN2 preview show, which ran in the weeks before the October premiere, was on the air twice before Lack pulled it, deciding it was too much like "SportsCenter." Then twenty-four hours before the network's launch, the entire rundown of the first day was revamped. Once "SportsNight" actually began, things did not go much smoother. Some of the shows were interminably long, at times lasting three hours. Olbermann and Kolber often ad-libbed their way through much of the night because there was little organization. It was so frenzied there were times the two anchors would cut to a commercial break not knowing what was coming up next. Scripts were often meaningless.

"The ESPN2 thing was chaos," said Olbermann. "Eighteen different people were told they were in charge. I was told I was in charge. John Lack told me, 'You are my eyes and ears here. You make the final decision. . . .' Everybody was told we were going to do a new kind of ESPN for the twenty-first century. . . . And they were crushing Suzy. They were squeezing her and taking time away from her and making her the butt of Mitch Albom jokes. And things like that. So I took her to dinner and I said, 'Stand up for yourself. I'll back you. Stand up for yourself.' So the first thing she did was go in and ask why I had so many on cameras and she didn't have enough. And I went, 'Not against me, against this idiot Albom.'"

"He would show up at four o'clock in the afternoon and talk to his book agent," Olbermann said of Albom, a best-selling author and award-winning sports columnist. "And he once said the word *nupitals* [meaning to say *nuptials*] on the air. . . . You hear a word and go, 'What is he trying to say? Don Shula is getting married, what are the nupitals?' Nupitals! And I looked into the prompter and it said, 'nupitals.' He had written it. He had this story about what Don Shula's wedding was going to be like. 'Nupitals!' There are some writers who can convert to TV and there are some writers who can't and there are some writers, with some help, who can and I think he was one of the latter. He could have been fairly big on TV. And instead they threw him to the wolves, too."

Kolber was granite amid the mayhem. She persisted through everything: the hectic schedules, the lack of planning and, she says, Olbermann's tirades. Kolber strongly disagreed with Olbermann's assessment. She said Olbermann is correct about the chaos, but she believes he was one of the major causes.

"I adored him, initially," Kolber said. "I thought he was great. He said, 'I'm the captain of this team.' Then the day before we launched, when everything got rocky, he quit. That was the first time I realized that he didn't understand what being captain of the team meant. He had never played a sport and really didn't understand what *team* meant, and certainly not being the captain."

Frustrated by an increasing number of changes with which he didn't agree, Olbermann walked out on "SportsNight" one day before it was scheduled to air. Management pleaded with Olbermann to return and he did. "That happened repeatedly during his six-month stay," said Kolber.

Kolber was enraged at how Olbermann would assure her the show was a fifty-fifty proposition, but then, she says, complain to management behind her back if she made the introductions before the top of the show and he did not. "I would go to management and say, 'You know what? If it's seventy-thirty, that's fine, but I'm not sitting out there to be his wallflower,'" said Kolber, who had been promised a coanchor position by management.

Olbermann's frustrations stemmed partly from what he felt were a number of reneged guarantees from ESPN executives. He was promised a Letterman-type role on what was billed as a major new station. Instead he served as the general of a dysfunctional army. Olbermann may not have been lied to. There was such confusion that executives probably forgot their promises.

Olbermann's contempt for his situation was so overt it poisoned the air at ESPN2. Kolber sometimes tucked herself away in the bathroom and cried, exasperated by her treatment and the mounting insanity. "I can't tell you how many times I saw that scene," said one producer. But Kolber always brushed away the tears, plodded back to the studio, and continued to carry on.

Things did not get better, however, with Olbermann. Whenever clips of alternative sports were shown on "SportsNight," off camera, Olbermann mocked the athletes, calling them losers, Kolber said. Olbermann even attacked the stories Kolber reported. "He came out one time and was busting on a piece I had done while we were on live," Kolber said. "Then they took a cut-shot of me and you could see the fire in my eyes."

An event in late 1993 probably infuriated Kolber more than any other Olbermann incident. Olbermann is a self-confessed fantasy-league junkie and at times he was a commissioner of multiple leagues. Olbermann was asked to film a spoof, for promotional purposes, in which he quit ESPN2—not for real, this time—to join a home-shopping channel to sell trading cards. The scene would be shot, taped, then used as a tease for the next night's show. It was written by Williamson, the coordinating producer.

As they were shooting it, Olbermann was in the bathroom, applying makeup, and he could hear Kolber voicing over the piece. Kolber, as part of the joke, said Olbermann was obsessed with trading cards. Olbermann heard the word *obsessed* and became enraged. He approached Williamson and screamed, "I can't work with her. I'm not doing the show with her."

Williamson tried to calm him down by explaining that he had written the piece. It didn't work. By now it was 8:50 P.M., ten minutes to air, and Williamson feared Olbermann would again walk out of the building. He finally pacified Olbermann, then said in Kolber's ear, about one minute before air, "Just go with it. Keith is going to do something live." Olbermann anchored the show from another part of the building while Kolber was on the "SportsNight" set. He refused to sit next to Kolber that night and would not talk to her for two weeks.

• • •

Kolber was asked why she and Olbermann didn't simply sit down and discuss their differences. "You couldn't talk to him," she said. "You couldn't have an adult, critical conversation. The few times I tried, afterwards, he wouldn't talk to me, and to have to work on a set with somebody for three hours who would not talk to you was not pleasant."

Wolff, the former production assistant, returned to ESPN after leaving in 1991 and sometimes worked closely with Olbermann. Wolff was one of the few people who understood Olbermann, and one of the few who could endure his outbursts. "Just an extremely bright guy. I think he was much brighter than just about everybody else at the network," said Wolff of Olbermann. "He was a guy who groused a lot. I liked him a lot. I got along with him wonderfully, but he was miserable in Bristol. He hated it and he made it clear to everybody. There are certain kinds of guys who are so smart they talk themselves into being miserable. That's Keith. He had too much information. He's a great guy, but he was just never happy."

Olbermann wanted out—soon. And he wasn't shy about saying so. "Toward the end of 1993, Keith was on the phone every day, talking to his agent, screaming at the top of his lungs, sitting next to me," Kolber said. "He would say to his agent, 'This is the worst situation. They're killing me.' He would yell his salary."

Kolber went to Howard Katz, a top executive at the network. Her anger at Olbermann could have powered a city. "You don't have to tell me if Keith is staying or going," she told Katz. "But it will help my mental well being. If he is going, then I know I only have a couple of months, but in the meantime, I may kill him with an axe."

Katz told Kolber, "Wait in line."

Olbermann returned to "SportsCenter" in April of 1994, reuniting with Patrick. He lasted just six months on "SportsNight." On her last day with him, Kolber decided it was time to let Olbermann know exactly how she felt. She pulled him aside and said calmly, "Look, I understand why you want to go back to 'SportsCenter.' I really do. And I know that they promised you things that they didn't deliver. I'm fine with all of that. But what I couldn't take was how you lied to me. You told me it was a partnership, but that's not what you really wanted."

After leaving the show, Olbermann and Kolber did not talk for several months. Their frosty relationship eventually thawed to cordial, but to this day, Kolber, although she has tremendous respect for Olbermann's talent, still cannot discuss Olbermann without irritation.

Olbermann thoughtfully responded, point by point, to everything Kolber had said. "I appreciate what she says about my being frustrated over being misled about my role," he explained. "We were all misled. They told her she was the show. They told Mitch Albom he was the show. They told me I was supposed to be Berman. On the air, I'd make an observation about something and she wouldn't just disagree with me, she'd correct me. 'Well, maybe Gordie Howe was good. But everybody knows every game has been elevated since the old days, so how good could he have been, really?'"

Olbermann confessed he did quit "SportsNight" before it was scheduled to air, but that happened a week to ten days prior to the first show, not the day of the show, as Kolber and others maintain. He said, "The one time I will admit to a completely staged, prima donna temper tantrum, we were supposed to be this cutting edge, new wave stuff. Instead, they took the most missionary-position producers in the shop . . . and brought in the sports editor of the *Boston Globe*, Vince Doria, to run it. And instead of cutting edge or satire or X-style sports, they were planning features on Doug Flutie, which was supposed to be cutting edge because he was in the CFL. And week after week as we moved through August and September toward the debut, this got worse. We had Nick Bakay do his [humorous] 'Tale of the Tape' segments at my suggestion, and Doria liked them, but he wanted to put a laugh track under them! On a news show! Every day we got farther and farther away from the stated goal. They didn't even have rehearsals or practice shows planned. Three hours a night, live, with an inexperienced coanchor and a guy with no TV experience or skills in Mitch Albom, and we weren't even going to rehearse. They were just going to have Steve Buckley do his baseball segment with a cap on backward and let it rip."

Then Olbermann added this striking piece of honest self-assessment: "So I thought I'd better blow up part of the building. And I quit. I mean, William Shatner was subtler at it than I was. I threw papers in the air. I called every member of management a moron. And I went and hid in an alleyway off the studio, sent my girlfriend flowers, smoked my pipe, and came back to the office. The whole thing took about two hours. At least we got the practice shows. What I should have done was actually quit. Suzy should've quit, too. And Albom."

"So was I shitty to people?" Olbermann concluded. "Absolutely. To Suzy? Probably, and she probably only deserved sixty percent of it. But the moment I walked back in after 'quitting,' I explained the point of the performance to her and either it didn't register or she didn't believe it because it's still an issue."

When Olbermann departed, Kolber, like the rest of the "SportsNight" staff, knew the show was doomed. It became official when Doria called Kolber to his office several months after Olbermann's departure and delivered the news that the show had been cancelled. "I'm sorry," Doria, always winsome, told her, "you worked your tail off. You deserved better." The staff was not given a cancellation date, so they continued to work as lame ducks.

In quintessential ESPN fashion, Kolber was not told her last day by a manager. Instead, she found out when she received her schedule, assigning her as anchor on the 6:30 "SportsCenter." Her final night on "SportsNight" was July 18, 1994.

"SportsNight" was one of the few programming blunders in the network's history. It never knew what it wanted to be. Was it built on hip jokes or serious journalism? Was it for eighteen-somethings or thirty-somethings? Was it mainstream or not? The entire episode humbled some ESPN executives. The network realized that to reach young viewers, women viewers, or a new, racially diverse audience, it couldn't have middle-aged white men calling the shots. As for ESPN2 itself, the network was, and remains, a major success, filling its day with a mixture of traditional and alternative programming.

Some good emerged from the debacle. Because of the deuce, ESPN discovered several new talents—Stuart Scott, a lyrical writer, and one of the few anchors of color; and Kenny Mayne, a Teutonic-looking upstart with a wry sense of humor and a controlled ego. Scott, Mayne, and Kolber became close friends in the final months of the show.

ESPN should have awarded Kolber a medal of honor for her stamina. After the cancellation, she handled a variety of assignments for ESPN, including anchoring the highly rated Sunday morning "SportsCenter." Then "Miss Launch" revisited her role. She anchored the first X-Games broadcast in 1995. Her work was again stellar, this time inciting the interest of Fox, which offered her a significant pay raise to leave ESPN. She accepted and became the first anchor for Fox Sports Net. In 1999 she returned to ESPN to coanchor "SportsCenter" and host the popular "Edge NFL Matchup" program.

Olbermann feels that Kolber has improved dramatically since her ESPN2 days, but off camera, he maintains, she is not the benign figure some portray her to be. Olbermann was in the temporary talent trailer at ESPN the day Kolber quit to depart for Fox. After she closed the door behind her, spontaneous applause followed. When it subsided, producer Mike McQuade, who had been trying to get Olbermann a computer for his temporary desk, turned and said, "Well, there is one good thing about her three years here. Now that she's gone, you've got your computer."

Olbermann was also in the Fox newsroom when, in early 1999, Kolber was saying her good-byes to some of the people she had worked with before returning to ESPN. When she left the area, Olbermann said, there was a standing ovation.

"So on the eternal line of sportscasters who treat people shitty, I'm on it, where I'm not sure," Olbermann said. "But from where I'm standing— using those two spontaneous moments as evidence—I can barely see Suzy she's so far in front of me."

14 The Mickey Mouse Network

Tony Bruno, the uncommonly talented former ESPN radio host, enjoyed celebrity status in Philadelphia where he had done a radio show for years, but after joining ESPN, he developed a national following. In 1994 the Arkansas Razorbacks were making their memorable NCAA Tournament championship run when First Fan Bill Clinton joined Bruno on ESPN radio. Bruno unwittingly gave Clinton an opening for a most memorable line.

"Ladies and gentleman, the President of the United States," Bruno said. "People might think that because I clown around a lot, we're pulling a fast one on the American public. But we're not."

Said Clinton: "I'm glad to be in a conversation where the American public thinks someone else is pulling a fast one on them instead of the president."

In October of that year, the most recognizable ESPN anchor, Berman, was wearing one of his trademark, colorful blazers when he began the five-minute walk from the press box down to the Rich Stadium field, where he would start work on the final wrap-up of the Bills' Monday night game. With eight minutes left in the game, the stands were packed with Bills fans, among the most passionate in sports. When Berman reached the field and began to stroll the sidelines, 20,000 people suddenly stood and cheered. Quarterback Jim Kelly thought the applause was for Thurman Thomas, the quick, darting star running back who had left the game with an injury and was now returning. Kelly was wrong. The fans were applauding Berman, who in Buffalo was as popular as many of the players.

Bruno's presidential pull and Berman's celebrity reflected ESPN's transformation into a national phenomenon. In January of that year, ESPN created an international sales unit to fulfill the demand for ESPN's programming overseas. In April the network won ten Emmys, and one month later started ESPN International, which began live service to more than twenty-five countries in the Middle East and North Africa. Then, on September 7, ESPN celebrated its fifteenth anniversary.

Despite the "SportsNight" misstep, Bornstein remained committed to the deuce. Others in management had their misgivings, but Bornstein steadfastly believed in its potential and was ultimately proven right. Bornstein's stubborn support was rooted in his core belief that ESPN had to reinvent itself every two or three years. ESPN2 was part of that process.

Bornstein usually shared his management philosophies and techniques in long discourses at the annual ESPN seminars, held on Cape Cod and attended mostly by the company's upper echelon. By 1994 Odjakjian, a regular at these meetings, had become the Forrest Gump of the network. Just like the movie character, played by Tom Hanks, who stumbled across every significant event of American history in the 1960s, the thoughtful and friendly Odjakjian had witnessed many of ESPN's pivotal events. Only "OJ" never accidentally stumbled across anything. He was too sharp for that. Odjakjian's contributions were based on his own ideas or those he helped someone else fully develop. He downplays his contributions to ESPN, which is his nature. The lack of arrogance and self-aggrandizement is what made him so popular around the network.

One late evening following a management session at the Cape, Odjakjian and programmer Ron Semiao, having downed a few drinks, started batting around a bevy of ideas for the second network. As the alcohol consumption increased, so did the zaniness of the ideas, which finally ended in the clouds, at least figuratively. "We should have a show with guys jumping out of airplanes and riding skateboards," Semiao said.

With that, the Extreme Games were born—with no ponderous ideas meeting or scientific marketing studies. It was vintage ESPN: Two guys sitting around, stoked by a little alcohol, dreaming up smart programming.

The next day, a sober Semiao and Odjakjian still liked the idea. Odjakjian had previously handled some Olympic-style programming and suggested using the Olympic Festival as a model for any such games. Semiao agreed. Shortly, their idea took shape, reaching the point where it was taken to Bornstein.

Bornstein believed people loved sports because of the aspect of drama, the suspense generated by not knowing the final outcome. The Extreme Games format fit that model. If it is difficult to predict the final score of a football game between two closely matched teams, certainly it is impossible to know the outcome of someone jumping out of an airplane or skiing down a slick mountain. Bornstein said if the network could get advertising for the games, it was a go. Eventually, so many advertisers wanted in, the network had to turn companies away.

On April 12, 1994, ESPN announced the creation of the Extreme Games, which would later become the X-Games, and air in 1995. (Several years later when NBC started its own X-Games, called the Gravity Games, ESPN officials allegedly warned the athletes that if any of them participated in NBC's event, they would be blackballed from the X-Games. Aghast, NBC confronted ESPN. The network denied the accusations. What is undeniable is that at the 1999 X-Games, the network tried to jettison a small group of attending NBC officials who were at ESPN's games.)

Semiao masterfully handled the most challenging project in ESPN's history, deftly meshing the dichotomous combination of stuffed-shirt advertising executives and off-beat athletes. Mainstream America, fat on sports like football and basketball, was intimately introduced to skateboarding and mountain biking. Before the inaugural games in Rhode Island, Semiao had sifted through a melange of sports, from rock climbing to boomerang throwing to greased-pole climbing. Most made sense, except one, which was inspired by a picture in *Details* magazine of a man soaring through the air, attached to a kite. Semiao added kite-skiing to the first games, but the man in the photo was found to be one of the few people in the world skilled at the sport. There were nine contestants in the kite-skiing category: One never left the water because he couldn't find a good current to sail. Another was able to finally fly but could not turn his kite; consequently, he sailed uncontrollably down the Rhode Island coast and disappeared from the cameras. He eventually made a bumpy landing and caught a cab back to the games.

• • •

Shortly before Odjakjian and Semiao's excellent adventure on the Cape, Christine Brennan and Lesley Visser were in the waiting room near the set of the Geraldo Rivera Show, preparing to tape a segment about women in the locker room. Brennan, the respected reporter for the *Washington Post*, and Visser, who began her career with the *Boston Globe*, were probably the top two women journalists in sports. They were also two of the most ardent advocates of women in the media.

While a makeup artist applied finishing touches, Brennan, Visser, and another guest, NBC's Hannah Storm, were chatting about the show's topic. Then, Storm uttered something that disturbed Brennan and Visser.

"I don't see why women need to be in the locker room anyway," Storm said.

Visser lightly kicked Brennan under the table. Expressing such an antiquated view was blasphemy to the two reporters. "Gee," Visser responded, "I didn't realize the enemy was among us." Most alarming, however, was the crack exposed in the unity among women sports journalists on the issue. To be sure, Storm was among a minority of women who held this belief, but Brennan's worst nightmare was a verbal boxing match erupting before millions of people, pitting woman against woman. "We cannot have a break in our ranks," Brennan said.

Brennan was a veteran print journalist who once covered the Washington Redskins, and although Visser was gravitating away from her newspaper roots, those days remained fresh in her mind. At the barely ripe age of twenty-one, Visser became the first woman NFL beat writer when she covered the New England Patriots for the *Globe*. Visser vividly remembered the time when women were not allowed in the locker room. After a chilly October game between the Patriots and Pittsburgh Steelers at Three Rivers Stadium, Visser was outside, scrambling for interviews. She approached gruff quarterback Terry Bradshaw and, holding her pen and pad in hand, was about to ask him a question about the game when Bradshaw snatched Visser's notebook and signed his name. He thought she was a fan who wanted his autograph. "Are you kidding me?" she said. "I'm a reporter."

Both women recognized the imperative need to be inside the locker room, especially for beat writers, because the best stories tend to emanate from there. No conscientious reporter would ever willingly give up such access. Besides, Brennan and Visser argued, too many women had fought too many battles to gain equal access to the locker room.

Brennan and Visser, with only minutes before the show's start, next displayed a classic brand of double-team defense. They asked Storm: Are you truly ready to publicly advocate that women should take a step back into the dark ages?

Once the taping of the show began, Rivera cocked his microphone to Storm for her opinion: Do women need to be in the locker room? "Of course we do," said Storm. Brennan and Visser winked at each other.

"That's Lesley," Brennan said. "She will get into the trenches and throw some elbows."

During the course of her long career, Visser has been subjected to her share of criticism, such as owning a racehorse with NBA coach Rick Pitino. Unlike the glowing reporting trio of Roberts, Kremer, and Mortensen, Visser was not a news zealot when she joined ESPN in 1994.

Nevertheless, because of her extensive background and connections throughout all of sports, she developed into a dominating television presence. She also never forgot her roots. Brennan, Visser, and several others started a scholarship fund for young women journalists and were instrumental in the formation of an association for women in the sports media. Visser may not have been there at the dawn of women covering sports, but she was certainly there when the sun was still cool. Brennan calls Visser "the queen bee of women journalists."

Visser's career began at Boston College. In her junior year, she earned a grant from the Carnegie Foundation. Other winners went into fields like archeology; Visser undertook the pursuit of sports writing, choosing to intern at the *Globe*. Before she left for the summer, the sports information director at the university told Visser, "Remember to wear a short dress."

Visser left the short dresses at home and embarked on her career, which was high-anxiety because she was a rare commodity. Women just did not go into sports writing then, but she plugged along fearlessly, and after covering high schools for two years, was assigned to the Patriots, becoming the first female full-time beat writer for an NFL team. Visser met Gayle Gardner in 1977 when she was a reporter for WBZ-TV in Boston. The women were not allowed in the locker room and sweated deadlines while waiting to interview players in the weight room, which they nicknamed "the wait room."

The newspaper was extremely supportive, as were most of the players, especially the black ones, because, as Visser said, "a black man in New England knows what it is like to be the awkward one in the room, and I could definitely relate to that since I was always the only newspaper woman around."

Wives of the players often viewed Visser suspiciously, wondering why a woman wanted to be around all those men. Her status as a professional reporter did not seem to matter to them. Coach Chuck Fairbanks, an old-school disciplinarian, saw Visser as a nuisance. Visser once asked Fairbanks to explain why he was starting one player at linebacker rather than another, a perfectly reasonable question. Fairbanks rolled his eyes. "Why don't you call my daughter for lunch," he told Visser, "you're about the same age."

Attempts to humiliate Visser were not confined to the Patriots. University of Houston coach Bill Yeoman told the press covering the 1980 Cotton Bowl that "I don't care about women's rights, I'm not having a woman in my locker room." Nine years later, tight end Mickey Shuler verbally abused Visser when she tried to enter the New York Jets locker room. He yelled to her when she got to the door that women were not allowed.

When she smiled, thinking he was joking, he shouted venomously, "Hey, no fucking women in the locker room!" Visser later received a written apology from the Jets player, which she hung on her wall.

Those kinds of ugly incidents would—and have—driven other women to leave the business. Visser persevered, spending three difficult but rewarding years on the Patriots beat and fourteen years at the *Globe*, where she covered ten Final Fours, twelve Wimbledons, five Super Bowls, five NBA Finals, two World Series and an Olympics. Few reporters—male or female—can boast of such a rounded resume. She could write about any sport with equal skill and loved the theater of language. It showed in her copy, and then later, on the air for CBS Sports.

After taking the job at CBS, she made several promises to herself. First, she would write her own material. Second, she would not become a statistic. Visser told CBS executive director Ted Shaker, "If you see me going down the rabbit hole, you have to tell me. Because I don't want to be one of those trivia questions who lasts a year."

Her first few steps into television were halting ones. On her first assignment for CBS, in the summer of 1985, Visser covered the U.S. Open championships in New York. That year Hana Mandlikova made a dramatic rise from near the bottom of the rankings into the top ten. She was the hottest story of the tournament, and after one of her matches, Visser tracked Mandlikova down and did a live courtside interview.

"To what do you attribute your sudden rise in the rankings?" Visser asked.

Mandlikova, in her thick Czech accent, said it was due to her new coach, but Visser, with a surprised look on her face, thought Mandlikova said "couch." Visser thought maybe the tennis player was sleeping better.

"Oh," Visser said, "did you get some new furniture?"

"Don't be ridiculous," Mandlikova said. "I said my coach, not my couch."

Visser quickly caught on, combining humor and her trademark good writing with a charming on-air presentation. She joined the CBS football crew of Gumbel and Bradshaw, and upon first seeing the former Steelers player, Bradshaw, reminded him of that instance in the tunnel when he autographed Visser's notepad. Bradshaw joked, "My autograph was worth more than any crap you were going to write anyway."

Visser can pinpoint the moment when her television training wheels came off. The CBS football crew traveled in a corporate jet all night—except for a stop in Des Moines, Iowa, so Bradshaw could buy ribs—to get to San Francisco for the 49ers game against New York on January 20, 1990. Visser had produced a feature on talkative linebacker Pepper Johnson and during the pregame show, while she was introducing the story live, the tape completely melted, sending the piece to the graveyard. Visser heard a panicked producer bark into her ear, "The tape broke. You're going to have to tell the piece."

There was no awkward moment as there had been with Mandlikova. Instead, Visser, calmly and gracefully, narrated the story of Johnson's outstanding season. "I had been in television for about six years at that point," Visser said, "but that was when I knew I could handle almost anything thrown at me."

In January of 1992, after the Redskins crushed the Buffalo Bills in Super Bowl XXVI, Visser became the first, and only, woman to host the presentation of the Lombardi Trophy. Many in television had been watching Visser closely, as she soon discovered after CBS lost its football programming to Fox. Visser wanted to stay in football reporting and started looking elsewhere. After flirting with Fox, Visser was approached by ESPN and ABC, under the same corporate roof, who pitched her a groundbreaking package. ABC would assign Visser to each of its highest-rated sports shows, particularly Monday Night Football; the Pro Bowl; figure skating, which consistently produced big numbers on television; and the Triple Crown. At ESPN, it would be football, all the time.

Walsh, who always admired Visser's work, met with her for lunch in 1994 at the Final Four. These were trying times for Visser. Her future, despite the offers, was still uncertain, as was her husband's, CBS announcer Dick Stockton. Visser was also coming off months of rehabilitation for a shattered hip, which she sustained after a fall while jogging in Central Park. What boosted her spirits were the words of Walsh.

"You will be a major player in our NFL coverage," he told her. "We want you, Lesley, and we'll basically do what it takes to get you." She joined both networks soon after that meeting.

Walsh liked Visser's star power. She was a magnet who attracted all kinds of viewers. Her addition was just one of several changes in what was turning out to be a hectic 1994 for ESPN. It had been almost two years since Tirico's suspension, and in that time, there had been no other complaints from women. In a cruel twist, ESPN management, which basically gave him a tap on the knuckles for his behavior, used Tirico's suspension against him in later years. This was a common tactic at ESPN, which shamelessly used whatever dirt it had on its employees to gain leverage against them, either during a contract negotiation or when management wanted them to take on additional responsibilities. Tirico was regularly reminded by managers how good the company had been to him. In exchange, they extracted their pound of flesh, requiring him to work a six-day week or an extra Sunday morning on the radio. In essence, the network was saying, "We could have killed you. We might still."

Tirico denied that ESPN ever used his suspension for sexual harassment against him, directly contradicting what some of his coworkers maintained. "Mike is a good and sincere man," said a male ESPN anchor. "He was humiliated by what happened and paid his debt, but the company kept a hammer over his head. Then something funny happened. His talent was so powerful, it overrode what the company was trying to do to him."

In 1994 Tirico lobbied management to give him a chance at doing golf play-by-play. At one time, there may have been questions about Tirico's character but never his talent. When Jim Kelly, the main golf announcer for ESPN, was assigned to cover the America's Cup that year, Tirico replaced him on two of the network's golf events. It surprised no one at ESPN that his pinch-hitting assignment resulted in a home run. Later that year, wholesale changes were made to ABC's golf coverage. Lead producer Terry Jastrow, who had been ABC's golf guru for years, was replaced by Jack Graham. The coverage itself changed as well. ABC eliminated its practice of using a central announcer and analyst who were stationed throughout the day at the 18th hole and were assisted by on-course reporters shadowing the leaders.

The last decision was to replace Brent Musburger as lead announcer with Tirico and add former golfing champion Curtis Strange as the lead analyst. The move was controversial. Originally, Patrick had been promised the plum assignment at ABC, but when management caught a glimpse of Tirico's work as a fill-in, it reneged, informing Patrick one hour before "SportsCenter" that he was not getting the job. Wounded and betrayed, Patrick turned to Olbermann, who was a shade beyond furious that his friend had been deceived. "You're angrier than I am," Patrick said.

No doubt Patrick would have handled the assignment skillfully, but Tirico proved an excellent choice. The moves made ESPN and ABC's golf coverage decidedly better. Tirico was in his element. Instead of droning on for hours, as the announcer sometimes did under the old format, Tirico worked a select number of holes and did what he does best, played traffic cop and offered quick, pithy insights.

ESPN experienced other changes. Anderson, for a short time, left for ABC. Wolff, the one-time production assistant, returned to write and produce for ESPN2. Still keeping Bristol in his rearview mirror, he worked primarily from Los Angeles, earning $1,000 a week. Brennan refined her role as an Olympics specialist for ESPN2. In July, the network hired Bonnie Bernstein, a reporter from a small station in Reno, Nevada, where she had written, produced, and anchored her own news show. Testing her immediately, ESPN assigned her to interview Nebraska football coach Tom Osborne after he had suspended troubled running back Lawrence Phillips, who had been charged with assaulting his former girlfriend, a Nebraska basketball player named Kate McEwen. Phillips was eventually forced to sit out six games, a decision roundly criticized by the media as too lenient.

After the Phillips's story broke, Bernstein received an after-midnight call from manager Jim Cohen. He wanted her to catch the first flight to the Nebraska campus, so she was on a plane at six that morning. Without a scheduled interview, Bernstein went hunting for Osborne around campus, with camera and soundman in tow. They found him at a luncheon, but he refused to give an interview. Osborne had coached many troubled football players at the university, and he was adept at evading the media on these kinds of issues. But Bernstein persisted. She followed him down a long spiral staircase and onto an elevator. Osborne finally capitulated. Bernstein got her interview, albeit a short one.

Cohen loved Bernstein's hustle. "You got him on an elevator?" he told her. "That's great."

Bernstein, as a Chicago bureau reporter, handled a mix of stories for ESPN, including the Chicago Bulls and NBA postseason games, baseball playoffs, college football and basketball, and two women's Final Fours. Bernstein was well-respected, until, according to a member of ESPN management, the network learned she may have become too close to an Atlanta Braves pitcher. Also, at an invitation-only, post–ESPY's party at the Omni Berkshire hotel in Manhattan, she was spotted by ESPN staffers sitting in the lap of baseball star Alex Rodriguez. Bernstein vigorously denied she was anything but professional.

"It used to really get me angry when I first got into the business," she said, "because if you are a woman and you are talking to an athlete, you are automatically viewed as sleeping with him. It was hard for me to hear the rumors that I was sleeping with athletes. It was a total lie."

"I understand now what was going on," she added. "I am a very private person and I never talk about my private life. I can't write and call and dispel the rumors, so I stick to talking only to my close friends."

Bernstein says soon after joining ESPN, she endured a terrible episode with a professional athlete she refused to identify. She says the player approached her once while she was covering a story and asked her on a date. When she rebuffed his advances, the player became vulgar, even physically threatening, she said. Bernstein says he continued to abuse her verbally when she would return to do stories on his teammates. When his behavior failed to abate, she contemplated suing him for sexual harassment. Bernstein decided against such action for fear it would imperil her career.

Bernstein now reports for CBS. There were times when Olbermann wished he were anywhere but ESPN. One such time occurred after he returned to "SportsCenter" on April 3, 1994, from what he acerbically considered the netherworld of ESPN2. When Olbermann and Patrick separated, "SportsCenter" lost a measure of its passion and identity. Reuniting them restored that immediately. The chemistry between them, the smirks and one-liners were as natural and as affecting as they had been when it was announced nine months before that Olbermann was leaving for ESPN2.

Some of their first shows after Olbermann's return were a bit too lively. There were numerous self-references. An extra "I" or "we" and maybe an unnecessary chuckle or two. This pattern worsened when Patrick left to cover the NBA Finals that year. When they were apart, the two men missed the show dearly and, frankly, each other. For Patrick, working with an analyst on the road did not inspire the same sublime moments he had with Olbermann, and for Olbermann, back in the studio, no one was Patrick's equal. "No offense to Kenny Mayne, but it wasn't the same thing," said Olbermann, speaking about the anchor who, among others, substituted for Patrick while he was on the road. "No offense to Bob Ley, but it wasn't the same thing."

When Patrick returned to the late evening "SportsCenter" after the finals, the two turned up the zaniness even higher, eventually pushing Walsh too far. He had a right to be angry because Olbermann and Patrick had indeed gone over the top. But so was Walsh's reaction. He summoned the two star anchors into Anderson's office. Anderson and Olbermann sat down while Walsh stood and Patrick leaned against the office wall.

Walsh was masterful at disarming his adversaries in these situations. He moved to take command of the room and was not above resorting to cheap tricks: Low-set chairs, a lot of misdirection, and a laugh as a means of derision. And he often played loose with the facts.

With Olbermann and Patrick, Walsh launched a twenty-minute, obscenity-laced tirade by blasting the two anchors for their increasingly unprofessional behavior on the air. As the tongue-lashing continued, Anderson burrowed lower in his chair, embarrassed by Walsh's declining composure, while Olbermann and Patrick burned, feeling Walsh was way out of line.

"You guys have to stop doing this clowning around stuff," Walsh yelled. "I don't want to hear any talking to each other."

"John, what do you expect me to do when Keith says something funny," Patrick responded. "Put my hand over my mouth?"

The more Olbermann and Patrick defended themselves, the more Walsh fulminated. "You know what you guys do? It's Nick and Hick," Walsh said, referring to the former CNN anchor team of Nick Charles and

Fred Hickman. "It's local news. It's embarrassing to me." Walsh then corrected himself. "It's embarrassing to ESPN."

"Maybe half of the stuff he said was correct," Olbermann remarked. "Maybe fifty percent of the fifty percent. But the infraction was a one and the reaction to it was a one thousand."

Even more puzzling to Olbermann and Patrick was that they were hardly the first anchors to yuck it up on the air. When footage of Olympic gold medalist Carl Lewis mangling the national anthem at a New Jersey Nets game aired on "SportsCenter," Steiner had laughed to the point of tears. Unplanned humor and unexpected laughter had become a "Sports-Center" tradition.

The dramatic, dark, emotional meeting ended, and Olbermann and Patrick walked out of Walsh's office, stunned and fuming. "Dan was red," Olbermann remembered. "He looked to me not on the verge of tears of sadness or embarrassment but of anger." Patrick returned to Anderson's office about an hour later, still incensed, and it took some time until Anderson could calm him down. Anderson then called Olbermann to apologize. "I don't know what Walsh was thinking," Anderson said.

"We got verbally spanked," Patrick remembered. "After the meeting, we walked out, and I said to Keith, 'We must not be any good. We must be terrible.' Keith was defiant, and this is where I give him credit. He said, 'That's bullshit. They don't want us to be big.' I really respected Keith for taking that attitude."

Walsh sometimes expressed his most important points through threats or intimidation. The episode was a classic illustration of this. Walsh could not brook Olbermann and Patrick's latest antics because they so flagrantly endangered his tightly constructed "SportsCenter" model: The show was the star, not the anchors. Such a danger clearly required his most effective means of response. Walsh's vitriol may have been directed more at Olbermann than Patrick, because it was Olbermann who was increasingly challenging management's decisions and openly defying those decisions, even mocking them.

"With Olbermann and Walsh, I have never seen two more opposite people," said Mark Mason. "ESPN and Walsh did not like the Olbermanns of the world, because Keith screwed up the network's mindset. ESPN's philosophy was to suppress the stars, and Olbermann had become one of the biggest in television. Not only that, Keith often spoke out against things, like the work atmosphere, and how tough it was for the PAs."

When asked about Olbermann for this book, Walsh contended that he was "a big fan" of the anchor, then commented more directly about him as a person. "He has a hard time finding happiness," said Walsh, "and I really wish he could be happy."

After offering that Olbermann has a "sensitive, sometimes fragile" personality, Walsh disputed the claim of Olbermann and others that he did not get the humor of Olbermann and Patrick. "I loved the humor, I got the humor, I loved the humor," Walsh said. "Sometimes it was too far inside the beltway. And I would say that to him, 'Who in the world is gonna know that reference?'"

As to his outburst in the meeting with Olbermann and Patrick, Walsh explained, "They were going so far overboard we had to say . . . as sports fans watching the show there was too little . . . sports." Walsh called the meeting "passionate."

Deeply affected by Walsh's harangue, Patrick licked his wounds and moved on, never betraying on the air the bitterness that consumed him for months. His ardor for ESPN wouldn't allow it. In the end, however, one fact was inescapable: That day was the lowest moment of Patrick's career. And he would never forget it.

The mercurial Olbermann was less willing to forgive. "I already had my doubts about how long I was going to stay there," Olbermann said, "because I had been through my ESPN2 experience. But after what Walsh said to us? That was it for me."

• • •

Although there was definite upheaval at ESPN in 1994, some things remained embarrassingly the same for the network. Its employees, especially the production assistants, were still subjected to horrific hours. Regina Wald,* working as a PA, was very close to her young niece and preparing to celebrate Christmas with her. It was the first time Wald's niece was old enough to understand the holiday and open gifts with the family. Wald desperately wanted to be a part of that experience, but she was scheduled to work on Christmas Day from five that evening to two in the morning. Wald sought a compromise, asking another PA, who was a friend and did not celebrate the holiday, if he could work for her from five to eight that night. She promised to make up the three hours on another day. He agreed.

A change even that innocuous required permission from Paradis, derided as "the Hammer" by some producers. But Paradis denied the request, adding, "I can't guarantee that you will be back to Bristol in time. What if it snows? Can't your family just videotape Christmas for you?"

Miffed and angry, Wald turned to her supervisor, Sacks, who brokered a sensible compromise: Wald's friend would work for her that entire day and she, in turn, would substitute for him on a day of his choosing. With the exception of a short vacation, Wald had once worked from mid-July to January without two consecutive days off, seemingly earning her some time away from the ESPN complex. She did get to see her niece, but only after considerable maneuvering.

An even more infamous, and disturbing, Paradis story involves "RPM 2Night" producer Martha Walker, who was enduring a difficult pregnancy. The at times oppressively sexist Bristol newsroom didn't know what to do with a pregnant employee, often treating Walker crudely and insensitively. One high-profile anchor called her "Fatso" and a top executive wondered "Who's the father?" It was the same later with anchor Linda Cohn, who once told a colleague that after she became pregnant some ESPN men avoided her, as if she were carrying a flu virus.

For Walker, though, the trouble was just beginning. A difficult delivery left her bedridden for eleven weeks. That did not stop Paradis from phoning Walker a short time after she had arrived home from the hospital. ESPN producers and others have a window in which to pick their vacation days and if they do not exercise that option during this time period, they lose their place, falling all the way to the bottom of the priority list. Paradis called Walker and insisted that she pick her days immediately, impervious to Walker's current hardship.

Walker had received tremendous support from her supervisor, Kevin Stolworthy, but the offensive comments from the newsroom and Paradis's poor timing vexed her. She reported the incidences to the company's diversity committee established by the human resources department, which took her complaints seriously and moved to ensure such treatment was eliminated.

When Wald arrived at ESPN in August of 1993, Jaffe never suspected that she would become the torchbearer for the women who had fought to improve conditions for their gender at the network. By the spring of 1994, Wald had already persevered through a series of sexual harassment episodes, and she was fed up. A tall, athletic, and mentally strong woman, Wald was impassioned, leather-skinned, and outspoken.

• • •

Most production assistants enter ESPN directly out of college, barely old enough to vote. Wald was a mature twenty-six, having arrived from a job at a movie studio. Other PAs might have first considered Wald a snob. She rarely attended the raucous ESPN house parties and did not appreciate the sophomoric atmosphere in the newsroom.

She soon noticed the difference in treatment between the male and female PAs, especially with regard to the sexual harassment policy. One coordinating producer informed incoming women production assistants that ESPN viewed sexual harassment as a serious offense and enforced the guidelines strictly. Yet Wald later discovered, from a male PA, that that same producer colored the harassment guidelines quite differently for the men. "All right, we have a sexual harassment policy," he would begin, "so basically if you see a girl with nice tits, be appreciative of those tits, but be careful about saying anything about them to the girl's face. Maybe after work you can tell her."

Ten days into her ESPN career, Wald attended her first, and subsequently one of her last, early-morning ESPN parties. This shindig, held at the house of a high-ranking producer, was attended by almost two dozen people, including some talent. Wald's supervisor, coordinating producer Dan Steir, who only a few days earlier had outlined the company's sexual harassment policy for her, was also there. Wald was standing next to Steir when she asked the party's host, a producer she had met only once before, if he had anything to eat. The producer replied, "If you want to eat, you go to Dunkin' Donuts. At my party, all you can do is drink. But you know what? Why don't you just get your ass in my bed and take your clothes off."

Steir said nothing. Wald was flabbergasted at the brazen producer and at the mute Steir. She left promptly. The next day, she called Steir and they met in the conference room. Unlike many new PAs, who are unduly deferential toward the company, Wald was not cowed by ESPN's numbing stature. She was not a typical woman newcomer at ESPN; nothing spooked her. Wald talked to Steir with an authority he had rarely seen in a PA.

"You sat here and you told me about the company's policies and how management would stick up for you if there was a problem," she told Steir. "At the party, you let me hang in the fucking wind. I don't care if it was on this property or off this property. It was a work-related party."

Steir was an excellent coordinating producer, with a conscience. The network, hoping to avert yet another sexual harassment problem, wanted to stop this one cold, so Steir ordered the producer to apologize the following day. He did, in a hallway, avoiding Wald's eyes the whole time. "I'm sorry you felt bad about what I said to you," he told her.

The incident was an eye-opener for Wald, revealing a hostility to women unusual in scope for a midnineties American company. She also noticed that the women coped with this environment in various ways, tending to divide into three groups. First, there were the women who used their feminine attributes to get what they wanted. Indeed, an occasional female PA did sleep with a male supervisor, or dressed provocatively, hoping it would please him and consequently help her career. Second, there were the women who de-emphasized their femininity in the hopes it would make them immune to harassment.

Wald fit perfectly into the third group: Women who were just themselves and refused to compromise any part of their soul or femininity to succeed.

Wald grew up around sports—her brother was an All-American football player. But Wald, like some others at ESPN, was not a sports trivia maven or intimately knowledgeable about every sport. She was once asked to get video of baseball player Alan Trammell, of the Detroit Tigers, for a "SportsCenter" feature but instead pulled clips from the Detroit Pistons file. The next day, someone taped a Trammell baseball card to Wald's locker, which gave her a good chuckle.

At one point, Wald was unsure of ESPN's plans to keep her beyond the harrowing six-month trial PAs must endure. Steir was lukewarm and Mc-Quade, one of the kinder people at ESPN, told her she was on the bubble, but that he liked Wald's work ethic and considered her upside promising.

Wald discovered her fate after arriving home from ESPN one night at 12:30. She had a message on the answering machine from Patrick, who had befriended Wald, and Dan Steir.

"Don't pack your bags," said Patrick, "you're staying."

• • •

Over the next several years, between 1994 and 1996, Wald moved through the ESPN maze, working in almost every part of the company. She cut highlights on "SportsCenter" and worked with Chris Fowler on the college football show. She stayed up well into the night as a production assistant for "SCAM," or "SportsCenter A.M.," on the weekends and even ventured to the other side of the building for ESPN radio. As Wald gained more experience, her confidence grew.

There were times when Wald wondered what required more effort, staying awake until three o'clock in the morning working "SportsCenter" or fighting a near daily battle against harassment at the network. Wald made several trips to the human resources department to file complaints against male workers and complained even more to her superiors. The accusations covered the entire ESPN harassment-and-obnoxious-comments spectrum. One of her superiors in radio made what Wald considered inappropriate inquiries into her private life. There was the editor who asked Wald if she was banging her boyfriend.

Ironically, Wald says that during her most difficult times at the network, Tirico was one of her staunchest supporters. He listened to her problems, and when she became seriously ill, missing a month of work, Tirico was one of the few at the network who called to see how she was feeling. Wald was aware of Tirico's past suspension for violating ESPN's sexual harassment policy—the two had had one serious conversation about the incident—but Wald never had any trouble with Tirico. She remains a fan.

Wald often sought advice from other ESPN women and from a few trusted men on how to handle the numerous harassment incidences. She was always urged to remain calm and not make an emotional decision she might later regret. During a rare vacation, while standing on the sideline of a Florida-Florida State football game, her mind wandered from the on-field action. Wald asked herself if maybe she was complaining too much or being too sensitive. "Maybe I should just stop fighting and keep my mouth shut," she thought. But that was not her nature. Like Ross and others before her, Wald was a battler.

One irritating moment, Wald says, occurred while she was working on "NHL 2Night" with on-air personality Bill Pidto, one of the most intelligent, likable, and caring on-air persons at ESPN. Pidto has had a solid career at the network, but he also had a peculiar habit. After one show, Wald explained, Pidto patted her on the rear end, saying, "Good show, good show."

Wald was livid and says she told him to never do it again. Pidto seemed astonished at her objection. "We're a sport, we're a team," he told her. "It's like a football player coming off the field."

"Do I look like a football player to you?" she said. "No. Don't do it."

But Wald says Pidto repeated his actions after a subsequent show. "I said no a little louder," Wald said. "Then he did it again. I screamed, 'DO NOT TOUCH ME ON MY ASS!'"

If Pidto had not gotten the message after three warnings, Wald decided, he never would, so she complained to her coordinating producer, who had a talk with Pidto and told him to never touch Wald again.

Wald's boss arranged a meeting in which Pidto and Wald could talk. Pidto did not apologize but instead defended his actions as nothing more than a symbol of camaraderie, an argument that only served to further annoy Wald. "Let me ask you something," she told him. "Where does your fiancée work?" Pidto told her and Wald made a logical connection. "What if she came out of a big sales meeting and the boss slapped her on the ass?" Wald asked.

Pidto objected that the atmosphere where his fiance worked was completely different from that of ESPN's. Pidto just did not understand why Wald was so upset.

Six years later, Pidto explained his actions by saying, "We'd do a show, and I'd hit people on the backside. To be honest with you, she told me one time to quit it and it didn't even register because I thought it was such an innocuous thing to do. And once I became aware that it really bothered her, it ceased. It was something that really opened my eyes, because it's not something that you really think about, that she would even be bothered by something like that. It was a totally innocent thing on my part."

When asked if he would have done the same thing to a more powerful woman at the network, say Robin Roberts, Pidto said, "Probably not."

• • •

There was no one incident of harrassment that led Wald to take action but a culmination of events. She was tired of dealing with what she deemed a largely ineffective human resources department. Sometimes her production bosses were sympathetic, other times they were not. She had few women allies—many were terrified of speaking up. Wald, however, remained fearless and felt some sort of public statement about the harassment needed to be made. She recorded her encounters of harassment on a day planner and during an afternoon meeting in the conference room, waited patiently while Bob Eaton, among other executives, discussed ordinary matters like the vacation schedule and production issues in front of a group of about thirty associate and feature producers, some of whom were women. Then Eaton, rather clumsily, addressed the fact that yet more women had complained about being harassed. He then made a side remark that insinuated some harassment problems were the fault of those women who had failed to follow proper procedures when filing complaints. That comment incited Brooks, still chafing at ESPN's ineffective handling of her problems with Tirico.

"How dare you blame us?" Brooks told Eaton defiantly. Brooks challenged Eaton for several more minutes, then a stifling silence followed. Then Wald jumped in with both feet.

She patiently read her notes aloud, detailing her own battles with harassment and those of other women. Wald concluded by pleading that

ESPN needed to take the complaints seriously, something she felt had not been done.

At that point, a flustered Eaton tossed it to the room. "Have any other women in here had these problems?" he asked. Slowly one hand went up, then two, and three, and eventually more than ten. Suddenly, a free-for-all ensued, as women, with building agitation, described their own harassment encounters. Male producers, incredibly, backed the women, acknowledging that harassment was a prominent problem.

ESPN's harassment problems had come full circle. Some six years after Ross forced the network to address sexual harassment, with her passionate speech before the entire staff in the company cafeteria, Brooks and Wald had done the same. It was yet another monumental moment for women in the history of the network.

• • •

By 1995 ESPN had an involvement in almost every major sport. The network was never more popular—or lucrative. ESPN contributed a robust twenty percent to the earnings of its parent company, Capital Cities. And some financial experts were projecting that ESPN's operating income would increase twenty-four percent, to $97 million, over the next two years. ESPN2 was reaching twenty million people, making it the fastest start-up cable channel in recent years. In total, ESPN pumped its product into sixty-seven million households in the United States and nearly one hundred fifty million around the world. Both networks combined were valued at $5 billion.

ESPN made money because it knew how to save money. A primary means was the heavy reliance on the extensive and cheap nonunion PA workforce. There were other ways the network controlled costs. Many of ESPN's reporters were hired from small markets, so the network could pay them as little as possible, often far below market value. Few balked at their skimpy paychecks or overwhelming workloads, and they tolerated the city of Bristol, because, after all, it was ESPN, the dream station.

"You work there and it cannot be underestimated what ESPN does for your career," said Brett Haber, a former anchor. "But you put up with certain things. The locale is horrendous, the pay is a joke, and the atmosphere is ulcer-inducing. But it's ESPN."

The cost-cutting applied to almost every level of management. Each ESPN coordinating producer works under an operating budget, and if the CP stays below that magic number, the network hands over a bonus equal to the amount held in reserve.

At times, ESPN has opted for poorer quality, thus cheaper, satellite feeds to save money, figuring the viewer wouldn't notice or care.

Some bureau producers spend $500 a year on ESPN merchandise like T-shirts and hats, doling them out to people who help the network throughout the year, such as the stadium electricians who keep the lights turned on for the late stand-up after the game or the groundskeeper who waits to mow the lawn until the reporter is done filing a story. Yet ESPN at times has refused to reimburse its own producers for the gear. That is not surprising because at one point, the network refused to purchase fax machines for its bureau staff.

The most effective cost-cutting vehicle is what one producer called the "road trip gang-bang." If a producer and reporter go to Florida to cover a baseball game, for example, they might stop on the way in Orlando to interview a Magic player for an NBA piece and then make a quick trip to Miami for a Jimmy Johnson interview. If a sit-down was arranged with a Marlins player, he might be asked about six different topics for other stories the network is preparing. Some athletes chafe at becoming a human sound bite.

When Jean McCormick was a researcher at "Nightline," the producers didn't flinch about using movie clips for a story. Cost was not a factor. At ESPN, such a move was considered too expensive.

The cost-cutting allowed ESPN to grow with few financial worries. Thus it avoided the major layoffs that have bedeviled some in the business. The staff had bulged to 2,300 by 1995, and Olbermann and Patrick remained the most popular of any of them. They were instrumental in the network's shift from a good cable station to a media superpower. Olbermann walked through airports and was stopped by fans who wanted to hear a throaty "from way downtown . . . bang!" Patrick was equally well known. He managed to get the home phone number of comedian and actor Jerry Seinfeld and on a hunch decided to ask the star if he wanted to tape a "Sunday Conversation," the network's in-depth interview format with top sporting personalities. He left a message on Seinfeld's answering machine and Seinfeld called Patrick back immediately. Instead of badgering him about how he got his number, Seinfeld was elated that Patrick had called, telling him how much he watched the show and that he quoted Patrick around the "Seinfeld" set.

Then Seinfeld went into one of his famous bits. "Now, Dan, do we have to do the 'Sunday Conversation' on Sunday or can it be Wednesday?" asked Seinfeld.

"No, Jerry, it can be Wednesday," Patrick said, playing along.

"Well, why isn't it called 'Wednesday Conversation'?" Seinfeld said.

Everything about ESPN—its incredible profit-making and cost-saving techniques, impeccable journalism, and star talent—made it a highly attractive property to Michael Eisner, the chairman of the Walt Disney Company. Eisner had bid within several billion dollars of purchasing Cap Cities in 1993 and remained fixated on it. Eisner felt the company, specifically ESPN, could play the pivotal role in Disney's expansion plans into sports. Just as Rasmussen, Evey and Simmons envisioned an ESPN that would one day be a major player in sports television, Eisner thought the acquisition of ABC and ESPN would give his company two blockbuster properties that could be combined to form the most powerful entertainment and media conglomerate ever. Eisner viewed ABC as a mechanism for planting Disney programming into most American homes, and he believed Disney could use its synergistic tactics to increase ESPN's reach even further. Additionally, Eisner liked the cross-promotion possibilities, a sort of one-two-three punch.

Eisner and Cap Cities chairman Tom Murphy stayed in contact for months after the initial near deal. By the summer of 1995, Eisner's team had estimated that buying Cap Cities would fall into the high-rent neighborhood of $19 billion. In July, Eisner's team suggested that figure should be offered, using a combined cash and stock sale. Eisner concurred, feeling that such an offer made the deal a lock. After weeks of face-to-face meetings and telephone calls, at the end of July, both sides agreed on a price. Each Cap Cities shareholder would get a piece of Disney stock, at the time trading for $57.38 a share, and $65 in cash for each Cap Cities share. It was a remarkable deal, with the final total standing at $19.08 billion. The agreement ran 125 pages.

Word of an impending deal reached some of ESPN's top executives. Nothing in the ESPN newsroom stays a secret for long and within hours rumors of the deal coursed throughout the building. Everyone had the same reaction: "What does this mean for us?"

In early August, Eisner and Murphy appeared on "Good Morning America" with coanchor Charles Gibson to announce the agreement. The transaction was one of the biggest deals ever, and the media spent the day in analysis overdrive. Later that morning in Bristol, the newsroom was being remodeled for what seemed the dozenth time, but talent, producers, and a handful of sleepy PAs ignored the commotion and gathered around the monitors to watch Eisner and Murphy's press conference live on CNN. Eisner called ESPN "the crown jewel" of the purchase.

Ley and Steiner sat next to each other, in disbelief, especially Ley, who remembered the days when the upstart network didn't even have a parking lot and had to beg cable operators to put it on the air. Now they were listening to a powerful media executive using words like "brilliant" and "synergy" to describe ESPN.

Steiner turned to Ley and asked, "Is he talking about us?"

• • •

After the storm of media coverage abated, Eisner made his way to Connecticut, and Bornstein gave the Disney chairman a personal tour of the ESPN complex. Wald was in a mostly quiet screening room when Bornstein and Eisner approached. She was introduced to him, and then Bornstein and Eisner moved along.

Eisner had met numerous top ESPN managers and high-ranking producers and was impressed with the network's operation. But he had just unknowingly met one of the company's unsung heroes in Wald, who left in 1997 to work for a professional sports league.

The number of harassment cases at ESPN began to steadily decline starting in 1995. The constant reminders, through education and other means, on the malfeasance of sexual harassment began to achieve the desired effect. Yet harassment still occurred. In the summer of 1995, a woman producer received an anonymous computer message from someone who said they admired the size of her chest. "I don't even have that big a chest," she said in an interview.

Said one male producer: "Being a woman there is like being a black guy in the Mormon Church. You're looked at as odd, strange, and all the guys wonder why you are there."

The "Up Close" producer who had been harassed and physically threatened by another producer consulted a lawyer and was strongly considering suing ESPN. She decided against it, fearing it would effectively end her career. ESPN did suspend the harassing producer and forced him to receive substance abuse treatment as well as counseling.

Some of the most haunting allegations of sexual discrimination and misconduct came from sales executive Linda Whitehead. She began working at ESPN's Michigan sales office on December 19, 1983, as a sales assistant and, according to court documents, as Whitehead moved up the ESPN chain, she was at times earning half the salary of her male counterparts. Whitehead claimed in court records that she and other women were routinely discriminated against because of their gender by supervisor Theodore Andrusz. She also claimed he routinely took clients to topless bars, which offended many women in the office.

Once Whitehead complained about her treatment, she alleged, the company violated additional state and federal laws by retaliating against her. The most disturbing assertion is that ESPN forged documents to portray her as a poor worker.

On August 24, 1998, Whitehead filed a lawsuit in a Michigan circuit court, which included six pages of allegations. ESPN quickly settled the case for an undisclosed amount. Whitehead's attorney, Lynn H. Shecter, said neither she nor her client could comment about the lawsuit because of a confidentiality agreement with the network. The Detroit ESPN office said Andrusz no longer works there.

Some details of the Whitehead lawsuit bore a striking resemblance to the case of Elaine Truskoski. For much of the early 1980s, Truskoksi was a loyal executive secretary to Scotty Connal in Bristol. She filed a legal complaint with the Equal Employment Opportunity Commission alleging sexual discrimination after Connal was demoted and Truskoski along with him from a grade nine (with a pay scale of $15,480 to $26,040) to an eight ($14,112 to $23,640). Truskoski withdrew the complaint after ESPN promised to keep her at her present salary. Part of the price for challenging the network, Truskoski claims, was a job photocopying all day, then a deadline of thirty days to find a job within the company comparable to her old one—even though none existed. She was finally fired. The network claimed Truskoski was offered three secretarial jobs at the same pay, but not as an executive secretary.

Truskoski believed ESPN was retaliating for her original complaint, a fear plaguing many women who contemplate taking action against the network. Truskoski refused to accept ESPN's decision meekly, filing a lawsuit in federal court, claiming ESPN unfairly retaliated for her complaint of the pay system. In the spring of 1993, she won her case, was reinstated to her position, and awarded $115,000 for legal fees.

Truskoski won, but not without bloodshed. In court documents, her attorney, Joe Garrison, said the network employed a "scorched Earth" policy by dragging out the trial with numerous motions, aiming to deplete Truskoski's financial resources. Garrison, billing at $225 an hour, his assistant, and a paralegal spent 659.9 hours on the case, court records show.

Several high-ranking ESPN officials testified against Truskoski, including company attorney Michael Schnipper. Yet at times she was not alone. Back in Bristol, whenever an article appeared in a newspaper about Truskoski's case, other secretaries posted the stories on the office bulletin board as a show of support. Management removed the articles and prohibited anyone at the network from discussing the case, not only with the media but with each other.

The harder ESPN pushed Truskoski, the more stubborn she became. They pressed her to settle. One afternoon Garrison and Truskoski met in his office. She knew what he was about to say. "I don't want to settle," Truskoski said. "You haven't even heard the amount," Garrison replied. "I don't care," Truskoski said. "You tell them to kiss my ass."

For the better part of sixteen years, sexual harassment and sexism dogged the network, a solution seemingly beyond its grasp. One man who worked quietly behind the scenes to achieve reform was human resources director Ricardo Correia, who quit his position in 1995, leaving a six-figure salary because he felt meaningful change was unattainable. During his three-year tenure, a steady stream of women complained to his department of ESPN's not responding effectively to the sexual harassment scourge.

At the time of this book, women who work at ESPN, even those who have denounced the network's past handling of sexual harassment, say ESPN now takes thoughtful and constant steps to prevent the problem. This may be the reason for the sharp decrease in harassment complaints in recent years, according to Walsh. ESPN circulates memos throughout the building, describing the exact nature of inappropriate behavior and warning that it will not be tolerated. Because punishment is more stern, an increasing number of men are finally taking the issue seriously. However, some men, such as a coordinating producer who supervises baseball, who women say is notorious for his sexually explicit remarks and advances (he has been chastised by management on several occasions but never seriously punished), continue to rise through the ranks despite past complaints from women. But after years of stupendous blunders by management and painful sacrifices by women, ESPN has finally started to tame its 800-pound gorilla.

Through all the backstage chaos, the network remained true to the journalistic standards Walsh had established years ago. In May of 1995, Kremer nabbed one of the biggest scoops of the year. When Jordan returned to the Chicago Bulls after a failed attempt to play professional baseball, every major media outlet was trying to snag him for a sit-down interview, from Barbara Walters to Peter Jennings. Kremer beat them all, lining up Jordan for a "Sunday Conversation."

ESPN radio's Nanci Donnellan, "the Fabulous Sports Babe," was earning $400,000 a year in 1995, and her show could be heard on one hundred fifty stations around the country. In June ESPN and ESPN2 began eight days and almost forty-six hours of "Extreme Games" coverage, with Kolber and Fowler hosting. The games were broadcast into one hundred countries in five languages.

One eventual defection was Wolff, the former production assistant and writer. He was working the NBA Finals with reporter Mark Schwarz when

Wolff's pager went off. It was his agent, wanting Wolff to call immediately. Wolff had been working on a movie script about a production assistant who uncovers a point-shaving scandal. "Just wanted to let you know that if you're thinking about changing careers, you can," his agent said.

Paramount Pictures had bought the script for $500,000. But instead of catching the first flight home, Wolff worked until the championship was over. "It was the PA in me," he joked. "I thought if I left before the games were over, I'd get into trouble."

The Gods of Sport

15

"Can We Cut Your Good-bye from 45 Seconds to 30?"

The Disney purchase made some reporters and anchors edgy. They joked that Eisner would force reporters to conclude their reports by saying "I'm going to Disney World!" The humor masked genuine concern shared by many at the network, except Bornstein—Eisner would practically write him a blank check to continue growing ESPN.

Even before Disney emptied its pockets to buy the network, Bornstein, working mostly from New York, was already plotting his next expansion. Bornstein wanted to take ESPN the company and make it ESPN the industry. In 1994 the network hired a Seattle-based Internet start-up company called Starwave. Bornstein envisioned the vast possibilities the World Wide Web held for expanding ESPN's brand. In only a short time, the ESPN SportsZone web page (later called ESPN.com) became the most popular sports site on the net. Eisner himself used the page to play in a SportsZone basketball fantasy league called the Duck Pond.

Another cable TV channel, ESPNews, launched two years later, was dedicated solely to highlights and sports news. Then, in 1997 Bornstein headed the purchase of Classic Sports, a cable channel that aired historic sporting events and profiles of legendary players. Vince Doria, who once headed ESPN2, was tapped to head the history network several years after its start.

It was only natural for ESPN to go into publishing, especially after *Sports Illustrated* and CNN converged in the fall of 1996 to start a cable sports network to compete directly with ESPN. CNN/SI hijacked some ESPN employees for its start-up, such as producer McCormick (who later left CNN/SI). Walsh, erroneously, as it turned out, thought CNN/SI would use the reporting muscle of the sports magazine and the resources of CNN to form ESPN's most formidable challenge. Instead, he was blindsided by Fox.

Sports Illustrated committed some miscalculations of its own. It never anticipated that a magazine backed by Disney and ESPN would pose much of a threat. ESPN wanted to differentiate itself from SI, which had dominated the sports magazine medium since the 1960s. The result: a magazine big in every way. It was several inches longer and wider than SI. Instead of printing weekly, the magazine was published twice a month, which saved money in the long run and forced it to concentrate more on feature stories than game recaps, looking ahead rather than back. What ESPN wanted with its magazine was a hip, young look accented with attitude.

In the spring of 1996, John Papanek was hired as editor-in-chief of *ESPN: The Magazine,* and he was the perfect man for the job. Papanek had spent twenty-three years at Time Warner, nineteen of them as a reporter, writer, senior editor and later managing editor at SI. A soft-spoken man, Papanek left Time on a bitter note. Shoved from his managing editor's spot and asked to head Time, Inc.'s new media division, Papanek proposed blending a general-interest magazine, television show, and Internet company into one potent, synergistic entity. Time, Inc. was not impressed. Frustrated, Papanek departed for the New Century Network and then was contacted by ESPN, who warmed to his media hybrid.

CNN/SI boasts a sparkling stable of reporters. Peter King, the professional football expert who made his mark at *Sports Illustrated,* rivals Mortensen in number of sources and propensity to uncover breaking news. Still CNN/SI is a mere blip, watched only, as SI writer Rick Reilly once said, on "the dark side of the moon and in parts of Fargo." Meanwhile, ESPN's magazine is biting into SI's $100 million annual profits, making the steep $75 million start-up costs for *ESPN: The Magazine* well worth it.

The keenest battles between *ESPN: The Magazine* and SI were over writers, editors, and production staff. ESPN offered big money to lure designer F. Darrin Perry, director of photography Nik Kleinberg, and managing editor Lynn Crimando from *Sports Illustrated.* SI was also forced to empty its wallet by offering enticing writing deals to retain Reilly, the best wordsmith in sports writing and Gary Smith, a yearly National Magazine Award nominee.

SI was not prepared for, nor could it compete against, *ESPN: The Magazine's* aggressive self- and cross-promotion, engineered by Disney. In February of 1998, ABC's Brent Musburger unabashedly ripped SI on the air as he did play-by-play for a college basketball game while praising ESPN's magazine. Then, ABC's "World News Tonight" anchor Peter Jennings hyped an exclusive *ESPN: The Magazine* story about University of Connecticut women's basketball player Nykesha Sales the night before the article appeared in the magazine's premier. The story questioned whether Sales had actually broken the all-time women's scoring record because of a scoring error. Although an interesting piece, the story hardly deserved mention on the national evening news.

ESPN's magazine has been a success, though it remains difficult to tell where the Tommy Hilfiger ads begin and the stories end. Walsh, a former *Rolling Stone* editor who birthed *ESPN: The Magazine,* hovered over it like a protective parent, often showing up on Friday before the magazine closed. Some staffers chafed at Walsh's meddling, but he has made sound decisions, among which was acquiring heavyweight writing talent such as Tony Kornheiser from the *Washington Post* and former *New York Times* reporter Tom Friend (who wrote a sharp piece on troubled running back Lawrence Phillips). Kornheiser's biting, engaging style is illustrated by this sample from the 1999 article on the woman who wrote term papers for the University of Minnesota basketball team: "She apparently got bored with the standard stuff and started writing about subjects that interested her, including PMS. Can you imagine the poor guy who mailed that one in? He probably thought PMS was a conference with an automatic NCAA bid."

The magazine also borrows the network's popular anchors. Dan Patrick's amusing interviews at the end of the magazine are one of its best features. And Mortensen, Seattle-based NFL reporter John Clayton, baseball writer Peter Gammons, hockey expert Al Morganti, and *Miami Herald* columnist Dan Le Batard all make solid contributions.

The magazine has experienced only a handful of problems, rare for a start-up. One problem, however, has been recurring clashes with the network itself. Often, the magazine sends a reporter along with a crew from the television station to cover a story, and vice versa. Usually this arrangement works fine; sometimes it does not. Tom Friend is a stubborn reporter and fishes for every detail to enhance his features. When working on a profile of Michael Jordan after the 1998 season, Friend was told that Stuart Scott had persuaded Jordan to sit down for a "Sunday Conversation." Friend figured he could listen in on the interview, which was being produced by Eric Lundsten, and pick up a few details, a reasonable request. Scott refused, arguing that space in the interview room was too limited, when that was indeed not the case.

When the Denver Broncos made a visit to the White House in 1999, an ESPN television producer, cameraman, and soundman, the latter carrying

an imposing boom microphone resembling the neck of a giraffe, were assigned to cover the ceremonies, as was, independently, a photographer
from the magazine. Only the photographer was not just any shutterbug
but the prolific Harry Benson, whose work has appeared in almost every
major magazine in the country. Benson is charming and friendly until
someone blocking his shot refuses to budge. Benson was standing behind
the ESPN cameraman and soundman, and neither would move after he
asked them. A nasty, almost physical, argument followed.

"ESPN treats photographers like maintenance men," Benson said.
"We're treated like serfs. And, by the way, if I had a brain defect, I would
be a soundman."

• • •

Eisner defines micromanagement, and Disney reflects his tendency to
pore over the smallest of details. Disney executives have been known to
call ahead to public relations firms helping with a Disney or ESPN event,
inquiring about the heights and weights of each member of the PR company scheduled to attend. If Disney deems a person too heavy, he or she is
asked to stay behind. When a Disney executive visits one of the company's
theme parks, he must wear a white starched shirt, shave all facial hair, and
be tattoo free.

The Disney way terrified some at ESPN, and they expected the worst
after the sale. Although Disney may have had little direct effect on ESPN
as a news agency, the indirect ripples still rocked some people's boats.
Soon after the purchase, actress Whoopi Goldberg hosted "Plays of the
Week." She made a few jokes, livening up the segment. Her appearance
was not coincidental. Goldberg was on "SportsCenter" only because her
vacuous movie *Eddie,* about a fan who becomes coach of the New York
Knicks, was premiering that week. The movie was made by Hollywood
Pictures, a subsidiary of Disney.

Goldberg's appearance infuriated some of the anchors, particularly Olbermann and Jack Edwards, two of the fiercest protectors of journalism on
the talent side. At an ESPN staff meeting after Goldberg's appearance,
both men voiced their displeasure, arguing that if Disney was going to use
ESPN to shill itself and its products, the network needed to make full dis-
closure to the viewers. That, they said, was the only honest approach to
take. Management said it would discuss the two men's concerns. No one
else at the meeting said a word about the problem, leaving Olbermann and
Edwards adrift in their own small craft.

ESPN, already efficient cost-cutters, learned a few more things from

Disney about keeping operating overhead to a minimum. ESPN Christmas parties, which before Disney's purchase were lavish affairs costing upward of $100,000, were scaled back. Instead of a beautiful engraved crystal dish as a holiday gift, post-Disney ESPN employees got tote bags or passes to a Disney theme park.

• • •

In 1996, David Aldridge, the longtime reporter for the *Washington Post,* added a heightened intelligence to the network's NBA coverage that paralleled the dramatic rise in the popularity of the sport. Aldridge, like many top reporters at the network, could tap a rich mix of sources, and he knew where to draw the line between being a reporter and being a buddy of the players. Some of the anchors who stepped out of the studio for interviews failed to comprehend or ignored this line, which often complicated the jobs of the straight-shooting reporters like Aldridge.

Aldridge's first assignment was to cover the NBA all-star game in San Antonio in 1996, which ended on an unusual note. Michael Jordan was awarded the most valuable player award but was booed by the crowd, who felt that center Shaquille O'Neal should have received it. Jordan's harangue by fans is one of those man-bites-dog stories. It never happens. After the game, Aldridge asked the superstar a logical question: "What was it like to be booed?"

Jordan eyed Aldridge warily, as if he were thinking, "You're asking me a tough question?" It may be nothing more than coincidence, but after that interview, Aldridge never went one-on-one with Jordan again.

Jordan will go to the same well if he knows a reporter or on-air personality will not ask the tough questions. That may be why Jordan developed such a close friendship with NBC reporter Ahmad Rashad and later with amiable ESPN anchor Stuart Scott. Scott's now immense popularity is ironic because he was once hesitant to join the network. Like other people of color, there was concern about living in the harsh cultural blandness of Bristol. He adapted to the city, however, and quickly rose to become a prominent anchor.

Scott made his name on ESPN2, where his poetical writing distinguished him. Management wanted cool—with Scott, that's what they got. There were times—many of them, actually—when management felt Scott went too far and wanted him to pull back. A few executives, including Norby Williamson, told Scott to reduce the slang. Another ESPN official, in an infamous move, asked Scott not to "talk so black." Scott fought the directive, thinking that if he diluted his writing, which he takes seriously, he would be selling out. Scott wanted to be for the black viewers what Olbermann was for the Yale audience. He wondered why Olbermann could quote "Beowulf," but he couldn't borrow from a John Coltrane lyric or a noted rap song.

In the end, Scott triumphed, and his writing remains as good as ever. "We talked about it all the time," said Kolber of Scott's battles with management. "He was put in a really difficult situation, because here is this network that was supposed to be hip, irreverent, a whole youthful image, but the guys running it could not relate to that. They wanted to try and reel Stu in, but they didn't know the right way to deal with it. I give him a lot of credit because he stuck with what he felt was right."

Others in the industry weren't quite sure what to make of Scott once he began doing the late "SportsCenter" with coanchor Rich Eisen, which reaired throughout the morning. Greg Gumbel, the classy ESPN original and a pioneer for blacks in sports broadcasting, was not impressed. "That overnight stuff?" Gumbel said. "The stuff that runs all morning? Awful. You don't know whether you're going to change the channel or put your foot through the TV before you change the channel."

Gumbel added, "Not everyone thinks a phrase from the latest rap song is cute and should be used every thirty seconds."

Scott's style may have had its detractors, but his popularity among viewers was widely acknowledged. This popularity, as with other ESPN anchors, conferred a celebrity status that often clouded his judgment. At times Scott acted more like a celebrity than a newsman, hanging out with players like Jordan at parties, palling around with them as friends instead of business associates.

Like the athletes they covered, many ESPN anchors developed an ugly sense of self-importance. Some took fame too seriously, with their heads swelling to the size of small planets. They started acting more infantile than the egotistical athletes they described on-screen. By the mid-1990s, in fact, some had become as arrogant as ESPN itself.

The anchors could exhibit odd, disturbing behavior. One called the New York Yankees public relations department for field passes for his wife and baby-sitter. The sitter wanted to meet star player Derek Jeter because she thought he was cute.

Chris Myers had replaced Roy Firestone as the host of "Up Close" from Los Angeles and did a highly respectable job. Myers was able to ask tough questions of his guests without losing their respect. Although management wanted Myers to be more confrontational, he resisted. His best interview was with former Heisman Trophy winner O. J. Simpson after a jury acquitted him of murder; that show was among the highest rated in ESPN's history.

Simpson unwittingly played another part in ESPN's history. More than a year before Simpson appeared on "Up Close" with Myers, a calm Jack Edwards, sitting near the newsroom before a remote-controlled camera called the "monkey cam," expertly described to viewers the high-anxiety spectacle of Simpson's infamous Bronco chase. During those hectic moments, Steve Anderson was ripping copy off the wire and getting people coffee as the long night dragged on. Anderson was as determined to get the story on the air as anyone in the newsroom, an action that helped solidify Anderson's reputation as a beloved manager.

Polished as Myers was in his role as host, off camera he was prone to tantrums. Some anchors said he had an assassin's heart and no aim. Myers sometimes wrote searing memos to Walsh carping that he deserved to replace this or that anchor at the network. When Myers left copies of the memos in the unlocked personal file of his computer, another anchor regularly went into the file and then, furtively, sent copies to friends on the ESPN campus. (That conduct led to yet another management memo, this one warning that anyone caught raiding another person's personal computer file would be severely disciplined.)

When Myers was interviewing Carolina linebacker Kevin Greene, the show experienced satellite troubles and Greene's image suddenly disappeared. Technicians restored the feed, but then they lost him again. By now, Myers was furious, and during a commercial break, he threw a mug full of water against a wall on the set, unaware of a makeup artist standing nearby. The cup barely missed her head, but the water ricocheted onto Myers's hair and suit. Before coming out of the commercial, a producer said sarcastically to Myers, "By the way, there's still a little water on your jacket." The network suspended Myers for several days.

Some misbehavior by certain anchors was a result of job pressure or of management's suppression of creativity. Walsh went to extremes in this pursuit and made it clear himself, or through his lieutenants, that ESPN valued the system over the individuals. And top station executives were not above attempting to humiliate the anchors into compliance, informing talent in staff meetings that focus group research showed viewers did not even know the names of the anchors. That was an obvious deception, because the anchors were among the most popular and powerful people on television. Few could walk into a restaurant or through an airport without being recognized.

Anchor Craig Kilborn, like Olbermann, refused to be boxed in by management, relentlessly testing the network with acidly funny on-air remarks. Kilborn and Haber, who became friends, knew they were not ESPN lifers and often sat at their cubicles in the newsroom dreaming of a future that did not include ESPN. They decided to use the network to get what they wanted because, after all, ESPN was using them. Kilborn played that role to perfection, using his sarcastic comedic talents to propel him out of Bristol and onto the set of a popular cable comedy show. Kilborn then went on to host a late-night talk show on CBS, the best-written of its ilk.

After a fruitful but rocky three-year tenure at ESPN, Haber left for a Washington, D.C., Fox affiliate. At ESPN Haber cursed at a cameraman, who left the film rolling and then turned it into management. Haber said his comments, while off-color, were meant in jest. He was suspended by the network. Haber later learned of management's intent to drop his contract when he saw an advance copy of an April schedule left in an insecure computer. Next to his name were those infamous blank spaces.

Haber holds no grudge against ESPN, summing up his experience in this way: "It's a tough place for a twenty-four-year-old kid to be thrust before America."

The bloodiest conflict between management and talent, of course, was between Olbermann and Walsh. The philosophical differences separating the two men would reach a critical point in the spring of 1997, the fallout of which is still being felt by the network.

• • •

In April 1996, eccentric billionaire Rupert Murdoch, who had a passion for sports and television, announced, in conjunction with Liberty Media, a plan for acquiring nine regional sports networks, connecting them, and then giving them a national presence. It was clearly Murdoch's first step toward establishing a counterpresence to ESPN. The problem for Murdoch was that few believed any media outlet could beat the more established cable station at its own game, which explains the announcement's lack of media attention.

Olbermann was stunned not so much by Murdoch but by an incident that occurred in late February inside ESPN. The coordinating producer for the baseball addicts' show "Baseball Tonight" was Jeff Schneider, who suggested to Olbermann that he coach first base for Edison College against the Minnesota Twins at Fort Myers, Florida. Schneider later microphoned two other first base coaches and then combined the Olbermann conversations with those running conversations for a story on the job of first-base coaches.

To Olbermann's dismay, the story ended up as a fill piece, meaning it would only run when "Baseball Tonight" or "SportsCenter" had to be expanded beyond its usual length. Wondering why, Olbermann asked Schneider what happened. Schneider reported that Walsh didn't like the piece "because there was too much you in it." The following year, in March of 1997, Olbermann came across Schneider at a tape machine going over a story in which Anaheim Angels coaches Dave Parker and Larry Bowa were microphoned. The Angels are owned by Disney. Olbermann asked Schneider, "We're doing this again?"

"Yep," Schneider said.

"I thought Walsh hated it," Olbermann said.

"Yep," Schneider said.

"Then why are you running this when they hated it last year?" Olbermann asked.

Schneider responded, "Because last year, I didn't have Michael Eisner calling Walsh asking when the story was going to run."

By the spring of 1997, the friction between Olbermann and Walsh had intensified. To Walsh, Olbermann was the antithesis of his ideal anchor. Olbermann thought Walsh didn't understand the dimensions of the show that made it special. One other thing bothered him. He felt Walsh, a stickler for decorum, at times treated people impersonally, almost cruelly.

Walsh was certainly not insensitive to everyone. He has been known to send gifts to families of newborns. Yet he does have a cold side. To illustrate his point, Olbermann told a story confirmed by ESPN producers involving coordinating producer Mike McQuade. McQuade was the line producer for the eleven o'clock "SportsCenter" from July of 1993 through September of 1996 and may have been the best the show ever had. In 1995 he resisted management's proposal to promote him to coordinating producer because he liked what he did. So McQuade requested to continue his current position, to receive a small raise, and to spend more time with his children. ESPN producers rarely receive a raise unless they get a promotion (which accounts for the glut of coordinating producers), but McQuade didn't want a promotion, which led to a stalemate lasting for months.

One afternoon McQuade had something to tell Olbermann. "You'll love this," McQuade said. "Walsh told me that the argument about spending time with my kids was irrelevant because a father doesn't really need to see his girls until they're seven."

Olbermann gave another example—again confirmed by producers from ESPN—of Walsh's chilly disposition. Tom Mees, the longtime, lovable anchor, died in a tragic swimming pool accident in 1996. The memorial service for Mees was attended by hundreds of mourners, many from ESPN. Olbermann and Patrick both adored Mees and cried at the service. The emotions prompted Olbermann to suggest that the new newsroom, then being built, be named for Mees. Everyone agreed, especially Berman, who was as close to Mees as anyone. Even Olbermann and Ley shook hands on the proposal—and they never agreed on anything.

Olbermann says he approached Walsh with the idea. Walsh, according to Olbermann, said, "Well, we'll consider it. But a lot of people had a bigger hand in making that newsroom what it is today." Walsh's indifference to Mees distressed Olbermann and others.

By April of 1997, the tenuous relationship between the two men had reached an all-time low. It took a turn for the worse during Olbermann's negotiations with the network to extend his contract. Howard Katz, then an ESPN vice president, was handling the talks, speaking mostly to Olbermann's agent, Jean Sage. Olbermann always believed that Walsh was directing the negotiations from afar.

On a Tuesday in April, Olbermann was on assignment covering the Jackie Robinson ceremonies at Shea Stadium when Katz asked Olbermann if he and Sage were close to a deal. Olbermann was irked by the place and the timing of the question, because he was working in a luxury suite ESPN was using as a remote studio, which offered no privacy. At various times, it was occupied by President Clinton, dozens of Secret Service agents, former slugger Reggie Jackson, Berman, Robin Roberts, baseball analyst Harold Reynolds, several producers, and more than a dozen ESPN staffers. Despite the rotating door of guests, Olbermann told Katz his impression was that no deal was pending.

Several days later, Olbermann appeared on Comedy Central's "The Daily Show," hosted by his friend and former ESPN anchor Kilborn. Olbermann was promoting his and Patrick's book, *The Big Show,* about life on the "SportsCenter" set. Olbermann thought he had permission from the network to reasonably promote the book on any media outlet of his choosing. ESPN required its anchors to request, in writing, permission before they appeared on another network. ESPN has suspended anchors for violating this policy. But Olbermann figured he'd tape the interview first, then write his request later.

Throughout the show, Kilborn joked that Olbermann was there without ESPN's consent. "Yes, that's right," Olbermann said. "Live and in color. You know the story with TV management everywhere, Craig. 'Don't ask, don't tell.'"

One reason Kilborn left ESPN was because he despised Bristol, and Kilborn knew Olbermann's sentiments about the city mirrored his. During a hilarious and now infamous "five questions" segment at the show's end, Kilborn asked Olbermann to "Name the most godforsaken place on the East Coast." Olbermann, smirking, responded, "Bristol, Connecticut." Olbermann knew almost immediately he had probably made a mistake, but, he reassured himself, this was a comedy show, and he wanted to play along with his friend Kilborn.

Olbermann was told by Comedy Central bookers that his taped interview with Kilborn would not appear for at least several weeks, giving Olbermann ample time to tell ESPN management he was appearing on the show. But that afternoon one of the Judd sisters canceled with Kilborn, leaving a programming hole that was filled with the Olbermann interview. It aired the next day. When ESPN management later heard about it, they did anything but laugh.

• • •

Later that month, Olbermann hand-delivered a memo to Katz in his office, expressing his displeasure with their conversation at Shea Stadium and offering some options to spur contract negotiations. Katz was not pleased. He promptly telephoned Sage, saying he was angered and hurt by the memo. "There will be no more contract negotiations," Katz told Sage, "until Keith apologizes personally to me for that memo."

Katz was not one to take abuse from anyone and he often handled his ESPN duties with the not-so-genteel style of a Marine drill sergeant. He was known for sometimes telling anchors before they went on the air: "Don't fuck up."

Katz and Olbermann exchanged fiery notes, during which Olbermann felt that Walsh was orchestrating ESPN's tough stance. Then on April 28, Olbermann sent a three-page memo to Katz so contentious in tone that any agreement from that point on would have been viewed as a huge upset. The memo read:

Dear Howard:

Disrespect?

"SportsCenter" wins its first Emmy since 1990, and Bob Eaton goes up and thanks you and John Walsh and Steve Bornstein by name and doesn't even collectively refer to those of us who actually do the show even as merely "the hosts"—and you write me a letter about disrespect?

The newsroom is louder than a bowling alley during a kids' party, our desks are located between coordinating producers who only use their offices to make loud phone calls and associate producers who play touch football in the hall, use our computers, and leave everything from peanut shells to banana peels under my desk; we virtually beg you for some place *private and quiet enough to write in* and you do nothing—and you write me a letter about disrespect?

You fire my best friend in the business one year, suspend and belittle another one of my best friends the next, and then fire a third the next (letting him find out in the most unprofessional way I've heard of, because someone left an advance schedule in an insecure computer)—and you write me a letter about disrespect?

Knowing full well that my agent is contractually obligated to tell me anything relevant to my job, you tell her the week before one year's Emmys that you are so dissatisfied with my conduct that you are considering buying out the remainder of my contract, and then you tell her the day of the next year's Emmys that you are considering suspending me—and you write me a letter about disrespect?

To a person who has presented you a show that has gained unprecedented ratings, and revenues, and media reviews gushing to the point of nausea, and whose work has gathered three Emmy nominations, a Cable Ace, and two other Cable Ace nominations—you begin negotiations a year ago by offering him an 8 percent raise—and you write me a letter about disrespect?

Having presented me with a series of three successive contract offers, the first being pulled off the table before we could respond, the second containing work hours worse than the first, the third containing a salary offer $150,000 less than the second, you approach me in the middle of a field assignment and hit me out of nowhere with the question, "Are Jean and I close to a deal?" This threw me to the degree that John Walsh said that there seemed to be something wrong with me on the air that night—and you write me a letter about disrespect?

Having asked me to leave a then already successful show to take the risk that was ESPN2, I am not only called "disloyal" by Al Jaffe for trying to negotiate a higher salary than you had offered me, and I am not merely subjected to the nightmare that was "SportsNight," but when you finally agree to let me return to "SportsCenter," you force me to sign a contract at reduced terms and for additional time—and you write me a letter about disrespect?

John Walsh calls Dan and me into a meeting in Steve Anderson's office in 1994—Anderson will be so upset that he will call both of us individually to apologize—and berates us in vile, unceasing, condescending, and inappropriate language for all of the eccentricities and style elements that have since elevated "SportsCenter" from a passable cable sports show to a highly regarded television program and gotten us deals on commercials, a book, and baseball cards bearing our likenesses—and you write me a letter about disrespect?

These last five years have been one continuous parade of disrespect—from you to me, from John Walsh to me, from management to the on-air staff, from management to the off-air staff. I have now worked for eight of the largest broadcasting companies in this country and never have I seen treatment of people approaching this. Even having written what I have written above, I know that I have been treated better than most of my colleagues—and that is why nearly all of my colleagues with any real skills or talents have left your employ, or are planning to do so.

And now I need to set the record straight on several points from your letter:

1. My agent had to change the nature of the work I might consider doing. You offered a radio/tv deal that seemed as if it had the germ of a basis for negotiations. Before I could formulate a response, you then withdrew this offer and re-presented it, having changed the most vital element of the offer—the time of the show—from the possible but not really desirable 1–4 P.M. slot to the infeasible 9 A.M.–noon slot. I wanted to work in the late afternoon and had no interest in working in the mornings. You had started at early afternoon and then bargained down from there to the mornings. At this point, with your having presented and then withdrawn not one but two radio offers, how do the negotiations continue at all if I and my agent do not change the nature of the work I might consider doing?

2. The issue of reduction of the workload is not merely a question of days—it is also a question of buttressing the staff to the degree where Dan and I do not have to be the last line of defense for *every* mistake made during the day. But the reasons you did not get a counteroffer suggesting that the three days of "SportsCenter" needed to be contiguous were: (a) I have no desire to live even three days of my life in some hotel or temporary accommodation here; (b) the money being offered was no more than one-third the value of the work required.

3. You have misunderstood my reference to the genesis of the one "SportsCenter"/four radio shows proposal. In my previous letter I referred to your having conceived of this idea, or at least one very similar to it, during our discussions involving Dan early in 1996. You have taken umbrage at an unintended slight; I believed I was giving you *credit* for creating this line of thinking. You may recall I brought it up anew last year, suggesting

the final year-plus of the contract be served out with me doing just radio from New York, a proposal you dismissed as infeasible and/or requiring a new long-term commitment from me.

Finally, I must tell you that whichever of the current newsroom snoops are quoting me as "counting the days until December 31st," and that "there's no way on earth I'm staying," what they have been reporting is in fact my general frustration over what is obvious to everyone in this company except its management. You have created a special set of rules to cover a few on-air people and favored members of middle management. The rest of us, no matter what our contributions here might be, are interchangeable parts whom you reward only when faced with competition for their services, whom you wear down or beat down at all other times.

My personal extension of this frustration, which has caused me to periodically make versions of the remarks attributed to me, reflects my simple astonishment at all of this. By a combination of a format, the pairing of two broadcasters, the input of a handful of producers, the hard work of the production staff, good timing, and sheer luck, you have been handed a television program that is a genuine phenomenon of current American culture. It is a program that is not merely a money factory; not merely the bulwark of the entire ESPN edifice, with the potential to remain such indefinitely no matter the gathering competition; not merely good, honest, and useful; but is also necessary the way the *Wall Street Journal* was necessary, or the way *Sports Illustrated* was necessary, or the way Cronkite or Huntley/Brinkley or Letterman was necessary.

And instead of doing anything and everything to keep happy the two people who are at the center of this program and who are its only public identity, you barrage us with petty complaints, lowball offers, a revolving door of support personnel—and letters about my disrespect.

I have been watching you dismantle one of the great media entities of all time, a process that dates back to Steve Anderson's departure, through Lenny Daniels', through the unwillingness to pay Mike McQuade more without promoting him, through Dan's many travails, and now to your embittering negotiations with me. Why shouldn't I be frustrated, angered, heartbroken? The gap between us that you referred to in your letter is one I have watched you build, stone by stone, since 1993. It's a damn tragedy, Howard, along the lines of the book *The Late Shift.*

Most of Olbermann's beefs were legitimate. His indignation at the treatment of people around him was genuine. Olbermann was one of the few who openly addressed problems. And he did it again in June of 1997, when Peter Vecsey, the vitriolic NBC and ESPN radio basketball analyst, accused Patrick, ESPN analyst David Aldridge, and the rest of the "Sports-Center" on-air staff of stealing his scoops. Not only were these serious accusations, they were made by Vecsey on ESPN radio. Vecsey had slandered ESPN employees on ESPN's own network.

ESPN occasionally takes credit for stories it does not directly break. However, Vecsey was wrong about Patrick, who clearly had given NBC and Vecsey credit for stories he broke. Because Vecsey refused to apologize to either Patrick or Aldridge, and management refused to discipline Vecsey or to remove him from ESPN radio, Olbermann angrily took action. On Thursday, June 5, he sent a memo to the on-air staff. "For my part, in light of management's refusal to do the only appropriate thing and remove Vecsey from any future ESPN radio network appearances," Olbermann wrote, "I have resigned from ESPN radio. Dan has asked for an on-air apology from Vecsey, which I do not believe is forthcoming."

"I am not encouraging you to take action because of this, other than what—if anything—your heart tells you to do," Olbermann concluded. "I just wanted you to know that when attacked, on our own radio network by somebody paid by our employers, our employers have thus far chosen not to defend us."

Olbermann's memo regarding Vecsey, but more important, the one he had written to Katz, illustrates his pluck. Olbermann enjoyed being a thorn in management's side. He also felt compelled to voice his opinion on issues because they needed to be discussed. And most of his complaints were valid. Management did at times play favorites. Management did at times treat many of the ESPN personnel shabbily, especially the production assistants. The network did keep the salaries of docile employees like anchors Bill Pidto, Karl Ravech, and Kenny Mayne mercilessly low—simply because they could. He watched women producers lose their shifts because they filed harassment claims. Many in management, with the exception of Anderson and a few others, did indeed lack basic people skills. In the mid-1990s, after the coordinating producers were assigned offices in the newly configured newsroom while the talent was forced to sit at small desks outside the CP's offices, Olbermann, Patrick, and Haber organized a petition protesting the new setup. Without Olbermann's stubbornness, the protest may have never happened. "Not to criticize my ex-colleagues," Olbermann said, "but one of the reasons salaries are so depressed there and the on-air staff is easily neutered is that even when there's blood in the water, they are usually far too timid."

Yet Olbermann didn't always know exactly when to apply the brakes. His memo also illustrates that.

• • •

On April 27, a Sunday, Norby Williamson, a senior coordinating producer, was asked by Walsh and Eaton to schedule an appointment with Olbermann for Monday afternoon. They agreed on four-thirty. Olbermann thought he could guess at a portion of the agenda, but he still wanted a clearer picture of what he was walking into. Patrick had phoned Williamson about his own schedule and then asked about Olbermann's meeting. Williamson said it was not disciplinary in nature but that Walsh and Eaton had a few questions. Patrick passed this information on to Olbermann.

That Monday, the meeting began with spare opening pleasantries. Walsh handed Olbermann two ESPN memos that had earlier been posted for the entire staff. Each one informed the reader that written permission from the company was required for any outside work.

Olbermann acknowledged he had received the notes. Then Walsh said, "I have to ask you about four events. Firstly, why did you appear on Craig Kilborn's show on Comedy Central without our advance permission? Secondly, why have you become a contributing editor to *Baseball America* without permission? Thirdly, why did you do the voice-overs for the public service announcements about chewing tobacco? And fourthly, when you were asked to do a sales promotional tape in May, why did you say you were refusing to do so?"

Olbermann retorted that he had been writing for *Baseball America* for years and that "The Daily Show" situation was a logistical error on the part of the show and he had always planned on telling the network.

"It is outrageous for you to be sitting there like a feudal lord talking to me like a serf, shoving these memos at me like this was the Star Chamber," Olbermann said.

The two sparred back and forth, with both men becoming increasingly agitated. Walsh finally ended the meeting, rescheduling another for the next day. On Tuesday afternoon, Olbermann met with Walsh in his office at three o'clock. Walsh took out a small index card with notes jotted on it and began reading what sounded to Olbermann like a prepared script. "We have decided, after reviewing the various issues, and considering how heated the negotiations have become, that the best course for all of us is to establish a two-week cooling-off period. During this two-week period, you will be on vacation. You will be paid, and this vacation will not count against your regular vacation time. Next week, after things have calmed down a bit, I'm sure Howard or I or both of us will be in touch with Jean to see if we can establish a framework for a new contract. We will also be glad to retroactively grant permission for the *Baseball America* articles, providing you make a written request and providing something can be worked out so that these articles can also appear on ESPN SportsZone."

"There really isn't much for me to say," said Olbermann, "as I gather from what you say that this is not a suspension, not a punitive act. This does not relate to some specific act or allegation? Am I right about that?"

"It's a two-week vacation," Walsh said. "A cooling-off period. A paid vacation."

The next five minutes were filled with uncomfortable tinkering about exactly when Olbermann's "vacation" would begin. Olbermann left the meeting and did not have contact with management the remainder of the afternoon. Management, however, did not remain quiet. Katz sent a memo to the entire on-air staff reminding them that anyone doing outside work needed permission in writing. The memo was clearly in reference to Olbermann's situation.

Olbermann later ran into anchor Gary Miller, who happened to be looking at the schedules, so Olbermann joined in. When the computer scrolled down to his name, Olbermann was surprised to see that beside his name were not the bold letters, "VAC," as was customary when employees took time off, but blank spaces.

A chill swept over Olbermann. The entire staff knew that blank spaces on the schedule meant disciplinary action. It had been that way with Tirico, Haber, Myers, Kilborn, and others when they had been suspended. Olbermann felt Walsh had misled him and called Williamson at home to seek clarification. Williamson left a long message on Olbermann's machine around seven-thirty the night of April 29. "Basically, your interpretation of this time," Williamson concluded, "can be anything that you want it to be . . ."

• • •

Olbermann announced his resignation from ESPN shortly after the start of his forced "vacation." Olbermann was accepting a position at the MSNBC network, where he would host a news talk show called "The Big Show with Keith Olbermann."

When Olbermann left ESPN in the late spring of 1997, the ratings for "SportsCenter" did not plummet, just as Walsh expected. All along, he had been saying that no matter who was at the anchor desk of "SportsCenter" or who piloted the network, ESPN had become too strong for the loss of one man to destroy it. Yet ESPN was missing a part of its soul without Olbermann. The overall intelligence of "SportsCenter" was lowered an octave. So was its mirth and edginess. Olbermann helped take "SportsCenter" to a place no other sports information show had been and probably never would go again. Away from the camera, he was one of the few inside ESPN with the clout and conscience to air legitimate grievances when others wouldn't. His departure would be felt in many ways.

In one move, Walsh had accomplished several things. Olbermann, his stiffest adversary, was now gone, and in the process, Walsh had set an example for others at ESPN with larger-than-life egos. If the network was willing to jettison one of its top talents, it was willing to dismiss anyone.

Walsh called Olbermann's final weeks and months at ESPN "sad and difficult," but he insists he tried to rescue the relationship until the very end. Walsh said the deal-breaker was Olbermann's wanting to work for ESPN as well as some of the company's competitors. That was unacceptable, Walsh said.

"By the end, Keith didn't have regard for any kind of management," said Walsh. "He just felt, 'There are different rules for me.' And we said, 'Yes, there are different rules for you, but when you go to do a commercial, just let us know you're doing it. If you want to go on Craig Kilborn, just ask us.'"

ESPN replaced Olbermann with a series of nondescript anchors who left a nondescript mark. Although Walsh continued to pan for top-reporting talent, such as Ed Werder, he limited his anchors to fairly safe, malleable choices, with the possible exception of Kolber, who returned to ESPN after a few years at Fox. None of the anchors Walsh recruited compared to Olbermann in ability. It was as if ESPN had traded away Joe Montana for an eighth-round draft pick.

Some, more than ESPN management will ever admit, were sad to see Olbermann leave, while others, like Ley, felt that he had worn out his welcome. Ley has denied saying this, but several ESPN anchors confirmed that upon hearing of Olbermann's departure, Ley yelled, "Our long national nightmare is over!" Friction between Olbermann and Ley stemmed from Olbermann's replacing him on the coveted 11:00 slot (some say Ley was bumped, others that he volunteered).

Steiner, who had worked with Olbermann in his radio years, said, "Keith is one of those tortured geniuses. That is one of the things that makes him good. But as an employee, he has a pretty short shelf life. He became bitter about ESPN after he left, which is insane because ESPN was as good to him as he was to it."

Patrick missed Olbermann immediately, but when Olbermann left and begin lobbing poison darts at ESPN in the media, Patrick became annoyed. "I used to tell Keith, 'Be happy where you are, instead of unhappy about where you were. Don't tarnish where you worked,'" said Patrick. "I got disappointed in Keith sometimes because he should be above taking shots at ESPN. If he's on your team, he's a great person to have by your side. If he isn't, you had better bring help. Bring the infantry."

"And you know what?" Patrick continued. "He was great to me, very, very beneficial to my career, especially on the air. He always had my back. For highlights, he would say, 'Did you know this fact?' He covered me. Was he quirky? For the lack of a better word, he is. But I embraced that and he never bored me."

Olbermann responded, "You have to start with the fact that THE one thing that made [their show] successful was Dan's competitiveness. Understand I mean all of this as a compliment. Dan is forever instigating, forever jousting, forever irritating your oysters, forcing you to make pearls. And I don't think he'd ever worked with anybody who could fence back at him. Three or four days after we started, I think he realized that the sparring we'd been doing since he replaced me at the CNN New York bureau in 1984 was the real thing, that it'd work on TV, too. He let his guard down, let me in, and we went straight forward from there. That's how powerful Dan Patrick's friendship and trust can be."

"But remember, too, that I left him," continued Olbermann. "Not once but really three times. I left him for ESPN2, and he called me from the all-star game in '93 telling me how many players were fans of the show, and said, 'You know, there's still time, you can change your mind.' And then I left him for real in 1997. [He said] 'You want me to say it? I have to actually say the word? Fine. Stay. Please stay.' And then apparently he was talking to Steve Bornstein [in 1998] about trying to bring me back. Something I knew nothing about at the time."

"So when Dan says I shouldn't trash my ex-employers, he means he takes it personally when I do," Olbermann said. "He supported me even though I left. . . . But he is competitive and I did leave him. And this produced a much greater conflict in him than it did in me."

• • •

On Olbermann's last day of doing "SportsCenter," he was sitting on the set several minutes before the show, lost in a sort of trance, in disbelief that this was really his last show. Then someone in the control room started talking in his ear. Olbermann had written a short good-bye but that someone had a request. "Keith, can we cut your good-bye from forty-five seconds to thirty?"

Olbermann just shook his head and then responded in typical fashion. "Can't you shave fifteen seconds from a volleyball highlight?" Olbermann said. "This is my last show, for Christ sake."

Olbermann got to keep those fifteen seconds.

16

Free Pizza

For the next several years, from 1996 to late 1998, the network made a series of smart moves and acquisitions. In 1997 it purchased the Classic Sports Network and Major League Soccer rights and began televising the increasingly popular WNBA, of which Roberts became a vocal proponent. A year later, ESPN signed another contract with its favorite brother, the NFL, to keep the Sunday night football package through the year 2005. It also officially launched *ESPN: The Magazine.*

Despite cloning and promoting itself, ESPN never forgot its roots, never deviated from its original mission, which was a love affair with sports. Live, the network broadcast baseball slugger Mark McGwire slamming his record 61st home run. And millions of sports fans showed their support by clicking their remotes to ESPN: During the McGwire–Sammy Sosa chase to break the home run record, ratings for the 11 P.M. "SportsCenter" over the first two weeks of September in 1998 were up 65 percent compared with the same period the year before. That means 1,341,000 homes were watching McGwire and Sosa blast baseballs out of the park compared to 819,000 the previous year.

And there was definitely a shakedown in the newsroom, complete with theatrical departures. New names made their way onto the Bristol campus. Jaron Jackson arrived from a Miami affiliate. Rich Eisen, a Staten Island native who came in April of 1996, started working with Stuart Scott on the late "SportsCenter." After Olbermann's departure, there were some anchors who felt that Eisen would take the coanchor chair next to Patrick. And Patrick did, too, since the two had done so many shows together. Patrick never lobbied for anyone—but he did go to dinner with Eisen in

Bristol and discussed how they would approach the show if he got the coanchor slot.

The other candidates were Mayne, Scott, and Linda Cohn, another good writer. Cohn distinguished herself in July of 1996 by skillfully handling a near riot at a boxing match. When the Polish Olympic gold medalist Andrew Golata continually punched Riddick Bowe below the belt, it led to a brawl in the ring between handlers and fans from both corners. Soon fans were throwing chairs as well as fists, as the fighting spread to the stands. ESPN was the first to show pictures from the match and the melee that followed. Cohn, anchoring that night from Bristol, smoothly related the details of what happened.

Scott had a similar experience when he coanchored the 2 A.M. show with Rece Davis the night a bomb exploded at the summer Olympics in Atlanta on July 27, 1996. Halfway through the show, Scott, Davis, and the crew decided to stay on the air indefinitely and were up until six-thirty that morning.

Mayne had made his own mark, though, in a more subtle way. When he once stepped outside the protective anchor bubble, he landed on ESPN's NFL pregame show for an interview with quarterback Randall Cunningham, whom Mayne knew when both were on the UNLV football team. When athletes speak about religion, most journalists change the subject as quickly as possible. Mayne, to his credit, probed the subject with Cunningham, who claimed he had undergone a religious conversion. Mayne asked if God really cares about game results. "Yes," Cunningham answered. "God knows who'll give him the glory. He can do that."

There have been fractious debates within ESPN over the reasons for Mayne ultimately getting the job. He was good. He deserved it. But some theorized that Mayne triumphed because he was devoid of ego and would be easier to control. Also, because he was not a household name, he could easily be jettisoned from the position if things did not work out.

"Kenny is funny, very sharp, very dry," said Patrick. "Keith was actually a little more predictable to work with in that you knew he was going to be unpredictable. I went from Bob Ley to Keith to Kenny. In my business, you can't find three more diverse personalities. But they all have one thing in common: They are very intelligent."

"Kenny took the right approach when he said, 'I can't be Keith,'" Patrick added. "He knew there was a shadow but it didn't scare him."

Chris Myers decided to join the parade of ex-ESPNers catching flights to Los Angeles and Fox. Myers feared ESPN was de-emphasizing "Up Close." When he told Walsh he was leaving, Walsh was caught by surprise. ESPN thought Myers would never leave.

"Do you really think this Fox thing will work?" Walsh asked Myers. "Yeah," Myers said, "I wouldn't be going there if I didn't."

Myers also saw something else developing. He says Walsh, who was involved in ESPN's television, radio, magazine, and Internet adventures, had too many responsibilities to be effective. Indeed, there were times when Walsh got some two hundred ESPN-related e-mails a week. He was clearly spreading himself too thin.

"I think that is one of the sad things I had seen happen," Myers said. "I was there ten years ago. I could just walk into John Walsh's office or call him on the phone and say, 'Hey, John, what about this guest or this situation,' and he was always very receptive even though he was in management. Then there was an ESPN magazine and ESPN in the Internet. Physically, he just couldn't get back to me, he couldn't be in touch with me and I assume other workers as well. And the people that they put in those places to deal with that didn't do it as well."

Walsh responded that while there was a period when his duties did increase because of ESPN's expansion into magazine publishing, he never failed to return any of Myers's phone calls.

Myers showed immediately he was willing to take chances at Fox that he would never have taken at ESPN—or been allowed to take. Soon after arriving, Myers said on the air that country music singer Garth Brooks was better off "shagging groupies" than attempting his planned tryout for baseball's San Diego Padres. Myers turned out to be right.

In early 1999, the night before Super Bowl XXXIII, Atlanta Falcons safety Eugene Robinson was arrested for solicitation of prostitution after propositioning an undercover police officer for oral sex. Robinson was the main topic of the game and of the postgame highlights after being beat for an 80-yard touchdown. Myers, while narrating the Robinson play for a late-night highlight show, said, "That gives new meaning to the phrase 'blown coverage.'"

Back at ESPN, Myers was replaced by Gary Miller, who won an audition between himself, Kremer, Roberts, and Mark Schwarz. (Schwarz, with a sharp sense of humor, describing the Los Angeles Lakers cutting of wacky basketball star Dennis Rodman, told viewers: "In the end, who would have thought Carmen Electra would get more out of her relationship with Dennis Rodman than the Lakers?")

Miller was a longtime ESPN anchor and reporter, known around the campus as gregarious and a big-time partier. Then came an embarrassing arrest when he was caught urinating out a bar window. Miller later reformed himself, eliminating his drinking and restoring his image at the network.

Miller's winsome style of interviewing contrasted with that of Myers, who rarely shunned the tough question. Once Myers bolted to Fox, the problem for "Up Close" was that the show was consistently outclassed by Jim Rome's copycat on Fox, "The Last Word." Rome had actually hosted an interview show in the early 1990s on ESPN2 and got into one of the most famous altercations in sports television history. Numerous times on his Los Angeles radio show, Rome had referred to Los Angeles Rams quarterback Jim Everett as Chris Everett, the female tennis star. It was Rome's way of saying Jim Everett was soft. When the football player came on the show, Rome called him Chris twice, and Everett warned that if he did it again, they would need to take a station break because things could get physical. Rome did not back down and called Everett Chris a third time. The 6 foot 5 inch Everett got up, tossed aside a table separating the two men, grabbed the much smaller Rome, and threw him to the floor. The entire episode was aired, and as Rome would say on his popular radio show, he got "jacked" by Everett.

The shuffling of ESPN personnel continued. On November 19, 1998, George W. Bodenheimer was named ESPN's fifth president (four months later, Bornstein was named president of ABC). Bodenheimer began in the ESPN mailroom and, unlike Bornstein, he was more personable with a manageable ego. Steiner continued in his laudable role as boxing reporter. By 1998 he had covered some fifty fights in ten years. But he was becoming bored with the sport, even offended by the continual scandals, which seemed to erupt once a week. When Mike Tyson bit a chunk out of Evander Holyfield's ear, Steiner had seen enough. He went to Walsh. "I can no longer be the cruise director of the Titanic," Steiner said. He wanted off the boxing beat, and his role on baseball play-by-play increased. Steiner got his wish.

The crush of work still played havoc with people's lives. In November of 1998, ESPN's baseball host Karl Ravech, an in-shape 33-year-old, was playing a pickup basketball game near the ESPN complex on a rare day off. Suddenly, he experienced pain in his chest and arms. Fellow on-air personality and friend Bill Pidto raced Ravech to the hospital twenty-five minutes away. "Hang in there, buddy," Pidto kept saying. Doctors told Ravech he had just suffered from a heart attack and needed angioplasty to clear a blocked artery. Ravech may have had his heart attack regardless of where he worked, but the stress of his brutal ESPN hours surely did not help.

No workers were treated worse than the production assistants. It was always a difficult job at ESPN, even when the network started in 1979, but considering the obscene money the network was now generating, much of it as a result of the undercompensated PAs, their treatment was particularly harsh. One PA said he had worked eighteen-hour days five times in his first few months. (The record is still believed to be about twenty hours in a single day.) A day off for a PA is a rarity. As senior coordinating producer Barry Sacks once told a PA: "If we call you on your off days and once or twice you say no, that's OK, but if it's three times, we start to take notice."

Breaks for production assistants are rarely put into their nine-to-twelve-hour shifts. A PA working on the weekend "SportsCenter" faced an even longer day, usually going nonstop from four in the morning to eleven at night. The company sometimes held office parties when management knew that most of the production assistants could not attend because of their schedules. That practice once drove an anchor to fire off a memo to management in support of the PAs. The pace for them is often so hectic that their version of dinner is scampering across the street to McDonald's between breaks in a game they are monitoring. They began to call this trek "the run of shame."

Just trying to get a day off is difficult for a production assistant. If a switch in the schedule is needed, a request in writing must be submitted. There was a time when PAs privately made switches on their own until a former one abused the system and then management stopped the practice cold. It got worse for the assistants when the network buckled down. One PA was not allowed to take the weekend off for his sister's wedding. Another asked for an off day four to five months in advance and didn't get it.

PAs usually undergo a temporary period of evaluation that lasts about half a year. During that probationary period, they are judged mostly by the highlight supervisors, or "hi-supes." A hi-supe can make or break a PA. They critique the shots a PA selects for highlights, time in the editing bays, attitude, and creativity. They then compile a daily report that is presented to the coordinating producers at the end of the PA's evaluation period. The CPs then vote on who stays and who does not. (David Brofsky, who appeared on a "SportsCenter" commercial, is best at retaining his people.) Politics and personality are often factors in who stays and who goes. And hi-supes still play favorites when making the proc sheet, which is the list of games to be cut. Rarely will a woman be given a big game to monitor.

An anchor can also play an important role in a production assistant's life. As a result, assistants are extremely opinionated about the talent, judging them on everything from their treatment of the PAs to the way they read the highlights the PAs slice up. PAs are required to create a clip reel of their best highlights, and if a talent mucks up a PA's best work, that hurts.

Most PAs want Dan Patrick reading their highlights. But if a PA gets a little too cute with his edits, Patrick can kill with a snide comment like:

"They're letting the kids get creative again." A smart-ass, seemingly frivolous line like that can, and has, prevented a PA from going beyond the initial trial period. Kenny Mayne is also highly popular, but he's not shy about vocalizing a PA mistake, such as the time he said that a player hit a home run "but of course we didn't see that." The PA had to explain why that particular play was not among the highlights.

Production assistants' opinions about the talent: Rich Eisen (arrogant on and off the air); Rece Davis (solid guy and good highlight reader); Steve Levy (always behind the action on the first shot); Stuart Scott (at times, difficult to match highlights with his on-air poetry); Bob Stevens (annoying voice); Linda Cohn (always reads her copy well); Pam Ward (knows her sports as well as anyone); Betsy Ross ("She should be used more, but she isn't because of that peeing-while-sitting-down thing"). Then there is Chris Berman, whom PAs consider the king of all highlight readers.

PAs wish the anchors, en masse, would forcefully address the at times depressing working conditions of the production assistants. Some talent have in the past, such as Olbermann and Jack Edwards, but PAs say that if all of the talent spoke up, the network could be a much more agreeable place to work. Realistically, PAs know such a mass demonstration will never happen, because their place in the ESPN hierarchy is somewhere between a desk lamp and a hamburger.

The tale that best illustrates ESPN's attitude toward some of its lower-level personnel is the disheartening story involving graphic operator Joe McGinn.

McGinn was well-liked at the network and worked closely with the production assistants. McGinn's popularity was due in part to his courageous struggle against liver disease. Walking with a limp and often fighting fevers and bouts of weakness, McGinn rarely complained or missed work. One day in early March of 1999, despite not feeling well, McGinn still made it into work but was forced to leave after only thirty minutes. Later, he died from a massive heart attack, which was related to his disease.

Those people who worked closely with McGinn were devastated. And because McGinn was a one-time manager for the University of Connecticut basketball team, Coach Jim Calhoun dedicated the school's NCAA Tournament run, which was just beginning when McGinn died, to him. Each player marked his pants with a black band in honor of McGinn.

Connecticut was a top seed in the NCAA that year, and when such a prominent school dedicates its postseason to a fallen manager, that is news. It appeared that ESPN was indeed planning to cover the tragic story and certainly mention it during their exhaustive tournament coverage.

One PA printed out almost a dozen stories on McGinn that were running on the wire and handed them out to the 7 P.M. "SportsCenter" producer Seth Markman, the 11 P.M. producer Cameron Penn, and Mike Moore on the assignment desk. Each said he was working on the story.

Nothing that day, or in the immediate days following his death, ran on "SportsCenter" about McGinn. UConn went on to win the NCAA title. When the team was cutting down the net in celebration, Calhoun ordered that one piece of string be left hanging for McGinn. It was then that Vitale and college sport anchor Chris Fowler addressed McGinn's death.

ESPN's handling of the news involving McGinn angered almost every PA in the building who knew him. To the production assistants, the lack of attention to McGinn's death reinforced their opinion of ESPN's regard for them—they were nothing more than replaceable parts, almost less than human, expendable and exploited. The coordinating producers involved in the decision not to air the story vehemently defended their actions, which angered the PAs even more.

Plans were already underway for PAs to form an organization, or even a union, and the McGinn fiasco served as an accelerant. More than a dozen PAs met quietly and created a list of demands, requiring the network to meet or a walkout would be staged. But the meeting became fractured and no definite agenda was created.

Still, the PAs remained highly motivated to better their working conditions, and a small group of PA representatives met with three coordinating producers. Their idea of creating a review board of PA representatives to meet monthly with management to discuss problems, especially the long hours, was promptly rejected. ESPN could not allow that kind of unified dissension, especially among a group of lowly-paid employees the company could not do without. The last thing ESPN wanted was for PAs to become a single voice that could then make demands.

The other ideas the PAs raised were met with an indifferent "We'll look into that." When one PA said that was the worst thing they could hear, they were told, "We'll look into that."

One request on the agenda ESPN did meet—a relatively cheap and simple request—was for a production assistant pizza night. Every other Saturday, the company springs for several large pizzas, and a giant sub on the odd Saturdays. So at least twice a month, the PAs don't have to make the "run of shame" to the golden arches.

Most PAs appreciated the free food, but they were not placated. Some remained bitter. One PA, soon after he quit, wrote a companywide e-mail expressing a number of frustrations. It concluded: "One more thing, just for the record, yes, Barry Sacks did accuse me of faking my back injury just to get a couple of months off. So you all have wild accusations to look forward to when you do leave."

• • •

While gambling at the network no longer reached the bizarre addictive levels in ESPN's early days, it was still a problem, no matter how much ESPN management tried to stop it. In March of 1998, during an NCAA Tournament game, Stanford was trailing Rhode Island by six points, with about one minute left. The oddsmakers had given Rhode Island five points before the contest, and several employees in the newsroom, some of whom had wagered $500 on the game, gathered anxiously around the monitors as the last seconds ticked away. Stanford, making a miraculous comeback and with less than ten seconds of play, had taken the lead by six points, thus covering the spread. Then a Rhode Island player made a wild half-court shot, which meant Stanford won by only four points. In the ESPN newsroom, some watching the monitors went ballistic, since the meaningless shot meant lost money. Suddenly, people were throwing things and kicking over trash cans in frustration.

The famous pools—for NCAA tournaments, Super Bowls, NBA Finals, even NASCAR—attract the largest number of ESPN bettors. At various points in the 1990s, management, fearing the numerous pools could affect ESPN's image if word of them ever got out, sent memos threatening that gambling of any type would not be tolerated. On August 30, 1991, Walsh distributed one memo to the production staff that read in part: "Our viewers will not tolerate the knowledge that a newsperson who is supposedly objective has introduced a bias into his work, based on how he has bet on a game. In fact, the simple knowledge that someone in ESPN's production department is associated with gambling, regardless of how the events have been reported, may well bring into question everything we have put on our air. Our credibility in this regard is vitally important and maintaining it is the responsibility of every person in every job in the department. We cannot allow ourselves to be compromised in this regard."

Four years later, executive Bob Eaton posted a similar note, warning that any type of gambling on company property could result in an employee's immediate dismissal.

None of those memos had any effect and the pools continued to flourish. In 1997 there was a "masters" golf pool in which the bettor picked five golfers, combined the score of those players, and the lowest won. One year the payoff was $3,000. In one NCAA pool, nicknamed "gold country," there were 125 entries, including several prominent ESPN anchors.

And then there's the macabre death pool. ESPNers throw in some money, pick a celebrity, and when that person dies, the winner collects the pool. The day Princess Diana was killed in an automobile accident, there was actually some cheering and high-fives on the Bristol campus.

• • •

ESPN's reporters continued to be the best at what they did. Jimmy Roberts had gained so much respect in the golf world that after Tiger Woods's stunning victory in the 1997 Masters tournament, Woods blew off CNN/SI and Fox to sit down one-on-one with Roberts. After the interview aired on "SportsCenter," it replayed on "Good Morning America" the following day. Kremer reported a dazzling and disturbing piece on NFL players' addiction to pain-killing medication. By 1997 Mortensen had at least one front office or player source on each of the league's thirty teams. Aldridge became the most respected television face in NBA locker rooms and executive offices.

ESPN's competitors had their talented reporters as well. Peter King, at *Sports Illustrated* CNN/SI, was among the best in the business. Ivan Maisel is a smart college football analyst for CNN/SI, and Stephen A. Smith did a solid job covering the NBA. On Fox, Sam Marchiano, the daughter of Sal and a one-time ESPN New York bureau producer, is perhaps that network's best overall reporting talent. Armen Keteyian of HBO and CBS is a respected reporter in television as is John Czarnecki from Fox.

Yet as the 1990s were coming to a close, the television decade belonged to ESPN—and it was the network's reporters that gave ESPN its edge. The anchors and their roles constantly shifted. They moved from 11 o'clock to 6:30, from weekdays to the weekend. The Kremers of the network, the reporters, did not. They were always there, dependable as Cal Ripken Jr., relaying information no other network had. Fewer viewers were tuning in to see the Patricks and Olbermanns because, well, there were no more Patricks nor Olbermanns. And never will be. It was almost as if the next ten years were shaping up to be the decade of the reporter, not the star anchor.

Epilogue: What a Story

In May 1999, ESPN temporarily ceased all hiring, not because it wasn't making money—it was still earning bundles—but because parent Disney was riding rough financial waters. Disney stock had dropped to $29.50 a share, down from $40.62 just several months earlier (Disney's stock is the subject of constant conversation at ESPN). Incredibly, the day had come when ESPN, shunned by Texaco after the Getty sale some fifteen years ago because the network was financially unattractive, was carrying Mickey Mouse on its shoulders.

As the year 2000 approached, Fox, which had spent more than $1 billion in the last part of the decade to build its regional sports concept, was closing the gap on ESPN, but ESPN still held a commanding lead. ESPN was reaching 76 million households, ESPN2 65 million, and ESPNews 12 million. Fox Sports Net reached 68 million total. The ratings showed that Fox's 11 P.M. highlight show trailed "SportsCenter" by a five-to-one margin. Fox counters that when the numbers are examined from 10 P.M. to midnight, they are much closer.

Olbermann was the effective reporter, and skilled writer, he had always been during his ESPN stint and most of his television career. And ESPN clearly remained threatened by him, as evidenced by several vicious—and anonymous—quotes about Olbermann from an ESPN executive in a late-1999 *Washington Post* story. Olbermann remains a highly visible target because he is so good and because he can be so polarizing. Olbermann's face remains plastered across many major league ballparks as a part of Fox's promotional campaign. In the ninth inning of an Atlanta Braves and Houston Astros baseball game in August of 1999, player Carl Everett smashed a double into left field, the ball careening off Olbermann's portrait. Braves broadcaster Skip Caray said: "Carl Everett just did something a lot of people in sports have wanted to do for a long time. He hit Keith Olbermann in the face with a line drive."

Fox was incapable of matching specialty shows like the impressive "SportsCentury" series, a yearlong project profiling the fifty greatest athletes of the past one hundred years. Patrick hosted the shows with a regal presence, while reducing his "SportsCenter" duties to one or two shows a week and increasing his ESPN radio duties. "I wanted to pull back," Patrick said, "because 'SportsCenter' is a young man's game." While Patrick voluntarily distanced himself from the show, Kenny Mayne, who had replaced Olbermann, was demoted in August of 1999 and no longer regularly worked the Sunday "SportsCenter." Instead, he was put on less prestigious weekday shows. He was told the news by management just several days before doctors induced labor on his wife. An ESPN spokesman denied that Mayne had been demoted, insisting that Mayne had simply had a shift in assignments.

(ESPN's timing was unfathomable when considered against the events of 1996. In that year Mayne's wife Laura gave birth to premature twins. One was Creighton, and he was stillborn. The other, Connor, weighed just 1 pound and 7 ounces. Connor died six months later. In August of 1997, Laura miscarried, and that tragic event was followed by another lost baby in 1998. Happily, the Maynes now have a healthy girl named Riley Hope.

Through all of ESPN's permutations, not only in recent years, but in its two-decade history, Berman still kept his childlike love of sports. When Berman began at ESPN, he could not believe someone was actually paying him good money to talk sports. He would get up in the morning, giddy, bouncing around his apartment, excited about the day ahead.

What has changed about Berman is that everything about him has become bigger—his talent, his ego, and his paycheck. One of Berman's favorite phrases is that he is "the pope of Connecticut." And he acts like it. The crew of the NFL morning show is supposed to rehearse about thirty minutes before air. Over the years, Berman has gone from showing up on time to appearing five minutes before rehearsal to making an entrance five minutes before the show and crowing, "Boys, how was rehearsal?"

And he is still likely to say anything on the air. During the 1999 NFL draft in April, the New England Patriots drafted center Damien Woody. That led the quick-thinking Berman to make the reckless quip, "Now the Patriots have a woody." When the Patriots later picked running back Kevin Faulk, a technician in the production truck joked, "Maybe Chris will say, 'Now the Patriots have a Faulking woody.'"

During ESPN's preseason broadcast of the San Francisco–Seattle game, Berman introduced reporter Melissa Stark by saying, "Hope you're staying out of trouble out there." Stark looked momentarily surprised by the comment but carried on with her report. Berman, who probably would have never made such a statement to a male reporter, apologized to Stark and viewers after a commercial break.

What has never changed about Berman is his bubbling personality and his genuine affection for sports. During the summer of 1999, Berman awoke in his hotel room in Cooperstown, New York, for ESPN's coverage of the Baseball Hall of Fame. It was seven o'clock in the morning, and the first thing he did was walk to the hotel window and open the curtains. After the sun hit him in the face, Berman thought, "You know what? This is going to be a great day."

Berman remains a simple man. He has no personal e-mail address, and his wallet is stuffed with little pieces of paper with phone numbers and names of people he owes return phone calls. And since Berman is one of the most recognized faces on television, his wallet sometimes bulges out of his back pocket with requests for his time.

Berman always has three things in his possession. A small picture of late anchor Tom Mees, a Juan Marichal baseball card, and the business card of Alan L. Bean, an ESPN fan and one of only twelve men to walk on the moon. "I keep that last card around," Berman said, "because it's cool."

Berman still has his critics both inside and outside the network. Few, however, will dispute the high level of talent he has maintained for the past twenty-one years. Berman has acknowledged the two biggest challenges ESPN faces: Ensuring its brand does not saturate the airwaves to the point of nausea, and keeping Fox at bay.

There is something else. The network has become grossly smug in its dominance. ESPN's position is that it answers to no one and that attitude manifests itself in a number of ways. It is not unusual for former employees, critical of the network in the press, to get a phone call from an ESPN official asking why they are making negative statements about the network, as if they had no right to speak their mind, despite the fact ESPN is "in their rearview mirrors."

This bold arrogance has also led to the watering down of the network's journalistic standards. Robin Roberts appeared at a political function in support of presidential candidate Bill Bradley, a terrific breach of protocol, especially since Roberts also does work for ABC News. Chris Fowler has attacked ESPN's incisive reports on the various abuses in college athletics, aligning himself more with the colleges than his own network. "Sports-

Center" is filled with stories of athletes driving drunk and with subsequent commentaries from ESPN personalities condemning such acts, yet Dan Patrick and Rich Eisen do beer advertisements for Coors.

ESPN's hubris also carries over to its business practices. When ESPN was bidding for the NASCAR rights late in 1999, the first portion of its written presentation was spent boasting about itself instead of addressing how the network would help the racing organization. A NASCAR official said ESPN's smugness was one reason that the organization changed networks.

There are other dents. In May 1999, ESPN sued major league baseball in Federal court to block baseball's termination of the network's regular-season deal after the 1999 season. Baseball was furious with ESPN's plan to move three Sunday night games in September to ESPN2 in favor of more popular NFL games. The network faced the frightening possibility of a baseball-less schedule, with a gap in its programming as large as the waist of an offensive lineman. The lawsuit was eventually settled and baseball remains on ESPN.

Then ESPN, outbid by NBC and Turner for NASCAR, was outbid by CBS for the rights to NCAA college basketball. CBS paid $6.2 billion for 11 years. Despite the bad news, Berman remains unfazed. He feels ESPN will stay on top forever.

And, despite its ills, he's probably right.

Says Berman. "Lately, there is a lot of revisionist history. People saying I'm out now only for myself or that ESPN isn't as good as it used to be. That's all hogwash. We were cult heroes once and I know those days are over, but look at where we once were, and look where we are now."

"What a story," Berman said. "What a story!"

Author's Note
Fall 2001

The National Football League's showcase game is the Super Bowl, and it is about excess. It is a week of glorious, ungodly excess, especially when a New York team is in the game, as the football Giants were in Super Bowl XXXV in January 2001. In this environment of $3,000 scalped tickets, celebrity parties, and fat cats in fat limousines, the network from the tiny city of Bristol, Connecticut, which at one point in its history could barely afford a parcel of land, showed even the biggest of spenders what excess is all about.

The media goes overboard in covering the championship game. But no media entity covers it as ESPN does. They treat the Super Bowl like it is the presidential inauguration.

This particular Super Bowl featured two unlikely teams: the New York Giants, one of the best franchises in sports, and the Baltimore Ravens, owners of the best defense in the history of football. The story lines from this game were not overly dramatic. In fact, some journalists expected it to be one of the most boring ever.

That did not stop ESPN executives from committing resources as Army generals readying for a worldwide conflict.

ESPN occupied more than 200 hotel rooms in the Tampa area, site of Super Bowl XXXV, dwarfing the number of rooms held by any other media outlet. Its overall cost of covering the game ran into the millions of dollars. Its reporters and anchors, dozens of them, swarmed over the various press conferences. The network covered the annual state of the league address from Commissioner Paul Tagliabue live on ESPN2. ESPN radio set up headquarters in the lobby of the Tampa Marriott, shuttling in guests and studio hosts.

The network's biggest names were all there: Berman, Kremer, Kolber, Mortensen, Tirico, Werder, Sal Paolantonio, Tom Jackson, and Scott, among many others. The number of personnel was simply crushing. "They send that many people not because it is necessary," said one reporter from CNN/SI, "but because they can."

This approach has its strengths and weaknesses. By bringing its best reporters to the Super Bowl, ESPN is assured of getting top material. Kremer had her annual smart Super Bowl story, this one on the security precautions teams had taken to ensure their players stayed away from the notorious strip clubs in the Tampa area, where police were strictly enforcing a six-foot bubble between the exotic dancers and club patrons. She is so trusted by NFL teams that the Ravens gave her a video they filmed of linebacker Ray Lewis addressing players in summer training camp only days after he was cleared of double-murder charges for the stabbing deaths of two people the night of the pervious year's Super Bowl. In fact, Lewis would be a constant theme in ESPN's Super Bowl coverage (Lewis graced the cover of *ESPN: The Magazine* with a first-person story, and network executives privately boasted about the scoop, with ESPN representatives even shoving the magazine under every hotel room door in the main Super Bowl media hotel), leading to an embarrassing incident involving one of its anchors.

Kremer also broke new ground in other ways. Her son William was born the previous Super Bowl. Kremer worked intensely while pregnant, even conducting meetings from her hospital room.

This time around, William was celebrating his first birthday, and mom refused to miss it. So she brought William with her to Super Bowl XXXV, and ESPN paid for a two-bedroom hotel room to accommodate mother, father, and son.

The network takes care of its stars, especially Kremer, who has produced more important stories than anyone in its history. However, Kremer and other female stars at the network, like Robin Roberts, have been lucky. They have not suffered the same indignities at the hands of male ESPN employees some ESPN women have.

Mortensen broke his usual scoops, including coaching news on Giants defensive coordinator John Fox and Ravens defensive coordinator Marvin Lewis. Werder and Paolantonio presented solid reports on both teams, and Berman and Tirico played skilled and gracious ringleaders to the various players brought to the set and numerous reports from the field.

It was, to be sure, from start to finish, an impressive production, but with a clear ESPN signature: overkill, overkill, and more overkill.

ESPN's Super Bowl coverage also showed what is sometimes wrong with such a blanket approach. Despite ESPN's mammoth staff, the much smaller cable sports network CNN/SI, which sent a fraction of the personnel ESPN did, often out-hustled ESPN to gain better, higher-quality stories, such as reporter Josie Carp's piece on Giants safety Sam Garnes, in which the two went back to Garnes's high school in the Bronx.

(CNN/SI also distinguished itself in another way. The network completely changed its entire presentation on its late highlight show. Instead of having two anchors interact only with a TelePrompTer and each other, the network has gone with a more creative approach. The thirty-minute signature show features the two anchors sitting in comfortable studio chairs, with another anchor standing on the other side of the set playing air traffic controller with stories, questions from telephone callers, and Internet inquiries. The CNN/SI duo of Fred Hickman and Vince Cellini are also less self-important than many of their ESPN counterparts.)

Additionally, ESPN is such a big family—with ESPNews, ESPN2, and ESPN Classic, just to name a few siblings—with so many mouths to feed that repetition is inevitable. And with all those minutes to fill, anchors and reporters often reach to fill time, such as when the normally able and serious reporter Solomon Wilcox quoted Robert Frost while covering the Hall of Fame ceremonies. The result was awkward and forced.

As often happens in such a high-profile setting as the Super Bowl, egos swell. This occurs in every form of journalism. Two sports columnists at the *New York Daily News* have actually gotten into bitter arguments over who gets the better seat in the press box. Since the stakes are higher in television, however, the egos are even more overwhelming, and there was no better example of this than an incident involving Stuart Scott and Ray Lewis on Super Bowl media day.

Media day is one of the biggest circuses in sports. Every media type covers it, interviewing players as they stand or sit in assigned areas and answer sometimes hundreds of questions. In this carnival atmosphere, it is difficult to stay neutral. Once, former MTV personality Julie Brown sat in the lap of a Buffalo Bills player, embarrassing herself as well all professional women journalists who are tarnished by such silly actions.

Anyone who covers a team or player long enough can develop feelings of friendship; the trick is to remain as independent as possible.

This is something many personalities at ESPN continue to struggle with. Berman is an unabashed homer for the Bills and San Francisco 49ers, sometimes polluting his words about either team with such corny affection that on those subjects he is practically unlistenable. Scott makes the same mistakes. He is a close friend of Michael Jordan's, despite the fact that as an anchor Scott must on occasion report on issues involving the former NBA superstar, who is now general manager of the Washington Wizards.

In fact, that is exactly what happened in February 2001. Scott sat down with Jordan for a lengthy discussion that ran in four parts on various ESPN programs. It was what print reporters call a "twinkie" interview— sweet on the outside, soft in the middle. Because Scott is a friend of Jordan's, he lobbed softballs at him, refusing to sternly challenge Jordan on his absentee style of management, even though Jordan has been criticized by his own players for rarely being around the team.

What Scott was thinking on Super Bowl media day in the minutes after Ray Lewis had finished a tense hour of interviews with over 100 reporters, only he knows. Lewis, whose double-murder charge and subsequent trial became one of the biggest stories of the NFL season—especially after he was fined $250,000 by the commissioner for lying to police—grew agitated over some of the questions and was clearly perturbed by the end.

After the session was over, according to an Internet reporter who posted the account on a CBS Sports web site, Lewis stepped down from his podium, and as he began to walk away, Scott met Lewis, put his arm around the Pro Bowl linebacker, and within earshot of several reporters, told Lewis, "Hey, Ray, fuck them, man." Scott was referring to the probing journalists. Scott's actions, more those of a friend than a journalist (didn't he realize that he, too, is "them"?) underscored the contradictions of the Super Bowl—and the biggest sports network that covers the biggest game.

• • •

A lot has happened to the proud—and paranoid—cable television network since the release of *ESPN: The Uncensored History*. Contradiction is indeed the word when it comes to ESPN, a network capable of producing both greatness and ugliness in the same instant.

In February 2001, in honor of Black History Month, ESPN ran a series of slick and heartfelt tributes to famous black sports figures like Jackie Robinson; filmmaker Spike Lee narrated. They were sharp-looking and smart—just what you would expect from Lee.

A short time before these spots aired, however, ESPN radio, which has dozens of employees in production but very few minorities or women, lost one of its only black producers. He quit out of frustration, feeling that blacks had little opportunity to advance into the upper echelon of the division. The handful of black production employees across the network have voiced this complaint numerous times.

ESPN also found itself involved in another controversy after the book's publication. In December 2000, an "Outside the Lines" investigative team followed baseball agent Jeff Moorad as he negotiated with various clubs, including the New York Yankees, for the services of his client, free agent Manny Ramirez. ESPN, in one of the more intriguing stories the network has ever done, shadowed Moorad through each of his negotiations, camera in tow.

During one session, Yankees general manager Brian Cashman, through a speakerphone and with cameras rolling in Moorad's office, tells Moorad the team has an interest in Ramirez. Neither Moorad nor, more importantly, ESPN told Cashman that their conversation was being recorded.

When the story aired, it was a fascinating bird's-eye view of the high-stakes world of baseball negotiations, yet for all of the story's passion and intelligence, it was a piece of questionable ethics. It is one thing for an agent to violate the trust of Cashman, but it is another for a professional network to do so. Cashman was outraged.

"I had no idea I was being taped," said Cashman. "I spoke to ESPN and Jeff Moorad regarding the issue. I handled it with the individuals involved and I'll leave it at that."

The Yankees were so angry that they investigated whether ESPN and/or Moorad had violated state laws that prevent taping a phone conversation without the knowledge of all parties. The club actually considered filing criminal charges against the agent and ESPN. But Moorad and ESPN did not violate any criminal codes, and in fact, even before the story aired, ESPN lawyers had cleared the story of any legal liability.

ESPN chose not to inform Cashman to keep the conversation genuine and catch the emotion of the moment. Of course, that is what any journalist wants, but ESPN grossly erred. In trying to capture a great story, it sacrificed a shade of its principles.

In defending itself, ESPN offered an end-justifies-the-means defense. Executives tried to say that everyone involved in the story agreed with the approach.

That was not true.

Behind the scenes, there was a tremendous debate, with some of the old-school producers vehemently objecting to the use of the Cashman portion of the story.

What few people outside ESPN know is that one of the story's key producers, thoroughly disgusted with the network's decision, asked to be completely disassociated from the piece.

ESPN executives, despite the questionable reporting tactics, were privately ecstatic with the story. The sordid way in which part of it was reported seemed to bother few of them.

ESPN even found itself entangled in a controversy involving its popular web site, ESPN.com. Rob Neyer is the hard-working senior baseball writer for the site and is as passionate a journalist as there is. And like many baseball writers, he is a geek when it comes to statistics. He loves them. Neyer recently wrote several stories about Babe Ruth's walk record and how it has been updated due to some lost walks. In another article, he decried the Elias Sports Bureau, the great statistical company that is partners with ESPN and the sports leagues, claiming that Major League Baseball had updated its records and Elias had not.

ESPN pulled Neyer's article off its web site without explanation, and Neyer responded by posting it on his own personal site, complete with an attack on ESPN for its lack of journalistic integrity. Neyer's main argument was that he should be allowed to criticize Elias but was censured because of ESPN's close ties to the statistical giant.

Neyer wrote: "A note to readers of my ESPN.com column. Said column will be on hiatus . . . I cannot discuss this matter further, so please don't bother sending me inquisitive e-mail messages, because I won't respond (unless you're my mom, and I'm not even sure about her). I'm in good health and in good spirits and I'll be back, as the column will presumably return next Monday. In the meantime, I hope to post a few random comments in this space, beginning with what you'll find below. Thanks for your patience and continuing support."

Speculation inside ESPN was that Neyer's column had been suspended; the network demanded that Neyer not publicly discuss the issue further.

There were additional headaches in ESPN's dot-com world. It is well known how harsh a workplace ESPN can be. The network pays its non-stars the television equivalent of minimum wage, and the hours are rough. People tend to develop a thick outer shell, which can lead to insensitive remarks and actions.

One manifestation of this happened in early 2001, when the network posted an atrocious item on its web site about the Oklahoma State men's basketball team. Ten members affiliated with the squad had been killed in a plane crash in February 2001.

The item ESPN posted suggested Pink Floyd songs that athletic teams could use as theme music and said the Oklahoma State's team song should be "Learning to Fly." The comment was in extreme poor taste and understandably angered some of the families of the people who died as well as members of the university.

ESPN removed the item and issued a statement: "The 'Learning to Fly' reference was not designed to be insensitive. Oklahoma State has just come off a serious tragedy and showed that with their win on Monday night they are able to focus on basketball by rallying together as a team to overcome adversity. We do see how this could be construed as insensitive, so we decided to take it down."

(Other than this major gaffe, ESPN's site is still remarkably popular and successful, at times attracting over five million viewers in a single month, far exceeding the numbers of any other sports web site, including competitor Foxsports.com. As ESPN was dealing with its embarrassing situation, Fox was making plans to thoroughly revamp its web site, including cutting back on staff. Yet some of the content on the site remains interesting even if few people are seeing it. Jim Rome's take on famed former Indiana and current Texas Tech coach Bobby Knight's commenting about the NCAA tournament for an Internet company was witty. "I can't believe that one of the greatest basketball coaches of all time is an Internet tout," Rome wrote. "I can't wait to see him on Saturday mornings, sitting on a set . . . giving me his five-star, triple-lock, guaranteed pick of the year and asking me for my credit card number.")

The network made news of a different kind when one of its own, reporter Melissa Stark, left the big stage of ESPN for the grand stage of ABC's "Monday Night Football." She joined Hall of Fame running back Eric Dickerson, comedian Dennis Miller, analyst Dan Fouts, and the steady Al Michaels.

Of course there was lots of synergy between ABC and ESPN in regard to "Monday Night Football." Miller was the subject of a "Sunday Conversation," and there were constant "Monday Night" tidbits in ESPN's glossy magazine as well as on ESPN.com. And no, the synergy does not stop with football. At the end of UCLA's upset of Stanford on ABC in February 2001, Brent Musburger, after the final buzzer sounded, exclaimed, "And UCLA moves to the lead [story] on 'SportsCenter!'"

While Miller attracted the most national media attention, it was Stark who attracted the demographics ABC was trying to reach: young men. Stark's attractive exterior is often the focus of viewers, but her reporting skills are solid. What Stark discovered was that while she had been a high profile personality at ESPN, it doesn't compare to the number of viewers who watch football on Monday night. Everything about her was severely scrutinized by fans and the media. Even ESPNers watched her every move, talking openly about everything from her friendships to her clothes.

Actually, according to an ESPN and ABC official, one of the top executives of "Monday Night Football" asked Stark to wear tight shirts and sweaters during the broadcasts to accentuate her figure. Stark obliged.

• • •

The sexual harassment allegations in the book drew the most rabid reaction from ESPN. Instead of admitting that mistakes were made and leaving it at that, ESPN went on the attack, sinking its teeth into anyone who had dared criticize the cable station. I was a troublemaker and unreliable. Women complainants were lying or exaggerating. Keith Olbermann was called the main source for the book, which is perhaps the single silliest thing ever stated about it.

The network privately threatened current and former employees with retaliation if they spoke to me about being sexually harassed. An anchor and coordinating producer chastised a former woman producer for granting an interview for the book.

John Walsh began making false claims that the book's publisher, Taylor, only publishes scandal books, a statement made to scare potential sources away from me and to discredit the book to the media. In fact, the company, which specializes in gardening and feel-good sports books, has never done the type of book Walsh described. When I confronted Walsh, he defended his statement by saying that is what he was told by someone else.

Just five weeks before the book's scheduled publication in April 2000, ESPN executives were so busy having meetings on how to deal with impending negative publicity from the book, it is a wonder the network was able to stay on the air. Walsh began meeting with female anchors, producers, and production assistants in small groups. According to several women who were participants, he again attempted to discredit me personally. He repeated the claim about Taylor (knowing that it was false) and said that I was a disreputable reporter and that the *New York Times* was about to fire me (I am still gainfully employed at the newspaper). He also asked that women not speak to the media or to me.

(In one of the meetings, anchor Linda Cohn exclaimed, "Hey John, I've never been sexually harassed!" to which one producer muttered, "Count yourself lucky, Linda.")

Around the same time, another top ESPN executive, Bob Eaton, met with coordinating producers, warned them about the book, and asked that no one speak to reporters after its release.

ESPN had, for almost a month, tried to get an early copy of the book. A few weeks prior to the April 5 publication, they did—many advance copies had been sent to potential reviewers, so the network could have gotten it from a number of sources. After reading through it, executives immediately went into an even more aggressive mode of damage control.

Eight days before the book was scheduled to hit bookstores, ESPN's human resources director, John T. Rose, sent a company-wide e-mail that included a copy of ESPN's sexual harassment policy. Rose claimed the network "periodically" redistributes the policy, though several employees told me that they had not seen it in the previous five years. In the book, several current and former employees, as well as the NAACP, are critical of the lack of blacks in key management and editorial positions. Some maintain blacks have routinely been passed over for promotions because of race. Rose would later, again via e-mail, send another memo, this one "reaffirming" the company's fair employment practices.

The ESPN hierarchy was not done. In the book I describe a female producer who, while working for ESPN radio in the early 1990s, was the target of a male coworker who made inappropriate sexual advances. When rebuffed, he became frustrated, and one day cursed at her in front of several members of the staff. He was eventually fired by ESPN (though Walsh rehired him in 1999 as an advisor for a special project).

Having read my account of the situation, Walsh and executive Rosa Gatti phoned the woman, now a freelance producer for ESPN, at her home in Florida. Both asked her to repudiate her claims in the book that Walsh had made derogatory remarks about her in a performance evaluation as retribution for her filing a harassment complaint against the man, who was a close friend of Walsh's. And that Gatti, at the time of the harassment episodes, had tried to talk the woman out of filing a harassment complaint against ESPN (she logged the complaint with human resources anyway). The woman refused to discredit the book.

Five days after rebuking Walsh and Gatti, in late 2000, she was informed by Eaton that a freelance assignment previously given to her had been assigned to someone else. She lost approximately $7,000 worth of work. ESPN insists the timing of her lost assignment was coincidental.

In the aftermath of the book's release, ESPN public relations officials phoned several media critics in advance, including Tom Hoffarth from the *Los Angeles Daily News*, asking him not to review it. He did anyway. Several media writers who wrote positive stories about the book received phone calls from ESPN public relations officials the day their stories ran, asking why they did not slam the book or why ESPN's perspective was not given more attention. In one case, Mike Soltys, who works with Chris LaPlaca in the ESPN communications department, went a step further. When Hoffarth quoted me, saying how stunned I was at the network's overall hypocrisy when it came to the book, Soltys sent the writer an e-mail stating that I had asked for ESPN's personnel records. That was a lie.

LaPlaca told me that ESPN would not use its resources to attack the book. That also turned out to be not true. With the network's permission, Patrick used his radio show, which reaches millions of people almost every day, to denounce the book.

"[ESPN is] twenty years old, we make mistakes, and we do not deny that [but] this is not a true representation of where I work," Patrick said on his show soon after the book's release, using almost the exact language Walsh, LaPlaca, Soltys, and others did. "This guy was taking any angle he could to get something juicy. A lot of innocent people [are] raked over the coals in this book [by] former employees."

The fact that none of this was true did not seem to matter to Patrick. The actual number of ex-employees used as source material for the book was very small, and of course Patrick never bothered to explain which "innocent" person was "raked over the coals."

He even attacked me personally, asserting that I was bitter because I had sought an on-camera position but was not offered employment. That was the same false statement executives at ESPN were making off the record to the media, and Patrick was simply parroting it on his show. In actuality, the network had contacted me about a job, not vice versa.

Some of the reaction from ESPN was just plain goofy: Bob Ley ripped the book while speaking to a group of college students.

ESPN's hypersensitivity was interesting, if not hypocritical. The network limited my access as much as possible, but when one of the major sports entities did the same thing to them, ESPN whined loud and long. Fox, NBC, and TNT snatched the broadcast rights to major NASCAR events from ESPN and other networks with a six-year, $2.4 billion contract. It was a move that stunned the network. At one time, the well-produced ESPN racing show "RPM 2Night" was a welcome sight inside every NASCAR event and the show often went on the road, broadcasting from various race sites. But after the network switch, NASCAR told ESPN that "RPM" was no longer welcome inside some major NASCAR events and that they would have to set up their production facilities far from the tracks—in some cases, a mile away from the course.

NASCAR's moving of "RPM" to the outskirts was so Fox's racing show, "Totally NASCAR," could set up inside and get the better access to the drivers.

Whoever pays the broadcast rights to a sport receives the better treatment. It has been that way for decades. ESPN and ABC paid billions for NFL rights and are coddled by the league, while NBC, which does not have the NFL, is all but ignored by it. It is common for ESPN reporters covering professional football to receive access print reporters can only dream of, and NFL public relations officials are not shy in saying that since ESPN helps pay the NFL's bills, they get better access.

Still ESPN, not used to being told no, acted with predictable petulance when NASCAR told them to set up their tents elsewhere. The network leaked NASCAR's plans to the media, hoping to embarrass the organization into changing its policy, with ESPN pit bull Soltys leading the attack. To its credit, NASCAR did not back down.

Soltys even went so far as to tell one newspaper that NASCAR's move would affect ESPN's "journalistic integrity," an absurd notion, especially for a media organization known to selectively apply journalistic integrity. For instance, during the winter of 2001, the NHL All-Star Game was being played in Denver's Pepsi Center and broadcast on ABC. The ESPN/ABC commentators would only say "Denver" when coming back from a commercial break, such as "Welcome back to Denver."

The reason "Pepsi Center" was not mentioned by the commentators was that Coke is the official soft drink of professional hockey.

Only a few days later, commercialism would again affect ESPN's news content. It happened during "SportsCenter," which on this night was being anchored by John Anderson and Rich Eisen. Early in the show, seconds after a Sacramento Kings–Milwaukee Bucks highlight, came a promotion for that month's *ESPN: The Magazine*, which featured a lengthy profile of superstar Chris Webber. The promo was not during a commercial but inserted in the middle of the highlight package.

Journalistic integrity? Imagine the *Washington Post*, in the middle of a story on the Redskins, three paragraphs down, inserting a paragraph reading, "Buy a subscription to our paper!"

• • •

Other factors contributed to ESPN's overreaction to the book. One of the axioms of the news business is that journalists are the most thin-skinned of all subjects. ESPN's armor has the consistency of toilet tissue. One reason lies in its history. The network was once ridiculed and several times in the 1980s nearly went bankrupt. For that reason, a sense of insecurity remains with some of the top executives who have been with the company since the beginning.

There is little chance the *New York Times*, which has been the subject of countless books, would react with the kind of venom ESPN did. One of ESPN's biggest complaints about the book was that it contained a disproportionate amount of material on its sexual harassment problems; however, fewer than fifty pages of the three-hundred-plus page work, some seventeen percent, focused on sexual harassment. By far the majority of the book details ESPN's emergence as a cultural phenomenon, documenting the network's rise to where it is now, the premier source for sports news.

Recently I spoke with former ESPN anchor Karie Ross, a hero to many women at the network after denouncing sexual harassment in a fiery speech during a company-wide meeting in the late 1980s. In the aftermath of her brave remarks, Ross says the network retracted a two-year contract extension. One producer—who is still at ESPN—called her at home so many times for dates she changed her phone number. An executive asked her out on a date; she said no. Ross later learned that, angry she had spurned his advances, the same executive had vetoed her for a prestigious assignment. That person is also still at the network.

Those and other indignities led to that now historic speech. "I got a reputation for being a troublemaker," she remarked. Ross has never been able to watch ESPN the same way since.

She's not the only one.

Since the book's original release, I have received a number of phone calls from various women employees—from producers to one anchor to secretaries to others—all relating their various experiences with sexual harassment at the network and asking that their names not be used. All the while, one of the larger misconceptions being floated by ESPN to the media was that their sexual harassment problems were currently nonexistent.

That could not be further from the truth.

In August 2000, around the same time ESPN was declaring itself a sexually deviant-free zone, one of its employees, John Spencer, a then-thirty-four-year-old on-air talent for ESPN International, was arrested for sexually molesting a fifteen-year-old girl.

Spencer played basketball at Howard University in the 1980s and professionally in China and Europe and was a well-liked member of the ESPN family. According to court documents, he was charged by the Morris County prosecutor's office with sexual assault and endangering the welfare of a child.

The accusations against Spencer surfaced in May 2000 when the girl told a teacher at Chatham High School in New Jersey that she was "kind of molested" by her "uncle" in the home of the Spencer family, according to an affidavit filed by a detective investigating the case. The girl was actually the daughter of a close friend of Spencer's.

The affidavit stated that Spencer was accused of kissing the girl on the lips, touching her breasts, and sexually touching her.

Spencer faced up to ten years in prison. In late January 2001, he reached a plea agreement with prosecutors, who dropped the sexual assault and endangering the welfare of a child charges in exchange for Spencer's guilty plea to criminal sexual contact. He received two years' probation, is considered a sex offender, and is subject to Megan's Law notifications. Neither his attorney nor ESPN will comment on his status with the network.

This is one of the more bizarre episodes involving an ESPN employee, but it is even stranger considering something that was happening in the sports world as Spencer's case wound through the court system. Green Bay tight end Mark Chmura, like Spencer a married man, was accused of sexually attacking his teenage babysitter after a night of drinking and sitting in a hot tub with her and other teenage girls. Though Chmura was acquitted of raping the girl, the entire episode was a sordid one.

Throughout Chmura's trial, ESPN football analysts railed against him, with many, including the normally tame Sean Salisbury, a former NFL career backup quarterback whom a colleague once called "the Michael Bolton of ESPN," ripping Chmura's bad judgment, saying Chmura should never have been drinking with teenagers to begin with. Indeed, the former Packers tight end did not make the smartest decision of his life that night.

But did anyone at the network stop and think for one minute: We have our own problems with men attacking young women; shouldn't we pull back, just for a second, from our perch of moral indignation?

ESPN continued to face its own usual sexual harassment problems. One of the network's most prominent on-air talents, who faced harassment allegations in the past, was again recently accused of inappropriate conduct. This time a woman claimed the man, who had met her only once or twice while both were on assignment covering a college basketball game, had called her at home around 1:30 in the morning and proposi-tioned her for sex. The scenario is all the more believable because it fits the previous pattern of this on-air talent: He usually harassed young, lower-ranked women who would probably be afraid to complain because of fear of repercussions from ESPN. Or, even if they did complain, that ESPN would ignore their pleas. Those fears are justifiable because ESPN has a history of mishandling sexual harassment problems the way a second-string point guard fumbles a no-look pass. This is exacerbated by the fact that ESPN is often reluctant to punish its stars.

There were other recent incidents. The network finally suspended a high-ranking producer with over a decade's worth of complaints against him from women, ranging from sexist comments to improper physical contact, after a woman complained about an inappropriate e-mail. An on-air talent was disciplined for a remark he made to a lower-ranked woman (though he vehemently denies he was disciplined for sexual harassment).

In the graphics department, a man was disciplined for sending porno-graphic e-mail to women.

After the publication of *ESPN: The Uncensored History*, the network plastered fliers throughout its Bristol campus, and even in some of its pro-duction trucks, warning that sexual harassment was a crime and would not be tolerated. To be sure, the working atmosphere at ESPN is better for women—because there is more awareness of the problem.

• • •

Despite some of the failures of its internal mechanisms as well as its su-persized ego and unabashed synergy, ESPN remains one of the more com-pelling choices on television. "SportsCenter" is by far the top daily highlight show (though Olbermann's Sunday epic "The Evening News with Keith Ol-bermann" can be just as good). The anchors rotate more than a pair of tires on a 1970 Chevy; still, the product remains sharp, habit-forming.

ESPN has also proven that while strong anchors like Olbermann and others are nice to have, they are not necessary for solid ratings. ESPN has been killing Fox, both in overall quality and ratings. The Fox network's approach of regional sportscasts simply does not work well because the quality of the local shows is subpar. Some of them, like the one in New York, look as if they were produced in someone's basement. Meanwhile, the evening "SportsCenter" is an intelligent and slick production. The look of the show is so glossy and professional, it rivals any of the network evening news shows.

ESPN misses the wit of Olbermann as well as the reporting skills of Jimmy Roberts, who left for NBC, but the network still has the best ideas, the best presentation, and the top journalists overall.

How the network handled the XFL, the upstart football league started by wrestling macho man Vince McMahon, is an example of ESPN at its best. Many other networks, including Fox and CNN/SI, took a snide approach to the league, mocking its wrestling roots.

ESPN reporter Curry Kirkpatrick did a smart story on the league, presenting just the right flavor of seriousness and fun. It was a tricky story for the network because its top sporting partner is the NFL, which thumbed its nose at the XFL and even encouraged some major media outlets to ignore the league. When the opening XFL telecast drew a 9.5 national rating, its largest national audience on a Saturday night for viewers between the age of 18 and 49 and one that doubled the NFL's Pro Bowl numbers, ESPN did the best balancing job of covering the league's various issues and showing highlights. XFL executive Dick Butkus even made an appearance on Miller's "Up Close."

The NFL was not happy with ESPN's coverage of the XFL and voiced its irritation to various ESPN officials. Still, the network covered the newsworthiness of the league, as it should, and took the occasional shot at the XFL, like other media outlets, such as when one "SportsCenter" anchor called it "male-chauvinist-pig skin football."

On November 30, 2000, ESPN celebrated one of the most significant anniversaries in its history by televising its 200th NFL game. It was an important moment for the network because in the early 1980s, a majority of NFL owners believed professional football should never be on cable television because it would not reach enough fans. Since it debuted in 1987, ESPN's "Sunday Night Football" has been one of cable television's highest-rated series.

ESPN remains solid because it has a core of good producers and the on-air talent level is deep. Since the book's publication, there has been some shifting of personnel, but not much has changed. Robin Roberts does an occasional "SportsCenter," but her career is headed for bigger things, like permanent cohost of a network morning show. She is definitely one of the classiest ESPN employees.

Tirico remains angry that his sexual harassment history was detailed in the book. While writing the book, I became convinced Tirico had matured and put these incidents behind him. And that's what ESPN officials would have us believe. Now, over a year later, and after more interviews, I am not so certain.

Patrick cut back on his television workload and now has his own radio show, which is slightly lowbrow; as *Sports Illustrated* media critic John Walters pointed out, ESPN's "The Tony Kornheiser Show" is "the better listen." It's easy to understand why: Kornheiser has managed the difficult chore of mixing wit with journalism better than Patrick has.

Walters captured Patrick's personality perfectly when he wrote that Patrick "comes off on radio as well-informed but too cute and, as when he somewhat facetiously chastised Charles Barkley for not inviting him to his New Year's Eve Party, a tad self-obsessed."

Patrick's name still has incredible marquee value. When Patrick shows up on the Sunday "SportsCenter," he commands respect just by his presence.

Kolber does an excellent job at whatever she does but is especially good as host of "Edge NFL Matchup." By far it is the best pure football show on television with its hard-hitting and in-depth approach. One show illustrated how Minnesota's electric wide receiver Randy Moss sometimes takes plays off, lazily refusing to block on running plays. Former NFL player Merril Hoge discovered the nugget after watching hours of game film, and it became a huge national story.

The cast of reporters is strong, especially Kremer, Mortensen, Jeremy Schaap (who did a wonderful job interviewing coach Bobby Knight after he was fired by Indiana), Shelley Smith, Paolantonio, Werder, David Aldridge, and John Clayton. Tom Jackson is the best football analyst on television next to Phil Simms on CBS. Anchor Pam Ward, who does double duty on television and radio, is the most underrated talent in sports television.

Walsh, like Patrick, has pulled back somewhat from the daily operation of the network but is still involved. Though Walsh will never be known as one of ESPN's best people persons—far from it—he will go down as one of ESPN's most valued executives.

Berman's name is still synonymous with ESPN. No sports television star of his status is friendlier or more genuine. When Berman does football highlights, it is a treat to watch. But he still irritates some people who believe his act—especially the nicknames—has grown tired. In an Internet column for America Online, sports novelist John Feinstein listed Berman's name under the headline "People Who Just Need to Be Quiet."

By far the most controversial personality in the book was Olbermann. Patrick, Walsh, LaPlaca, and others at ESPN portrayed Olbermann as a quasi ghostwriter for the book. Though not true, the move was a smart one because they know how polarizing Olbermann is.

Since Olbermann's departure, ESPN has attempted to demonize him and has made insinuations that it is better off without him. As harshly as Olbermann treated some people at ESPN, the network was just as cruel to him when he left, mainly behind his back.

As for his value to ESPN, what the network did in the days after his departure speaks volumes about its true feelings. In June 1997, some forty-eight hours before his departure, Olbermann, while in the office of an NBC News vice president, separately phoned both Walsh and former president Steve Bornstein to inform them he had signed with NBC. Bornstein told Olbermann, "It'll never be as good without you. Thank you."

Even after Olbermann had signed with NBC, his old network was trying to get him back. Walsh called Olbermann at home one Monday in the weeks after he had left ESPN. "Howard Katz and I have just spoken to [ABC president] Bob Iger, and he wants to present a proposal to you involving a primetime assignment with ABC News and some continuing work for ESPN." Nothing ever came of the desperate move by ESPN, but Iger did tell Olbermann, "Feel free to come back."

Olbermann's presence in the book reflected reality. He was a huge part of the network's explosion in the late 1980s and early 1990s, regardless of how determined ESPN may be to diminish his contributions today. He was one of its stars. And he is also one of the most engaging, cordial, and entertaining people I have ever met. Show me an ESPN reporter who walks into the Dallas Cowboys locker room and asks to interview the most boring player on the team or the third-string tight end. That's Olbermann. Other reporters want the sexy names who will say the most interesting things.

At Fox, he left his anchoring position to host his own Sunday night sports highlight show on the same network, "The Evening News with Keith Olbermann." It is consistently strong, mainly because of Olbermann's writing and wit. Fox executives enlarged Olbermann's staff, and when he wasn't working on his show, Olbermann was working on several books, including one tentatively named *The Kate Chronicles*, about a sports anchor and a murder.

Olbermann's show was the constant when Fox Sports Net underwent a dramatic lineup change in February 2001. The old format had a 10 P.M. national report with two hosts, an 11 P.M. regional broadcast with two hosts, Jim Rome at 11:30, and a midnight national sports report again with two hosts.

Fox shifted to a 10 P.M. regional sports report with two hosts and a 10:30 national show—cut from one hour to thirty minutes—with one host and a panel format that includes guests. It was the fifth different format change since December 1999.

There was another significance: By ranking the lower-quality regional shows ahead of the "National Sports Report," Fox was officially surrendering the ratings war for news supremacy to its nemesis ESPN.

"SportsCenter," and in some ways ESPN overall, emerged supreme in its bitter fight with Fox.

That was no surprise. ESPN has been a part of people's lives for too long to lose such a war. I wonder if there will ever be a serious challenger to the network.

• • •

ESPN's founders remain some of the most interesting figures in the network's history. They watch ESPN with a combination of pride and disbelief. They are stunned at how large their baby has grown. Bill Rasmussen still remembers clearly how he put some of the start-up costs for ESPN on his Visa credit card. Now, the network earns billions.

The lives of the founders have changed since those hectic but wonderful days when they built the network with their bare hands. Chet Simmons is retired and living in Savannah, Georgia. He is still a fiery personality, as evidenced by his recent views regarding the XFL on NBC. Simmons has unique insight into the subject because, before becoming president of ESPN in the early 1980s, he was the first president of NBC Sports. Then, after ESPN, Simmons was the first commissioner of the United States Football League, which offered professional football as a sincere sports venture.

What does the former chief of NBC, ESPN, and the USFL think of the hyped-up XFL on one of his old networks? He told the *New York Post*: "I watched (the opener) on NBC and I was frightened. I saw exactly what they were selling—a little boy holding up a sign that read 'I'm here to see the cheerleaders,' close-ups of cheerleaders acting like strippers, the vulgar comments and sexual innuendo out of the mouths of the announcers. The cameramen obviously were directed to find and promote the most antisocial things they could find, like all the young men in the stands with a beer in each hand.

"I thought to myself that it doesn't matter if it's staged or real, or whether some of it's staged and some of it's real," Simmons said. "Either way, it's frightening. Is this the way NBC chooses to generate ratings? Is this what NBC Sports has become? Is this what NBC wanted young viewers, especially kids, to perceive as sports? I was disgusted and depressed.

The pride I always held through my association with NBC was gone. We may not always have succeeded, but we always tried to present classy productions. But NBC's relationship with the XFL is clearly designed to present sports in a lowlife form."

Added Simmons: "I started thinking about some of the great sports production people at NBC, people who have passed away: Scotty Connal, Ted Nathanson, Harry Coyle. I know that they would have been ashamed and depressed, too. When I was with the USFL and we had a deal with ABC, Roone Arledge called to complain that one of the team's names was the [Houston] Gamblers. But the XFL directly encourages gambling. And it's aimed at kids. What good can come of that? And it's an NBC property. It's a bad dream, beyond belief."

Simmons sent NBC President Bob Wright a personal letter via e-mail to express his disgust with his old network's association with the XFL.

No, not even all these years later has Simmons lost his edge.

The only worse nightmare Simmons can imagine is if his other love, ESPN, begins an XFL-like league. That likely won't happen. But Simmons would have hated part of the network's highlight package during one slow February, when ESPN showed highlights of "drag queen soccer" from Brazil. It was a distasteful bit and showed that ESPN is not immune to the overall lowering of decency in sports.

Stuart Evey, the former Getty executive who helped give ESPN its first major influx of cash, is living in Spokane, Washington. He is active in community affairs and serves on the boards of directors of two companies headquartered in the city.

Evey remains proud of his efforts to convince Getty to back ESPN financially, something that was considered extremely risky, even foolhardy, at the time, but Evey's foresight was brilliant.

"The growth and dominating position in sports television attained by ESPN over the years has been a source of great pride for me," said Evey. "In 1979, it is likely that the launch of ESPN would not have been possible without Getty Oil Company. The relationship of major networks with their affiliate networks precluded their making major investments in cable, and left a small window for non-network companies to consider investments in this new industry. Getty recognized early on that our corporate management, comprised of oil executives and directors from the financial community, did not have the flexibility or personalities to react in a timely manner on major decisions, most notably, the rights acquisition process. Also, the need to make continued investments to enhance the value of ESPN.

"As ESPN grew, these occasions became more frequent," Evey said. "The successor companies to Getty were Capital Cities/ABC in 1985, followed by the Disney company in 1996. These ownership companies brought totally different management styles to ESPN, and the sequential timing of their ownership was key to its uninterrupted growth and success."

Evey added, "Today I am a great fan of ESPN. With the proliferation of competition, the management seems to stay ahead of the pack with content and on-air personalities. ESPN has name recognition unparalleled in sports broadcasting, and as stated by former chairman of ABC Leonard Goldensohn, ESPN may be the most successful story in broadcast history. A great deal of gratitude is owed to the financial, legal, and administrative staffs at Getty, which played a major role in assimilating ESPN into the corporate structure of Getty. This became a source of constant irritation to the management of ESPN, but also prolonged the interest and investment by Getty."

Scott Rasmussen, Bill Rasmussen's son, who did as much legwork as anyone in ESPN's early days, is running a polling company called Rasmussen Research, which developed a system for collecting statistically reliable telephone survey information for a lower cost than traditional methods, mainly by using the Internet. *USA Today* has used his service.

As for the creator of ESPN, Bill Rasmussen, he still lives a low-key life. He is involved in various entrepreneurial adventures and still goes through each day with a smile on his face.

He said recently: "I'll never forget my days at ESPN. That was one of the most exciting times of my life."

Acknowledgments

I first decided to write a book about ESPN in the summer of 1994, after the network called me about becoming one of its reporters. I had a tryout in Central Park and it was one of the worst experiences of my life. I was awful.

I always had great respect for the reporters of ESPN. While covering the National Football League, I was constantly bumping into Andrea Kremer and noticed no one more tireless, thorough, and talented. Chris Mortensen was always on the telephone ringing sources, or they him. Now I had my close encounter with ESPN and was even more fascinated by the great network, despite my sweaty and stuttering audition. My curiosity, spurred on by countless thrilling stories from ESPNers, turned into years of research and more than two hundred interviews.

Actually, this book is the third link in a chain of inspiration. I read Michael MacCambridge's history of *Sports Illustrated,* entitled *The Franchise,* and he had been inspired by Robert Draper's history of *Rolling Stone* magazine. I only hope my book is on the same level as those two excellent works.

Three key people helped lay the foundation for *ESPN: The Uncensored History.* Bill Rasmussen sat down with me for two days in Boston and endured my countless phone calls and e-mails. For his patience, I am eternally grateful. Scott Rasmussen was also a major help. Chet Simmons is one of the smartest people I have ever met, and his vivid descriptions added color to those early days. Stuart Evey has become the forgotten man in the network's history. Without him, there might not have been an ESPN. His notes were extremely helpful, as were the recollections of his daughter, Christine Evey.

A number of people helped me reconstruct the early days of ESPN, but key contributors include George Conner, Stephen Bogart, Bob Pronovost, Sal Marchiano, Gayle Gardner, Greg Gumbel, George Grande, Steve Sabol, and Bob Gutkowski. Former NFL broadcast guru Val Pinchbeck and Baltimore Ravens owner Art Modell took me inside the negotiations during ESPN's first television contract with the NFL. Also Tom Odjakjian, a most important man in ESPN's history, who held a variety of production jobs, lived up to his reputation as one of the kindest people on the planet.

Dozens of current and former production assistants, producers, directors, talent, and management personnel all helped me understand life in the modern ESPN. Former producer Mark Mason provided insight into ESPN radio. Dan Patrick, who wore out his cell phone one night, was extremely candid and friendly. Chris Berman phoned several times from airports and a few more instances from his palatial estate in Connecticut. Anchors such as Robin Roberts and Charley Steiner opened up their professional lives. Other anchors and on-air personalities also helped, but asked not to be identified. Suzy Kolber's thoughts on those chaotic ESPN2 days were indispensable.

Numerous ESPN staffers appraised their network with surprising candor. Many did not want to be named. For their assistance, I am grateful.

I want to extend particular thanks to the many women heroes who have helped me piece together the difficult portrait of life then and now for women at ESPN. Many risked their careers to speak to me, fearing reprisal from the network. Former human resources director Ricardo Correia also risked the wrath of ESPN, and I am equally thankful to him for his courage.

By far, the most difficult part of this book was navigating through ESPN's paranoia. There was a concerted effort by members of ESPN management to prevent current and former employees from speaking to me. Officially, the network's stance was that it was not cooperating with the book in any way. ESPN even refused to supply photographs of the network's campus or of its key personalities. In the end, however, a number of people did cooperate, some against ESPN's wishes.

The most disappointing part of the process was dealing with John Walsh, who oversees the newsroom. Walsh is considered a top journalist in sports, yet at first, Walsh refused to cooperate unless he could remove material about ESPN that he considered negative. In other words, Walsh wanted to censor the book. Walsh eventually submitted to several interviews, but only after the manuscript had already been turned in, leaving limited time to digest his responses, which may have been Walsh's plan all along.

Walsh did distribute a memo throughout ESPN in late 1999, permitting interviews of anyone who wanted to cooperate with the book—a complete reversal of policy—but only after the manuscript had been submitted. Thus the memo's sincerity must be questioned.

Also, no interviews were conducted with anchor Bob Ley, who considers himself the top journalist at ESPN. Ley refused to do an interview, saying he was writing his own book on ESPN, a claim he has made for years.

Ironically, when I spoke to Walsh, he said to me, "You can't trust anything Keith Olbermann tells you." Because of the warning from Walsh and others, I triple-checked every word that Olbermann said during an interview in his Los Angeles office. The extra precaution was unwarranted because Olbermann turned out to be utterly honest, both about himself and his old network.

Fox publicity men Vince Wladika and Dennis Johnson, as well as anchor Chris Myers, extended particular hospitality, as did public relations executives LeslieAnne Wade from CBS and Mark Mandel from ABC.

The writings of Richard Sandomir from the *New York Times,* Bob Raissman of the *New York Daily News,* and Phil Mushnick from the *New York Post* were extremely helpful. Sportspages.com was also an invaluable research tool.

My agent, Randy Voorhees, was essential to this work. I will forever be grateful for his ideas but most of all, his faith. The smartest decision I ever made was hiring Susan Thornton Hobby as manuscript overseer.

I could not have undertaken this book without the benefit of my mother, Alice, who showed me a long time ago what it takes to be great. Or Kelly, who deserves my deepest thanks for her patience and support.

Index